T0244289

Dogwhistles and Figleaves

Dogwhistles and Figleaves

How Manipulative Language Spreads Racism and Falsehood

JENNIFER MATHER SAUL

OXFORD
UNIVERSITY PRESS

OXFORD
UNIVERSITY PRESS

Great Clarendon Street, Oxford, OX2 6DP,
United Kingdom

Oxford University Press is a department of the University of Oxford.
It furthers the University's objective of excellence in research, scholarship,
and education by publishing worldwide. Oxford is a registered trade mark of
Oxford University Press in the UK and in certain other countries

Published in the United States of America by Oxford University Press
198 Madison Avenue, New York, NY 10016, United States of America

British Library Cataloguing in Publication Data

Data available

Library of Congress Control Number: 2023942417

ISBN 978-0-19-287175-6

DOI: 10.1093/oso/9780192871756.001.0001

Printed by Integrated Books International, United States of America

To all the communities, virtual and in-person, that sustained me through the writing of this book. And to those who have tried so hard to sustain all of us through this ongoing pandemic period—fighting the surprisingly interlinked plagues of Covid, misinformation, and hatred. Finally, to my Dad—who I like to think would really have enjoyed this book. And who would definitely have liked the orange cover.

Contents

Contents

Acknowledgments

I first began working on the topics central to this book in the UK, in 2014, when the world looked very different. As I approached my post-Head of Department sabbatical, due in 2015–2016, I planned to write on dogwhistles and other devices for subtle racist messaging. "Oh good," I thought to myself, "there's a US election coming up—there's always lots of subtle racist messaging!" (Because I'm originally American, my knowledge of such campaigns in the US goes painfully far back.) At that time, I wasn't even thinking about the Brexit campaign, which seemed wildly unlikely to succeed.

The year 2016, as we all now know, changed everything in both of my countries. It also changed my research. I became gripped by the question of why such *unsubtle* racism succeeded on a national scale—all the predictions of political psychologists would suggest that it wouldn't. That's when I began to think and write about figleaves, devices which allow for a shifting of norms, by making (some of) the audience think that *maybe this racist-sounding utterance isn't so racist after all.*

I thank all of my wonderful colleagues at Sheffield for discussing this material with me, and for making me the person and philosopher that I am—especially Jules Holroyd, Rosanna Keefe, Steve Laurence, Stevie Makin, Komarine Romdenh-Romluc, and Bob Stern. As always, my decades of philosophical conversations with Chris Hookway continue to be one of my largest philosophical influences. I'm also grateful to all the Sheffield tree campaigners, for giving me another fight to throw myself into—and for making it a shockingly winnable one.

In late 2019 I moved to Canada, initiating one of the most disruptive periods of my life. It began with the sale of our UK house falling through, leading to a period in which we spent months living out of suitcases in Mary Hardy and Phelim Boyle's spare rooms. I owe an enormous debt to them for their incredible generosity and warm welcome (as well as many great evenings of ranting and wine). Just as we finally moved into our house and got our finances in order, the pandemic lockdown hit.

This book is a product of the pandemic, mostly conceived and written during Ontario's long lockdown. In my desperation for connection, I joined or started roughly a million reading groups. I'm grateful to all of them—Nikki Ernst's Words Workshop (a truly remarkable pandemic creation and force for social and political philosophy of language), WOGAP, ROGAP, Sheffield Feminism, Waterloo Feminism, Social Epistemology, Language in the Trump Era, and probably others. The most important for this book's subject, though, was the Conspiracy Theories reading group, and one of the most important things about that group was Brian Montgomery's insistence that we should not just read academics writing *about* conspiracy theories, but also look at videos made by conspiracy theorists. This had an enormous influence on my thought about the topic, as did the wonderful, careful, supportive discussions with this group. But I am not sure I would have written the book at all if it weren't for a different reading group, the tiny accidental one that somehow lasted and turned into a writing group, sustaining me through all of this time. Thank you.

My students at this time (both grad and undergrad) were also a vital connection to the outside world—and discussions with them were enormously important not only to my thoughts on these topics, but also to my psychological health. But it also turned out that two classes I was teaching—on Misinformation and on Pandemic Philosophy—required me to think about conspiracy theories. It was through this that I came to notice the use of dogwhistles and figleaves by conspiracy theorists, and the book doubled in scope.

The international community of philosophers became more important to me than ever—and it had always been important. I am so grateful to all the groups of people who gave me feedback on parts of this book, either in person or on Zoom (and even the ones who made me use Teams), at: the Eastern APA in Montreal; CNRS Paris; the Hate Speech Conference in Genoa; the Norms of Public Argument Workshop in Lisbon; the Social Epistemology Workshop in Berlin; the Meaning and Reference in Social Context Conference in Taipei; the CHIPS Conference in Barbados; the Language and Power Conference in Barcelona; the "Who's Got the Power" Conference in Reykjavik; the Conference in Logic, Epistemology, and Philosophy of Science in Bogota; the ARCHE Postgrad Conference in St. Andrews; the ZAS Conference in Berlin; the GAP Conference in Cologne; and the Media Ethics Conference in Leeds; the Joint Session WOGAP, ROGAP, The Words Workshop, the Penn/Rutgers Race Reading Group; as well as invited talks at Tampere, UC Irvine, UC Santa Cruz, Hamburg, Tuebingen, Arkansas, UNAM, Glasgow, Guelph, Sheffield, the University of Saskatchewan, Vienna, the University of Southern California, Washington

University St. Louis, UQAM, Rutgers, Durham, KCL, Seattle University, Cambridge, the Central European University, Valencia, Umea, Stockholm, Purdue, the University of Connecticut, Oxford, Liverpool, St. Mary's, Southampton, Nottingham, McGill, Hannover, Humboldt, New School, Wayne State, Waterloo, the University of Vermont, Warwick, Lund, Harvard, and Indiana.

I have discussed the issues in this book with far too many people to remember them all, but I know I've benefited from conversations about it with Kyle Adams, Tasneem Alsayyed, Sari van Anders, Greg Andres, Louise Antony, Eleanor Aurora, Al Baker, Elizabeth Barnes, Susan Brison, Gerry Callaghan, Ross Cameron, Laura Caponetto, Patrick Connolly, Josep Corbi, Greg Cote, Matthew Cull, Shannon Dea, Molly Dea-Stephenson, Esa Diaz Leon, Matt Doucet, Ray Drainville, Theo Drainville-Saul, Maren Ebert-Rohleder, Barrett Emerick, Carla Fehr, David Fisman, Keith Frankish, Doreen Fraser, Miranda Fricker, Katy Fulfer, Manolo Garcia-Carpintero, Iz Gonzalez-Vazquez, Tobies Grimaltos, Alex Gruenewald, Sally Haslanger, Larry Horn, Katharine Jenkins, Gabrielle Johnson, Maria Kasmirli, Madeleine Kenyon, Anna Klieber, Rae Langton, Lisa Leutheuser, Alice MacLachlan, Elin McCready, Teresa Marques, Neri Marsili, Mirelle Martin, Pepe Martinez, Elin McCready, Nadia Mehdi, Eliot Michaelson, Mari Mikkola, Nadia Miller, Carlos Moya, Deborah Muehlebach, Kate Norlock, Nick Ray, Martina Rosola, Joe Saul, Julie Saul, Naomi Scheman, Jason Stanley, Heather Stewart, Alessandra Tanesini, Lynne Tirrell, Peter Thurley, Pepa Toribio, Jose Torices, Jordi Valor, Chris Wass, Jon Webber, Alex Wiegmann, Kimberly Witten, Audrey Yap, and Lori Young. Tim Kenyon was an especially important influence on my thoughts about bald-faced lies and bullshit, and I'm grateful that he was happy for me to use ideas from our co-authored paper in this book. I'm also extremely grateful (as ever) to Peter Momtchiloff for overseeing the editing of this book, and for decades of beers at the Joint Sessions. The team from OUP (Chris Bessant, Hayley Buckley, Amarnath Kalaimani, and Jamie Mortimer) have been extremely helpful and patient. I also had the impressive assistance of Madeleine Kenyon as an additional proofreader, who did an absolutely stunning job of catching an embarrassingly large collection of ways I could express myself more clearly! Finally, I'm deeply thankful for the careful, helpful comments from some fantastic anonymous referees. They've greatly improved the book.

The most important community through the writing of this book was my family—both those I was locked in a house with, and those I was kept away from behind a closed border. I learned that even after two years locked up together I still have tons to talk about with my partner Ray and my son Theo. Indeed, Ray and I discovered just how many ways our interests intersect—we wrote a paper and a successful funding application together, and look forward to writing many more papers about dogwhistles and figleaves online. Theo has yet to co-author a paper or a funding application, but I never knew a teenager could be this interesting and fun to talk to—about the topics in this book, and beyond. Throughout my life, my mother, Julie Saul, has been one of the wisest and most insightful people to talk to. Though the pandemic kept us apart, it also gave us our first chance ever to be in online reading groups together. And of course the constant flow of examples, analysis, and swearing from her had a huge impact on this work. My brother Joe has also always been a steady source of quiet support and great examples. Although my Dad wasn't around for this book, he certainly helped to shape me into someone who wanted to write it. Finally, thanks also to Odysseus, Gilgamesh, and Enkidu—without whom life would be much more boring (and less covered in cat hair).

Content Note

THIS BOOK DISCUSSES AND QUOTES VIOLENT AND RACIST RHETORIC.

Typographical Note

I have struggled a lot with the choice of whether to use capital letters for "White" and for "Black." As I write this, it's clear that we as a culture have not yet reached a consensus on what to do about this choice. The same is true even if we look only at the views of racial justice advocates: some argue for capitalizing neither, some for capitalizing only "Black," and others for capitalizing both. I have decided on the latter course, because I've been convinced by the arguments of leading philosopher of both race and language Kwame Anthony Appiah (Appiah 2020). Appiah argues that capitalization of both draws attention to the fact that they are socially constructed rather than natural. In English, we capitalize adjectives that are derived from proper names ("American," "English"), which is something we don't do with most adjectives. In particular, it's not something we do with color terms—so capitalizing words like "White" and "Black" helps to make clear that we're not just talking about color. But that's not all, according to Appiah:

> We routinely name and capitalize entities (the Middle Ages, January, the Pacific Ocean, Copenhagen) that reflect human interests or actions. On the other hand, we tend *not* to capitalize "natural kinds"—that is, categories that track with inherent features of the world, independent of our interests or doings. Einstein, the physicist, is capitalized; einsteinium, the element, is not.

Capitalizing, then, calls attention to the socially constructed nature of "White" and "Black"—reminding us that they are like nations, cities, or months—human inventions. Only capitalizing "Black" would suggest that whiteness is somehow more of a natural kind, which is not only false but a pernicious myth to perpetuate.

For me, a further reason for capitalization is that I am exploring parallels between attitudes towards groups like not just Blacks and Whites, but also Muslims and Mexicans. Since the latter *must* be capitalized, it seems to me wrong not to capitalize the former.

As Appiah also notes, we cannot know how things will turn out with respect to capitalization. It may be that in a few years (or perhaps sooner), one usage or the other will fall firmly into place. If my usage here turns out to no longer carry the meaning that I hope it now does, I apologize in advance for any confusion and ask the reader to bear in mind the reasoning that led me to make the choice that I did.

To be true to the sources I quote, I have retained original capitalization within quotations.

Introduction

Trump's 2016 presidential victory revealed some quite obvious divisions in the United States—between those who loved his crass racism and sexism, and those who hated it, for example. But even among his opponents there were divisions that his win laid bare. One of these is brilliantly illustrated by a *Saturday Night Live* sketch[1] showing a group of anti-Trump voters watching election returns at a party. The White viewers find his victory unimaginable, while the Black viewers clearly expected precisely this. The White viewers are shocked and horrified by the fact that racism still exists. The Black viewers shake their heads in bemusement at the White voters' ignorance and lack of self-knowledge.[2]

The received wisdom in political psychology would have predicted much of this: that many White Americans would be blissfully unaware that Obama's election hadn't ended racism, and also blissfully unaware of their own racist sentiments. It would also have predicted that Black Americans would generally suffer from fewer such illusions, either about the country or about the White people at the party with them. It would even have predicted the resounding success of a politician who played to White Americans' racist sentiments. What it wouldn't have predicted, however, was that such success could be achieved by *openly and brazenly* appealing to these racist sentiments. Trump's success was thoroughly at odds with what had seemed to be the well-established predictions of political psychology (e.g. Mendelberg 2001: 99; Hurwitz and Peffley 2005). Since the Civil Rights Movement, this orthodoxy held, overt expressions of racism were unacceptable in national political discourse—they would doom a campaign.[3] But Trump ignored all this, and did what was supposed to spell the end of a national quest for office: he said blatantly racist things, so blatant that they were readily recognized as such and criticized for it in the mainstream media.

From day one of the Trump administration, blatant falsehoods also took on new prominence. There had been plenty of large falsehoods during the campaign, but not like what came after. The side-by-side pictures shown everywhere made it more than clear that the size of Barack Obama's inauguration crowd dwarfed that of Donald Trump's. And yet Trump insisted, and his spokesperson Sean Spicer insisted, that Trump had had the larger crowd. This lie was shocking both for its obviousness and for its pointlessness: it wasn't an important matter, and yet even when caught in the lie, they would not back down (Palmeri 2017). And the obvious lies continued, morphing into support for conspiracy theories even less plausible than Trump's longtime advocacy of the theory that Barack Obama was really born in Kenya (Barbaro 2016). There was the stunning spread of QAnon, a conspiracy which holds that a "deep state" insider has been putting coded messages on social media about (putting it briefly) a grand conspiracy of Democrats and celebrities abusing children by draining their adrenochrome, among other things—and Donald Trump's secret heroic efforts to end the abuse. And it grew even more shocking as QAnon adherents won Republican primaries and then became congressional representatives. These weren't just falsehoods, but the sorts of falsehoods that would previously have ended any careers associated with them. All of this, of course, built up to the conspiracy theory holding that Donald Trump really won the 2020 election. This conspiracy theory, and the support that it got from Republican politicians, directly led to the violent assault on the US capitol on January 6, 2020, by people carrying confederate flags (Associated Press 2022) and wearing T-shirts with anti-Jewish slogans (Sarna 2021), an event that dramatically brought together the blatant racism and wild conspiracism. And, of course, all this continues even though Trump is no longer President: Republicans who deny the stolen election claims become pariahs in the party.

These dramatic rises in blatant racism and obvious falsehood are what is sometimes called "saying the quiet part loud."[4] It is definitely not the case that the racism was new, or that politicians had always been truthful before. The quiet part had always been there, and it had always been deeply damaging and dangerous. (And of course through much of history the quiet part had been very loud indeed.) But something had indeed shifted: the unsayable became sayable. And not only did it fail to ruin careers, it seemed to help them. This matters: increasingly hateful language is often a precursor to violence and even genocide. As Lynne Tirrell writes:

The genocide of the Tutsi in Rwanda in 1994 is a cautionary tale for the rest of the world, warning of the ways that one group can be pitted against another through differences entrenched in practices of speech, reference, and categorization, to the point of murder. Anti-Tutsi speech was a chronic social poisoning that then catalyzed into an acute outbreak of violence. (2017: 117)

Her work is building on that of Victor Klemperer, a Jewish linguist who chronicled the linguistic changes of the Nazi era, and their effects.

Nazism permeated the flesh and blood of the people through single words, idioms, and sentence structures which were imposed on them in a million repetitions and taken on board mechanically and unconsciously.
(Klemperer, with Brady 2000: 15)

It is no small thing, then, for previously unacceptable expressions of racism to become ordinary. Normalizing increasingly blatant racism is a dangerous step—one we need to notice, understand, and fight. These are key goals of the present book.

I am far from the first to ask how the changes of the Trump era happened. But the approach in this book is quite different from others. One of the differences is that I am examining the spread of explicit racism and blatant falsehood together. Most authors have focused on the racism, *or* on the spread of obvious falsehoods, but I think there is much to be gained from looking at parallels between them.[5]

Given that racism is, if defined in terms of claims, basically a collection of falsehoods that should be obvious, this point needs some explaining. Racist falsehoods have a sadly very long history and are well entrenched in widely accepted White supremacist ideologies. There is nothing new about the acceptance of racist falsehoods. Nor, tragically, is their falsehood obvious to much of the country (though it should be). Again, White supremacist ideologies are widespread, and underpin fervent belief in these falsehoods. As Charles Mills describes it, this is an ignorance "propagated at the highest levels of the land, indeed presenting itself unblushingly as knowledge" (2007: 13). My focus here, in terms of racism, is on how this already widely accepted racism has come to be so openly expressed. My focus, in terms of falsehood, is largely on different claims—those that are widely seen as obviously false and ridiculous, such as the QAnon conspiracy theory. (Although racist claims *should* be seen in this way, they are not, due to the entrenchment of racist ideologies.) My claim is that similar and connected techniques have led to the rise of openly expressed racism and widespread false and conspiracist beliefs. Examining these together sheds light on both phenomena.

Another difference in my approach is that I am not focused primarily on Trump's most ardent supporters, asking how it is that they have come to so fully embrace his blatant racism, or asking what it is that has moved his base to so fervently support wildly implausible conspiracy theories. (The most popular answers to these questions invoke either broad features of our current moment, like anti-immigrant sentiment (Margalit 2019); or particular features attributed to the character of Trump supporters, like a tendency to authoritarian thinking (Pettigrew 2017; Womick et al. 2019).) Instead, this book offers a careful examination of the way that current political rhetoric is simultaneously directed at a variety of different groups in society, and all the complex and interactive ways that this rhetoric affects these groups. Some of these people, obviously, are committed Trump supporters. But in a way they are the least interesting. It's no surprise that they like what they hear in terms of blatant racism and falsehood. It's much more revealing and important, it seems to me, to look at why other people put up with this—or even support Trump—despite finding it at least somewhat disconcerting. These people are crucial. One reason is that they may themselves be persuaded to become blatant racists and conspiracists. But even if they aren't, they may well be persuaded that the worrying statements are not actually so bad. They may go ahead and support these candidates, or at least fail to oppose them. They might pass on their messages in a spirit of uncertainty—but still pass them on. All of these actions and non-actions are crucial to the rise of blatant racism and wild conspiracism.

A primary focus of this book, then, is the rhetoric that allows for the persuasion or reassurance of this malleable group. It does so by achieving a deniability which allows members of this group to convince themselves that deeply held norms against racism and untruthfulness are not being violated, don't apply, or are not so important in this instance. The techniques for achieving deniability with respect to both racism and obvious falsehood have certain key points of similarity that I will explore here. Their similarities lie not just in the way that they lend deniability, but in the ways that they contribute to the pitting of various groups against each other.

Properly understanding this requires a careful look at political rhetoric, and this requires a somewhat new approach to philosophy of language. To grapple with it, we must examine the ways that divisions between groups are exploited (and enhanced) by public speech. Traditionally, analytic philosophers of language have tended to focus either on context-independent elements of language, like linguistic meaning and semantics; or on small face-to-face conversations, for those more interested in context and pragmatics. Neither of these approaches is well suited to fully understanding the complexities of public speech designed to exploit divisions among groups, though of course each one provides valuable insights that can be drawn upon in developing a way to think about this sort of political rhetoric. Recently, there's been increasing interest in political speech, which is clearly directed at a larger group. However, these two broad approaches have continued to hold sway to a surprising extent, with most theorists focusing either on the workings of particular terms, or on power dynamics in ways that are modeled on small group conversations.

The sort of manipulative language that is crucial to our current situation, I argue, makes crucial use of divisions among a vast audience. I will argue that the same sort of segmentation of the audience plays a vital role in both the spread of explicit racism and the spread of obvious falsehood. In considering these groups, two key factors will be how the groups respond to the utterances that are made, and how they relate to the social expectations that have in the recent past constrained the expression of explicit racism and obvious falsehood.

I will argue that the best way to capture the social expectations which previously constrained speech is to see them as extremely vaguely defined norms which many (crucially, not all) people try to follow. As I formulate them, these are the extremely vague norms captured by the invocations *don't be racist* and *be truthful*. The vagueness in formulation allows for individuals to select their own understanding of what these norms require, which is crucial to explaining the many ways that people attempt to circumvent the norms, or to convince themselves (and others) that they are indeed still following them. These norms, and the flawed ways that they are applied, will play a crucial role throughout this book.

I am especially interested, then, in the ways that various groups in the population differ from one another. There are three main groups (outlined below) that will aid in our understanding of the spread of blatant racism and falsehood. Importantly, people do shift between groups from subject to subject and context to context. Someone who opposes the norm against racism, for example, might accept the norm against untruthfulness. Someone who thinks it's acceptable to be racist against one group might think it's not acceptable to be racist against another group. Some violations of norms will be easier to recognize than others, and sometimes this will be affected by one's own group membership and convictions. And people's opinions can, of course, change over time.

The first group is the norm opposers. It is probably not a surprise to realize that such people exist in the case of norms against racism. They are the explicit racists, the people who join the Ku Klux Klan and hang out in

White supremacist groups online. It may seem a little more puzzling to suppose that there are also people who oppose the Norm of Truthfulness. But substantial groups of people enjoy the flouting of even this norm, at least under certain circumstances. A recent study, "The Appeal of the Lying Demagogue" (Hahl, Kim, and Zuckerman Sivan 2018) revealed that when people feel sufficiently aggrieved by the establishment, a person whom they recognize as lying can be appealing precisely for breaking this norm.

The second group is the people who accept the relevant norm, but can be relatively easily convinced not to worry too much about it. This may happen in several ways. It may be that a claim can be phrased in such a way that it is not recognized as violating the norm. For some of these people, this may be very easy—they may simply be bad at recognizing violations. For others, this will require more care. Alternatively, a claim may be phrased in such a way that doubt is raised about the violation of a norm. Or, as we will see, some additional utterance may provide enough reassurance or raise enough doubt that some of these people refrain from judgment. People of this second group may be persuaded to support politicians who make their racist or false utterances *in the right way*; or alternatively they may be persuaded simply not to oppose them so strongly; or to pass their messages on in the spirit of "asking questions." The main thing is that these people would be likely to oppose the obvious racist or liar if they recognized them as such, but they can be caused not to recognize them. These people will be a particularly important topic in this book, as the language used in addressing them makes an enormous difference to how they receive the claims that are made. In particular, the use of rhetoric that lends deniability has a substantial effect on these people.

The third group is the strong norm supporters, who not only support the norm but are good at recognizing violations of it. These people are not persuaded by just the right phrasing into doubting whether the utterances in question violate the norms. To them, the violations are obvious. The use of deniable rhetoric is important with respect to this group too, however: members of this group will condemn claims that have been made using deniable rhetoric, but it is more difficult to get uptake for this condemnation, and so the condemnation itself can be used to sow division. As Ian Haney López writes, "[Trump's racism was] audible by design to those in the political know but not to his supporters…[He calculated] that he could parlay charges of racism against him into aggrieved outrage among his supporters" (2019: 35).

Being explicit about these divisions helps us to work through the complexities of some powerful manipulative utterances. We will discuss all this in much more detail in the chapters to come, but an example will illustrate the general form of what we will see in greater detail later.

Consider, for illustration, Trump's call (during the 2016 election campaign) for "a total and complete shutdown of Muslims entering the United States until our country's representatives can figure out what is going on" (Johnson 2015). This is widely (and correctly) seen as blatantly racist. Blatant racism used to be seen as something that was unacceptable in political speech. Yet Trump succeeded. Let's look at how the various groups outlined above seem to have reacted.

The group that supports anti-racism norms and is good at recognizing their violations recognized this for the racism that it is, condemned it, and considered such a level of racism to mean that Trump was not an acceptable candidate for President.

Unsurprisingly, those who oppose the norm against racism may well be very happy to see themselves and those they support as racist. These people are the ones who warmly embraced the thought of a racist candidate, and who liked the racism of utterances like this one.

The really interesting group, for our purposes, is the one made up of people who would be moved by the very specific way that this utterance is phrased. The end of the utterance is the key here: it is what I call a figleaf, a bit of speech that provides cover for what might otherwise be easily recognized as racist. The fact that the ban is to be *just until we figure out what's going on* provides some cover for racism—a racist, some think, would expect whatever the problem is to be a permanent one, not one to be solved by a temporary ban. For this group, the figleaf may raise just enough doubt about the utterance's racism that they are reassured.

The careful phrasing induces the persuadable group to go along with it, or at least to be uncertain about opposing it. But this isn't all that it does. Both the racism and the manipulative utterance fuel the (rightful) anger of those who strongly support the anti-racism norm. This anger helps to foment division. As fascist leaders have known for some time, making one's followers feel under threat from others is a powerful technique to motivate strong loyalty (Stanley 2018). The mere fact that some people will make accusations of racism helps to motivate those who have come to support Trump, whether because they are proud racists, because they have been convinced that there is no norm violation, or because they are uncertain about whether there is a violation. The careful phrasing plays a key role here: if the racism is at least somewhat disguised, then some will see the reaction against it as inappropriately judgmental. Opposing this may move them from uncertainty to defensive support for the person who made the racist utterance.

This book is very focused on the rhetoric used in public speech that has succeeded in making blatant racism and obvious falsehood a surprisingly effective political strategy. A part of what we will be trying to understand is how individuals may be motivated to support, or at least not oppose, a candidate spouting blatant racism and falsehood. But a crucial part of this project is to reject a strict dichotomy between individualistic and structural approaches. What happens to these individuals is not just a matter of their individual psychology, but a matter of the forces that act upon them in their society and social subgroup. And the results of these effects upon individuals are very much felt at societal and structural levels. When enough individuals become convinced of a conspiracy theory which holds that Donald Trump really won the 2020 election, for example, they may band together to stage an insurrection. And perhaps even more importantly, the widespread belief that the election was stolen serves to underpin efforts to disenfranchise voters of color on a massive scale. If successful, these moves will enhance the already massive structural barriers against any effort to reduce oppression. (For more on interactions between the individual and the structural, see Madva (2016).)

Below, I summarize the overall shape of the book with a chapter breakdown.

1. White Racism, White Racial Folk Theory, and White Racial Discourse

Chapter 1 provides essential background and scene-setting to understand the racial rhetoric that will be explored in Chapters 2 and 3. It explores the deeply flawed folk theory that many White people subscribe to about race (Hill 2008; Bonilla-Silva 2002, 2018). This theory allows its subscribers to think of themselves and those they support as not being racist. One part of this theory involves setting a very high bar for what is required to be racist and combining it with lots of excuses for why apparently racist behavior or speech might not really be racist. This goes hand-in-hand with a conception of racists as a kind of moral monster, to be feared and reviled, but also probably so rare that we would not encounter them much in everyday life. This fits well with the fact that political discourse since the Civil Rights Movement was (until recently) thought to be governed by what Tali Mendelberg (2001) called the Norm of Racial Equality, which rules out open expression of racism. At the same time, however, White people continued to harbor high levels of what psychologists call "racial resentment". Politicians who could find a way to appeal to that racial resentment while not being too obvious about it have long been able to do very well in US politics. Until the election of 2016, in fact, it was widely believed that a politician openly expressing racist sentiments could not longer succeed on a national scale in US politics. This state of affairs helped to give birth to the sorts of deniability-seeking mechanisms discussed in Chapter 2.

2. Racist Dogwhistles

Chapter 2 explores one of the most-discussed techniques for appealing to racial resentment without running afoul of the Norm of Racial Equality: the dogwhistle. (The metaphor is derived from special whistles used for dogs, which cannot be heard by humans.) The account of dogwhistles developed here differs from others in the academic literature by insisting on a bifurcated approach (building on Saul (2018, 2019; Drainville and Saul, forthcoming).[6] Racist dogwhistles, I argue, come in two main varieties that work very differently.

- Overt Code[7] racist dogwhistles work like a secret code, designed to be understood by one group (those who don't accept norms against racism) and not recognized by the others. A paradigm case of this would be codes—like "88" to mean "Heil Hitler"—used by White supremacists on the Internet to communicate with each other in such a way as to evade detection by hate speech algorithms.
- Covert Effect[8] racist dogwhistles act on some of the people who accept the anti-racism norm without their awareness of this, causing them to base their decisions on racial resentments. One way of doing this, which we will discuss later in the book, is to avoid racial terms, but use racialized imagery. We will see that words like "welfare" have also been shown to work in this way.

Dogwhistles are, importantly, also propagated and spread by those who are not aware of what they are doing—who, for example, use an item of White supremacist code without realizing that is what it is. This is a crucial part of the functioning of dogwhistles. It helps them to spread, and it also is the foundation for deniability. If one *might* use a dogwhistle innocently, there is so much more plausibility to claiming that this is what one has done. Moreover, disputes over whether something really is a dogwhistle both derive from and feed the division that is so central to our discussion. This chapter, then, explores some of the complexities of this deniable mode of communication.

3. Figleaves for Racism

Chapter 3 tackles the pressing and difficult issue of how it is that blatant racism has recently become so much more mainstream in US politics. I argue that a key mechanism is the use of what I call "racial figleaves" (Saul 2017, 2019a, 2019b, 2021). Figleaves' artistic namesake is used by artists to literally cover the body parts one is not supposed to show in public. Racial figleaves are additional bits of speech which provide metaphorical cover for utterances that would otherwise be seen as clearly racist.[9] These sometimes immediately accompany the racist utterance, as in "I'm not a racist, but…." And they sometimes appear at a different time, often when a speaker is accused of racism ("But some of my best friends are Black" is a classic choice for these times). Figleaves, of course, are not for everyone. The proud racists are not bothered by the racism and the strong supporters of anti-racism norms will mostly not be convinced by them. But they can be effective with the middle group—those who don't want to be racist, but can be convinced that the utterance wasn't racist after all; or maybe just come to doubt its racism enough to look the other way.

Figleaves have been particularly important to Donald Trump, who uses them regularly. They even played a role in Trump's announcement of his candidacy, in which he suggested that Mexicans were rapists but bizarrely added, "And some, I assume, are good people" (Phillips 2017). This strange addition did valuable work for Trump as a figleaf. Unsurprisingly, White people's immensely flawed understandings of racism play a crucial role in the working of figleaves, as does the vagueness of the anti-racism norm. Together, these make it very easy for many White people to convince themselves that they (and those they care about) are not making racist utterances.

And even when they do not convince themselves of this, they may succeed in raising just enough doubt that they don't feel the need to abandon a candidate they feel drawn to. This chapter explores the nature of figleaves in detail, arguing that they are especially important because of their capacity to shift understandings of what counts as racism.

4. The Rise of Blatant Falsehood

In Chapter 4, I turn my attention from blatant racism to blatant falsehood. As already noted, another shocking feature of our present time is the current prevalence of extremely obvious falsehoods in political discourse. These include wildly implausible conspiracy theories, of the sort that would previously have ended the political careers of anyone endorsing them. I am far from the first person to attempt to make some sense of this situation, and in Chapter 4 I lay out important features of the ways that my conceptualization differs from others. Once more, a key difference will be my attention to the importance of recognizing different reactions from different groups in the population. I argue, for example, that a claim cannot simply be classified as a bald-faced lie, one so obvious that its utterer knows that they will not be believed. For almost any political claim that we are tempted to call a bald-faced lie, there will be some who find it believable. Similarly, I resist the impulse to make sweeping claims about the thinking of conspiracy theorists, since there are important variations among these. This recognition of differences across the population turns out to play a crucial role in understanding how politicians who propagate blatant falsehoods and conspiracy theories can succeed. It also plays a crucial role in key rhetorical moves that are used in propagating these falsehoods, as discussed below.

5. Figleaves, and Dogwhistles, for Falsehood

Just as they facilitated the rise of blatant racism, dogwhistles and figleaves have facilitated the rise of blatant falsehood. Chapter 5 explores their functioning, against the background of the Norm of Truthfulness. Starting with figleaves, we see how the many available interpretations of this norm give rise to a wide range of figleaves. These figleaves—such as "lots of people are saying" or "Im just asking questions" have played a vital role in helping to move wild conspiracist theories into the mainstream of US politics and political discourse. They have helped to normalize ideas that would once have been so far outside the bounds of the reasonable that any politician who took them seriously would have lost their election. Figleaves have helped to convince people that maybe the claims are worth considering after all; or that perhaps this is a joking context where truth doesn't matter; and so on. As we will see, the use of figleaves has allowed people to feel just comfortable enough with messages widely seen as false that they are willing to support those who utter them, or to pass on the messages as worthy of consideration. As was the case with blatantly racist speech, those with this attitude of half-hearted acceptance have played an important role in the propagation of blatant falsehood. Figleaves, I argue, have been crucial to this.

Dogwhistles have also played a role, if a somewhat lesser one. The QAnon Conspiracy theory, based around the idea of coded messages revealed and spread online, is perfectly suited to the use of Overt Code dogwhistles. And indeed these have played a clear and documentable role in the spread of the theory—sometimes through deliberate and actual use of dogwhistle terms, and sometimes through (almost certainly) false attribution of coded messages.

6. Obvious Falsehoods without Deniability

Importantly, not all of the blatant falsehoods of the Trump era have required figleaves. As elsewhere in the story I'm telling, divisions between groups play a crucial role. Some groups genuinely believe the blatant falsehoods and therefore do not require figleaves at all. Others thoroughly reject the blatant falsehoods, and are not moved by figleaves. But others are much more puzzling—these are the people who recognize the falsehoods as bald-faced lies, and yet continue to support the liars. Chapter 6 delves into the question of how this can be, and argues that the answer is to be found in the work that bald-faced lies do for authoritarian leaders.

7. Dogwhistles, Figleaves, and the Fight against Racism and Blatant Falsehood

This final chapter turns to the difficult but important question of how to respond to the rhetorical moves that have been the topic of this book. It is of necessity a somewhat speculative chapter, since responses to figleaves have not been studied empirically. However, some things are clear. It is clear that the kinds of responses to dogwhistles that worked in the past—for example, discussing the racist message openly—do not work now. It is also clear that the divisions which have been central to our discussion mean that simple factual corrections of blatant falsehood will rarely succeed. Finally, it's more than clear that dogwhistle and figleaf phrases—which have both innocent and less innocent uses—cannot be dealt with via any automated moderation online.

I argue that dogwhistles and figleaves are almost certainly best dealt with by the sort of pro-active solution known as inoculation. People need to be taught to recognize and understand how these techniques work, and given an awareness of how they are used to manipulate them. For example, it is all too easy to suppose that if someone mitigates an otherwise appalling utterance with some phrase that seems to backtrack a bit (that is, a figleaf), this makes the entire utterance less dangerous and concerning. If what I have argued here is correct, it may in fact make the entire utterance far *more* dangerous and concerning. Realizing this could lead to an important shift in how people view political discourse, and hopefully also in what they are willing to tolerate and amplify both in face-to-face conversations and on social media. Importantly, though, even here more detail is needed. Developing and testing techniques that will work for such education is no trivial task. My hope is that this book can serve as a catalyst for doing so.

As I write this, Joe Biden is President and Donald Trump is facing a large number of indictments. But that does not mean this topic has ceased to matter. Even if the current state of affairs meant that explicit racism and blatant falsehood *were* on the retreat, this project would be worth doing: it would be worth understanding their rise so that we could avoid facilitating it in the future. But that is not our situation. As I write, the overwhelming majority of Republican voters say that they believe a conspiracy theory holding that Trump actually won the 2020 election. The stolen election claims have been used to institute measures that suppress the Black vote across the country. Republican politicians who dare to oppose this theory have been forced out of leadership roles, Donald Trump is universally accepted as the leading candidate to be Republican nominee for President in 2024 and recent polls show him roughly tied with Joe Biden. And authoritarian leaders continue to rise around the world, using strategies of division, racism, and wildly implausible conspiracy theorizing. This topic remains all too relevant.

But I nonetheless want to end this introduction on a slightly more hopeful note. The very blatantness of the racism and falsehood has also galvanized extremely strong social movements against those propagating them. The people pouring into airports in instant response to the first attempted Muslim ban (https://www.theguardian.com/us-news/2017/jan/29/protest-trump-travel-ban-muslims-airports) contrasted sharply, for me, with the near-total absence of opposition to the equally xenophobic British Prime Minister at the time, Theresa May. May's policies were at least as anti-immigrant as Trump's, but she cultivated an air of respectability that made it all too easy for many people not to notice what she was doing. This was not Trump's approach. His racism and falsehood were (and were likely meant to be) extremely obvious not just to his strongest supporters but also to his strongest opponents. (As we have seen, it was for the people in the middle that he engaged in deniability tactics.) This overtness was a highly successful way of exploiting and deepening divisions. But it also meant that the racism and falsehood were out in the open and—to a large number of people—undeniable. The strength of the movement against him as a result provides a kind of hope. If we can understand what has happened, and how to fight it, there are many who are more than ready to join in the battle.

I
RACISM

1
RACISM

1

White Racism, White Folk Racial Theory, and White Racial Discourse

Hard as it may be to imagine from our current vantage point, there was a time not that long ago when it seemed, even to experts on the subject, as though racist sentiments were being driven further and further underground. They by no means believed that racism itself was dying out, but rather that the social acceptability of expressing it openly had been decisively defeated. Indeed, experts predicted that the subtlety would be ever-increasing. Here's one such prediction, from Hurwitz and Peffley:

> One must wonder if the norm of political correctness and the fear of being accused of racialization have driven racial appeals even further underground, possibly to the point where virtually any presentation of race—in audible or printed narrative or in pictures—has become practically verboten. If so, the racialization of politics will increasingly take place mainly at the level of code words, or words that are fundamentally non-racial in nature that have, through the process of association, assumed a strong racial component...We may pre-suppose that modern battles will be far less obvious in nature and will rely instead on the subtle introduction of strategic words or phrases with racial connotations. (2005: 101)

It's a bit of an understatement to say that Hurwitz and Peffley's prediction was wrong. It is important to pause and appreciate just what a shift took place between 2005 and 2016. Hurwitz and Peffley predicted that racial appeals would become ever more subtle and underground, and instead we found ourselves with Donald Trump, who launched his campaign with this infamous utterance:

> When Mexico sends its people, they're not sending their best. They're not sending you. They're not sending you. They're sending people that have lots of problems, and they're bringing those problems with [them].

They're bringing drugs. They're bringing crime. They're rapists. And some,
I assume, are good people.   (Phillips 2017)

Not much later, Trump announced his desire to ban Muslims, calling for
"a total and complete shutdown of Muslims entering the United States
until our country's representatives can figure out what is going on"
(Johnson 2015).

What happened? How did this fail to doom his campaign? As we have
seen, experts were predicting a need for ever more subtle expressions of racism, and things went in entirely the opposite direction. Were the experts
always wrong about what one could get away with? Or did something about
the country change, making it possible to win elections while being much
more openly racist? In order to answer these questions, I'll begin in this
chapter by explaining why it is that political psychologists like Hurwitz and
Peffley made the prediction that they did. This will involve a close look at
political psychology, and especially at the deeply flawed ways of thinking
about race that are common among White people. (Although our focus will
be primarily on those who adhere to the deeply flawed White Folk Theory
of Racism, the fact that other White people hold different views will also be
crucial to our discussion.) In the next two chapters, I will use this understanding to explain how the carefully coded communication Hurwitz and
Peffley were familiar with took place, and to explore the nature and extent
of the changes that have occurred since.

1. Norm of Racial Equality

Hurwitz and Peffley's comments were part of an effort in political psychology to understand the phenomenon of implicit racial communication. Their
research followed on from that of Tali Mendelberg (2001), who was trying—in the early 2000s—to understand the ways that politicians made use
of White voters' racism in ways that were more subtle than they had been
prior to the Civil Rights Movement of the 1950s and 1960s. (This research
program will be central to our discussion of dogwhistles in Chapter 2.)

Prior to the Civil Rights era, Mendelberg argues, open expressions of racism were very much commonplace. During the slavery era, even abolition-
ists used vile language, describing slaves as "brutish, ignorant, idle, crafty,
bloody, thievish, mistrustful, and superstitious" (Mendelberg 2001: 30).
Widespread acceptance and use of such rhetoric, especially in political

speech, is what Mendelberg refers to as the Norm of Racial Inequality. During subsequent US history, this norm waxed and waned in force. At various points in time, one party or another moved away from such racist rhetoric. Also, at various points there was sufficient agreement between the parties on racial issues that these topics receded from prominence in political campaigns. An important change took place, however, with the attention that US national media gave to campaigns against lynching led by Black activists and especially the National Association for the Advancement of Colored People in the early twentieth century.

Opposition to the Norm of Racial Inequality began to grow in White (especially northern) society. Mendelberg considers the 1940s and 1950s to be the point at which a different norm, the Norm of Racial Equality, *began* to emerge. Early on, the gradual emergence of this norm made no difference to southern White political speech. Congressional debates included such people as Senator James O. Eastland arguing that even African-American troops were "lazy, irresponsible, and 'of very low intelligence"' as well as guilty of raping White European women (Mendelberg 2001: 71). As the Norm of Racial Equality came into force, however, southern White politicians began to temper such rhetoric. The Democratic Party started to split over racial issues, and the wing which defended segregation called itself the States' Rights Democratic Party (also known as the Dixiecrats), referring to the right of states to maintain such institutions as slavery or segregation. This was an important moment in the development of what will turn out to be a very influential dogwhistle, as we will see in Chapter 2. Right now, the main point to make is that there was at least *some* half-hearted effort to brand the point of this party as not being about race. Still, the party's platform advocated segregation, and members of this party struggled to remain on message in terms of avoiding explicit racism. Its presidential nominee, Strom Thurmond, still said things like "all of the bayonets of the army cannot force the Negroes into our homes, schools, churches and places of recreation" (Mendelberg 2001: 73). While the Norm of Racial Equality had begun to make some appearance, then, it was not very strongly entrenched, and even among many of those who made some effort to follow it the effort was rather half-hearted.

After the Civil Rights era, however, the Norm of Racial Equality became much more fully accepted, and indeed Mendelberg argues that it came to govern national US political discourse. It forbade open expression of support for legally enforced racial segregation, legally permitted racial discrimination, and explicit claims of biological racial inferiority.[1] Extremely blatant expression of racism became a barrier to the election of a national politician. The claim here is not that all White voters adhered to the norm, but rather that enough of them did that national politicians felt the need to show some respect for it. A significant enough number of White voters adhered to the norm that politicians came to believe that they should try not to violate it. (The focus in this chapter is on the White voters who tried to follow this norm, but the ones who rejected it are important to bear in mind, and will matter in chapters to come.)

It's also well known, however, that White people displayed high levels of what psychologists call "A blend of anti-Black affect and the kind of traditional American moral values embedded in the Protestant Ethic...a moral feeling that Blacks violate such traditional American values as individualism and self-reliance, the work ethic, obedience, and discipline" (Kinder and Sears 1981: 416). Racial resentment is measured by level of agreement with items like the following:

> It's really a matter of some people not trying hard enough; if blacks would only try harder they could be just as well off as whites.
>
> (Mendelberg 2001: 131)

Initially, it may seem puzzling that the same people could display high levels of racial resentment and simultaneously care about the Norm of Racial Equality. However, the racial resentment items are actually carefully constructed in such a way that they do not include things like support for legally enforced segregation or discrimination, or open claims of biological racial inferiority. If these are all that is ruled out by the Norm of Racial Equality, then it's not so puzzling that one might both endorse the norm and display racial resentment. Still, this tension does make one want to know exactly what the content of the Norm of Racial Equality is. Unfortunately, Mendelberg never states the content of this norm.

I hold that the content of the norm is best understood very simply.

Norm of Racial Equality: *don't be racist.*

Understood in this way, the norm is indeed widely accepted and strongly held. But it is also extremely vague and open to interpretation. Unsurprisingly, people have a tendency to adopt interpretations that let themselves and those they care about off the hook. The bar for racism that is set by most White people is very high indeed, one that allows them to endorse racial resentment items while thinking that they are not being racist.[2] To understand more about how this works, it will help to have in place some of the work of sociologists and sociolinguists on how (many) White people think about race, which is what we will examine in the next section.

First, though, I want to consider the possibility that the norm is really something like: *don't be seen as racist.* The idea behind this formulation is that White people following the norm are more concerned with how they are seen by others than with how they actually are. I think this has to be considered a live possibility. Indeed, psychologists have long distinguished between internal and external motivations to control prejudice. An especially important discussion of these differences comes from Plant and Devine (1998). According to them, an internal motivation comes from "internalized and personally important" convictions, while an external motivation comes from "social pressure to comply with nonprejudiced norms" (Plant and Devine 1998: 813). They develop an influential scale to distinguish these, but note that they are difficult to tease apart, and that much research fails to do so. It needs to be borne in mind, then, that White people may follow and interpret the norm in ways consistent with either internal or external motivation. They may be concerned with *not being racist* only when they think this might be observed; or they may privately see the norm as only about *appearing* racist.

2. White Folk Theory of Racism

2.1 Basic Tenets of the White Folk Theory of Racism

Sociolinguist Jane Hill (2008) and sociologist Eduardo Bonilla-Silva (Bonilla-Silva and Forman 2000; Bonilla-Silva 2002, 2018) have studied the deeply flawed ways that White Americans tend to think about race. Hill calls this the White Folk Theory of Racism, and Bonilla-Silva describes it as the theory of Color-Blind Racism. Although there are differences between the ways that these two theorists describe this belief system, what matters for my purposes is to draw out a broad understanding based upon the work of both of these scholars.

According to the White Folk Theory, races are a matter of biology (Hill 2008: 6; Bonilla-Silva 2002: 42), and to be a racist is to believe "that people of colour are *biologically* [emphasis mine] inferior to Whites" (Hill 2008: 6).

A person who makes claims of *cultural* inferiority, then, will not be a racist. This is why, Bonilla-Silva notes, Whites tend to hold that explanations of racial inequalities should be given a cultural explanation (Bonilla-Silva 2002: 42). Moreover, it is not possible to be racist against groups that are not biologically defined, since they are not races. We can see this theory at work in the following anecdote:

> A supporter at a recent rally defended Trump against the charge of racism by insisting, "He didn't say nothing about the color of somebody's skin." By implication, if Trump attacks people's culture, religion or country of origin but avoids mentioning biology, it's not racism.
>
> (Haney López 2019b)

The White Folk Theory makes very restrictive claims about what is required to be racist. It includes what Hill calls "personalist ideology."[3] With respect to racism, this means that "racism is entirely a matter of individual [conscious][4] beliefs, intentions, and actions" (Hill 2008: 6). But what people say or do may misrepresent their real self with regard to racism. According to this view, the truth about what a person believes, and so about whether they are racist or not, is to be found in their *heart*. It is difficult to access this truth, and therefore tricky to be sure whether someone is racist or not. This is especially the case because people's *heads* often lead them to carelessly say things that sound racist despite their non-racist *hearts*:

> Language that comes from the "heart" is the authentic voice of a person's intentional core, but when we hear the "head" we hear only superficial and fleeting expressions that can include "mis-speaking", "blundering", "mistakes", and "poorly chosen words". (Hill 2008: 105)

Hill illustrates the functioning of this White Folk Theory by discussing an incident which temporarily derailed the career of politician Trent Lott. While Majority Leader of the US Senate, in 2002, Lott attended an event in honor of Strom Thurmond, and referenced his time as presidential candidate of the States' Rights Party:

> I want to say this about my state: When Strom Thurmond ran for president, we voted for him. We're proud of it. And if the rest of the country had followed our lead, we wouldn't have had all these problems over all these years, either. (Hill 2008: 99)

It is very difficult to read this utterance as anything other than a statement that we would have been better off if the country had chosen a segregationist for President. As a result, a firestorm of controversy built up, and eventually forced Lott out of his leadership role (though he did subsequently move into other major roles in the party). The defense of Lott made repeated reference to the head/heart distinction. Lott himself said that he had made "a mistake of the head, not of the heart" (Hill 2008: 103). Defenders of Lott made the same claim: "I think this was a mistake of the head, not of the heart" (Representative J. C. Watts, quoted in Hill 2008: 104). They also referenced the great difficulty of knowing whether someone is racist or not, on the assumption that this is a fact about their heart that may not be apparent: "one should be very hesitant about ascribing bigotry. It is hard to discern what someone feels in his heart of hearts" (Charles Krauthammer, quoted in Hill 2008: 104).

As a result of this head–heart distinction, and the very restrictive view of what is required to be racist, there are many things that can serve as evidence that someone is not racist, according to the White Folk Theory. For example, if someone has friendships with members of a racialized group, this will often be cited as evidence that they are not racist. The same goes for other evidence of positive behavior or attitudes toward individual members of a racialized group. Both Bonilla-Silva and Hill mention these conversational moves as parts of the theories of racism they discuss, but they do not state a particular belief that underpins them. It seems to me likely that these moves are underpinned by the belief that a racist would have negative beliefs about or attitudes toward all members of the group that is the target of the racism. The general picture we have drawn also fits well with findings from psychology about "lay theories" of racism:

> Because of the uniquely polarizing and controversial nature of ideas about race…people's theories of racism tend to be constructed in ways that allow them to maintain a safe distance from any appearance of personal bias.   (Sommers and Norton 2006: 119)

If a person accepts the folk theory of racism described above, it may be very easy for them to become convinced not to worry about an utterance—or even an action—that might at first seem to be racist. If they think, for example, that only people (and not utterances) can be racist, convincing them that the person who made the utterance was not racist is enough to make them stop worrying about the utterance. And we have seen that it is very easy to do this. One might simply insist that they are not racist in their heart. Having a friend of another race absolves one of worries about racism. And so on.

2.2 The Exonerating Image of the Racist

It is no surprise, given all that we have seen about the White Folk Theory of Racism, that on this theory racists are believed to be very rare. Hill writes that according to this theory racists are "ignorant, vicious, and remote from the mainstream" (2008: 6).[5] The idea of the racist as "vicious and remote from the mainstream" is highly reminiscent of the effects of the widespread conception of rapists as monsters. Susan Brison notes that while rapes by intimate partners are often not seen as crimes at all, those rapes which are recognized (generally those by strangers) are seen the actions of "a psychopath, a monster, 'not one of us'" (2006: 263).[6] Barrett Emerick and Audrey Yap argue that the conception of the rapist as a monstrous figure serves as a barrier to recognizing that non-monstrous people may be rapists:

> After all, the idea that there is a type of person that commits sexual assault
> implies that people who do not fit into that category are correspondingly
> not that kind of person...the step we want to avoid is the inference from
> the fact that sexual violence is a serious matter and can do immense harm,
> to the claim that the perpetrators of sexual violence have a particular kind
> of irredeemable, inhuman, or otherwise monstrous nature. As mentioned
> earlier, a close association between sexual violence and a particular kind
> of moral character makes it too easy to dismiss any claims against people
> who do not seem to have that type of character.
>
> (Emerick and Yap forthcoming: 3)[7]

In the case of racism, the dynamic is a similar one. And the language used is similar. Famously, Hillary Clinton characterized many Trump supporters as a "basket of deplorables":

> "You know, to just be grossly generalistic, you could put half of Trump's
> supporters into what I call the basket of deplorables. Right?" Clinton said.
> "The racist, sexist, homophobic, xenophobic, Islamophobic—you name it.
> And unfortunately there are people like that. And he has lifted them up.
>
> (Reilly 2016)

On this understanding, racism is not a mainstream phenomenon with which all of us will have had personal experiences. Instead it is relegated to the "deplorables." This sort of language can make it difficult to recognize one's coworkers, neighbors, friends, and even self as harboring racist attitudes. In short, if one's paradigm case of a racist is a hood-wearing KKK member who supports legally enforced segregation and openly uses the very worst racial slurs, one may have difficulty recognizing anyone less obvious than this as a racist. Any evidence that a person does not fit this paradigm will allow for the dismissal of claims of racism.

This extreme view of a racist, like that of a rapist, serves as what Emerick and Yap call an "exonerating image": "Exonerating images function to ensure that members of the dominant group cannot be recognized (and responded to) as wrongdoers" (forthcoming: 11). We can extend this idea, when considering racism, to note that exonerating images are not just about wrong *actions*. Such images may also ensure that members of the dominant group are not seen as racists or makers of racist *utterances*. This exoneration is what Shen-Yi Liao (2016) refers to when he suggests that racists are made into unicorns:

> Racists are now made into unicorns. Well, at least the word "racist" is made to be like the word "unicorn". Of course, unlike unicorns, racists are still with us. But at least our language has been untethered from reality so that we can no longer talk about them.

The adherence to this paradigm of racist as monster has the apparent advantage of taking seriously the importance of racism. But it has the unfortunate effect of keeping us from seeing its ubiquity. Michelle Moody-Adams (1994) discusses a similar dynamic that Hannah Arendt draws attention to in her famous work on the banality of evil, and how difficult it can be to appreciate Arendt's point:

> Hannah Arendt insisted that "the trouble with Eichmann was precisely that so many were like him, and that the many were neither perverted nor sadistic, that they were, and still are, terribly and terrifyingly normal." Arendt wanted to convince us that ordinary citizens can do evil—even extraordinary evil; moreover, they can come to view such evil, and their participation in it, as "routine." Some of Arendt's early critics were deeply troubled by her now-famous assertion of the "banality of evil" because

they thought that it threatened to trivialize the horrors of Nazism. But in their distress they overlooked a central point of that assertion. Arendt wanted to reject, as a barrier to understanding, the all-too-common assumption that only "sick" or "monstrously insane" people could commit the terrifying evils of Nazi concentration camps.

A crucial part of the flawed understandings of racism that are prevalent among White people, then, is the idea that racists are rare and monstrous figures. On this kind of a view, it is impossible to understand that good people can do racist things, that racism is ubiquitous, and that racism can be found in structures and institutions, not just the hearts of Klan members.

2.3 What's Wrong with the White Folk Theory of Racism?

While the White Folk Theory of Racism is widely held among White Americans, it is not an understanding of racism that any serious scholar on the subject would embrace. There is substantial disagreement over exactly how to define "racism,"[8] but there is no serious theory of racism which functions like the White Folk Theory does. In particular, it is clear that any reasonable theory of racism must allow for the following:

- It is not just individuals who can be racist, but also, among other things, words (like the n-word); institutions (as in the findings of the Lawrence Inquiry (Macpherson 1999) in the UK, that the Metropolitan Police were "institutionally racist"); or laws (like voter ID laws that systematically make it more difficult for some racial groups to vote). Indeed, it is widely accepted that the current global order—wealthy countries, so-called "developing countries," and the international organizations that regulate their interactions—is racist.[9]
- Individuals can be racist without being monsters who hate all members of the racial group against which they are racist (a very explicit racist might genuinely like the server who waits on them, for example).
- Individuals can be racist without seeing racial groups as biologically defined.
- Individual racism is not just a matter of conscious beliefs, but can also be a matter of less conscious phenomena, or of other attitudes.

Among scholars of race and racism, none of these are remotely controversial views. I will treat them as established. In this book, my focus will be on the ways that the White Folk Theory of Racism interacts with certain linguistic mechanisms to aid in the rise of explicit racism in political discourse. In order to understand this, we don't need to decide on one of the many definitions of "racism" that there are. It is enough to know a bit about what racism is not. And racism is decidedly *not* what the White Folk Theory takes it to be.

2.4 An Objection

It is important to my picture that the Norm of Racial Equality is widely accepted, even amongst people who adhere to the deeply flawed White Folk Theory of Racism.[10] And this does, I think, have a great deal of intuitive plausibility: after all, many of these people would sincerely say true things like "it's important not to be racist." However, these people are also seriously misguided about certain other important matters. If they think, for example, that racism requires a conscious hatred of all members of a group, they are simply wrong about racism. So does it really seem right to say that they accept the norm *don't be racist*? For comparison, consider the norm that *one should remove one's muddy shoes before entering a house*. Now imagine a person who thinks "shoes" means *gloves*, and who would never remove their muddy *shoes* when entering a house. We would not describe this person as accepting the norm of removing their muddy shoes. By parallel reasoning, consider the person who thinks it's not racist to believe that Black people just need to try harder, and who claims to think it's terrible to be racist. One might well insist that they are simply not talking about racism— due to their deep misunderstanding of what racism is.

However, this move is too fast. The people with differing understandings of racism are not using the term as differently as the person who thinks "shoes" means *gloves*. They are all meaning *something* having to do with thought or treatment connected to race. Those who accept the Norm of Racial Equality may well further agree that this is wrongful thought or treatment. This is well captured in standard dictionary definitions of "racist," which offer a fairly broad range of things which might count as racist.[11] Anyone who uses the word "racist" roughly in accord with one of these meanings is—by the standards of our shared language—talking about racism, even if they are making some false claims about it. (This contrasts sharply with the person who uses "shoes" to mean *gloves*: that person seems deeply confused about the language.) Importantly, they are also likely to believe some true things about racism: they agree that a person who hates all members of a race is a racist, and that one who deliberately discriminates against members of a race is a racist. Despite considerable disagreements, there are also important areas of agreement.

There is an important difference between misusing a word so badly that one has changed the subject and saying false things about the subject matter. We need to be able to say that someone who says "you're not a racist unless you consciously intend to discriminate" is making false claims about *racism*, rather than talking about something else. If we insist that the people who accept the White Folk Theory of Racism are talking about something other than racism, we lose the ability to say that—by accepting this theory—they are wrong about racism. We also lose the ability to recognize that they are in other ways right about racism. If they're not talking about racism, then identifying areas of agreement and disagreement makes no sense: they're just talking about something else. For all these reasons, it seems right to insist that—within a pretty broad range—those with a variety of views about the nature of racism all do count as talking about racism. The people who sincerely say "it's wrong to be racist," then, do count as accepting the Norm of Racial Equality, even though they are wrong about what it is to be racist.

3. Other Prejudices?

A fairly wide variety of prejudices are frequently referred to as instances of racism. These include religious and national prejudices—particularly perhaps if the nationality or religious group is stereotypically thought of as dark-skinned. Yet it is not straightforward to consider these to be racial groups, on the White Folk Theory of Racism. After all, these groups are not biologically defined: people can convert to a different religion, or become citizens of a different country. Nonetheless, they are frequently considered racism, and they loom large in discussions of Trump's racism.

In fact, there is substantial controversy over whether religious or national prejudice constitute forms of racism. Anna Sophie Lauwers (2019), for example, distinguishes between anti-Muslim *racism* and anti-Islam religious bigotry. The latter is not racism, she argues, because it does not involve a commitment to innate and unchangeable characteristics. On the other hand, Anya Topolski (2018) traces the origins of the European concept of race to argue that concepts of race and religion have historically been deeply intertwined, and that it is a mistake to view racial and religious prejudice as wholly distinct. Modood and Sealy argue for the importance of recognizing cultural racism, "in which issues or groups come to be understood through racial meanings, construed as processes of essentialism and determinism that pick out not just—or not even—aspects of physical appearance, but aspects of cultural or religious beliefs, practices, values or behaviour" (2022: 3). They argue that this is vital to understanding the ways that racism works, in particular with respect to religious groups and prejudice against eastern European immigrants in the UK.

But we don't need to delve into these issues here. What we need here is to understand what *commonplace* understandings of racism look like. And it seems clear that these do make room for at least the possibility of religious or national prejudice constituting racism. This wouldn't be the case if it were just academics or a small number of activists who consider these forms of prejudice to be racism. But what we have seen in discussions of Donald Trump makes it clear that it is very common to call these prejudices racism. Importantly, victims of these prejudices frequently describe them as racism. And those who hold these prejudices may well see the relevant groups in ways that are generally thought to be racializing—as sharing innate traits, as possessing similar appearances or ancestry, and even as biologically defined. Nonetheless, it also very common to encounter the idea that religious or national prejudice should not be thought of as racism.

These sorts of prejudices are, then, a kind of borderline case for adherents to the White Folk Theory of Racism. Some will see them as clearly forms of racism, while others will strenuously disagree. Yet others will harbor some uncertainty, which can be—we will see—exploited.

4. White Ignorance

The White Folk Theory of Racism will often lead to ignorance about whether oneself or someone else is in fact a racist. This is, arguably, a form of what Michelle Moody-Adams calls "affected ignorance—choosing not to know what one can and should know" (1994: 296). This sort of ignorance, according to Moody-Adams, "hinders understanding of how wrongdoing begins, and engenders a self-deceptive complacency about the potential each individual human being has to support and engage in morally culpable conduct" (1994: 299).

The White Folk Theory of Racism described by Hill, combined with the exonerating image of a racist as a hood-wearing Klan member, is a perfect example of the sort of false theory that props up the broader system that Charles Mills has called White Ignorance: "a non-knowing, that is not contingent, but in which race—white racism and/or white racial domination—plays a crucial causal role" (2007: 20). Two of several key mechanisms Mills discusses for maintaining White Ignorance are the use of flawed concepts and false reigning theories. The White Folk Theory of Racism is clearly a deeply flawed theory, and the concepts of *racism* and *racist* being used are immensely distorting and damaging. This theory and these concepts allow White people to avoid facing up to racism even when it is very blatant. The maintenance of this sort of view of racism is no accident. As Joé Medina notes, there are some things that privileged people need "not to know" (2013: 34). That one is oneself a racist, or that a loved one is, or even an admired political figure, is just the sort of thing that many people need not to know.

Medina describes people who hold this sort of view as suffering from epistemic vices. They "can be blamed not just for lacking particular pieces of knowledge but also for having epistemic attitudes and habits that contribute to create and maintain bodies of ignorance" (2013: 39). But Medina is also right to maintain that this is not just a matter of individual decisions to have some false beliefs. It is important to contextualize these individual epistemic vices by understanding their social situation:

> We become active participants in collective bodies of ignorance typically without knowing it and apparently without much conscious effort on our part, but this is because there is a complex set of social structures, procedures, and practices that encourage us to go on with our daily business without taking an interest in certain things, without challenging certain presuppositions and stereotypes, and without even learning to ask questions about distortions that are simply taken for granted automatically and habitually in the way we think and act.   (Medina 2013: 145)

The image of the racist as monster is not one that White people are often encouraged to challenge. The White Folk Theory of Racism is a comfortable one, one that provides a helpful reassurance that one is not after all one of those monstrous racists. These help to sustain each other, in concert with a social milieu in which they are widely accepted and often seen as common sense.

Importantly, the White people who subscribe to the White Folk Theory of Racism and the exonerating image of racists as vicious Klan members *do* have the ability to learn otherwise. In fact, they may well have been exposed to arguments against these views, over and over again. Certainly arguments in favor of recognizing racism that does not fit these models have had a prominent place in our public discourse, at least in recent years. People of color, moreover, have been arguing against these claims for a very long time. And yet these arguments have failed to get purchase for many people. A key reason for this is likely to be what Gaile Pohlhaus (2012) calls willful herme-neutical ignorance: the active refusal of dominantly situated people to make use of the hermeneutical tools that have been developed by marginalized people, which would help them to understand the world more adequately. Usually, this is because these tools would reveal things that the dominantly situated people don't want to see.

The upshot is that White people who subscribe to the false theories just outlined can be very easily convinced that they themselves are not racist, and that those they admire or support are not racist. This is important, because large numbers of White people also subscribe to the Norm of Racial Equality, and therefore want to avoid thinking of themselves, or those they support, as racist. The deeply problematic theories of racism that many White people hold make it possible for politicians to manipulate this desire, as later chapters will make clear.

5. Division

It is important to emphasize that the claims being made in this chapter about White thinking on the topic of race are not claims about all White people. The views described are ones that are very common among White people, common enough to be characterized as mainstream White thinking by political psychologists, sociologists, and sociolinguists like Mendelberg, Bonilla-Silva, and Hill. But it's actually crucial to the sorts of manipulation we will discuss in this book that White people are far from monolithic in their thinking about race.

The first point to notice is that not all White people accept the Norm of Racial Equality. This has not been much discussed in the literature that makes use of this norm. But that makes sense, since the focus of that litera-ture (as we will see in Chapter 2) has been on how it is that people who accept this norm may nonetheless be manipulated by appeals to their racial resentments. In the broader discussion that I am undertaking, however, it is very important to note that there are people who do reject this norm, even when formulated as simply as "don't be racist." These are the people who are quite happy to be racist. Some of them do wear hoods and join White supremacist organizations. Others, however, are not active in this way but nonetheless hold these views, perhaps only admitting them to a few close friends or relatives. For people who reject the Norm of Racial Equality, racists are not monsters; they believe that those who think racism is bad are deeply misguided. These people are obviously crucial to the rise of both Trump and explicit racism, and they perpetrate enormous harms, including acts of great violence against people of color. However, racist politicians can communicate with them very straightforwardly, without any careful linguistic constructions or maneuvering. They are a vital part of what has been happening, and will be important for our discussion. But the motivation for the linguistic maneuvers that are our primary focus comes from those White people who accept both the Norm of Racial Equality and the White Folk Theory of Racism. These people are manipulable by politicians who want to play on their racism, but this manipulation must be more carefully performed.

White people also deviate from what we have discussed thus far, in the other direction. They vary in their levels of racial resentment, with some White people displaying low levels of racial resentment, or even none. Importantly, many White people actually reject the White Folk Theory of Racism described in this chapter. It is increasingly common for White people to recognize the existence not just of conscious intentional racism, but also implicit racism and structural racism. Very many White people do not think of race as a biological category, and reject the use made of the head–heart dichotomy. Finally, White people increasingly recognize the ubiquity of racism, and that one does not need to be an unusual moral monster to act or speak in racist ways. Particularly since the rise of the Black Lives Matter movement, there has been increasing awareness among White people of both structural racism and implicit bias. Books intended to teach White people how to be less racist have shot to the top of the bestseller lists, and White people have increasingly joined in anti-racist actions and protests.

There are, then, increasing numbers of White people who reject the White Folk Theory of Racism. These people recognize that racism may be structural, and may not be conscious and intentional. They know that people without bad intentions or conscious racist beliefs play a crucial role in perpetuating and facilitating racial power structures. They recognize that racist language may be used by those who do not intend harm and may not understand the harm that they are doing. They think it is important to interrogate and understand all the ways that our actions and institutions may be racist, especially where this is not obvious to us. These people are obviously very important to the resistance against the rise of explicit racism. But they have also been skillfully and nefariously used by those who want to foment division and aid in the rise of explicit racism, as we will see in subsequent chapters.

We will see that the existence of these groups is a part of what helps the strategies explained in Chapters 2 and 3 to be so successful: pitting the groups against each other has played an important role in the rise of explicit racism in political discourse.

2

Racist Dogwhistles

In Chapter 1, we saw that the US norms of political discourse shifted over the course of the Civil Rights Movement to the point that the Norm of Racial Equality came to hold sway on a national scale. This norm meant that many White American voters did not want to see themselves or their preferred candidate as racists. Nonetheless, many of these same White American voters tended to harbor high levels of racial resentment. This meant that they could be reached by racial appeals, as long as these appeals did not fall foul of the Norm of Racial Equality.

Fortunately for politicians wanting to make such appeals, the White Folk Theory of Racism made it easy. Recall that according to this theory racists are quite rare monsters, and there are a large variety of ways to deny that any person, action, or utterance is racist. The situation was ripe for exploitation and it was—not surprisingly—exploited. A key strategy was the use of dogwhistles, which played upon racial resentments in ways that went unrecognized by at least a large proportion of voters. Although, as we have seen, dogwhistling went back well before this time, one of its most talented users was Republican mastermind Lee Atwater. We have particular clarity about the campaigns that Atwater engaged in, due to a surprisingly frank interview that he gave:

> You start out in 1954 by saying, "[N*****, n*****, n*****]." By 1968 you can't say "[n*****]"—that hurts you, backfires. So you say stuff like, uh, forced busing, states' rights, and all that stuff, and you're getting so abstract. Now, you're talking about cutting taxes, and all these things you're talking about are totally economic things and a byproduct of them is, blacks get hurt worse than whites..."We want to cut this," is much more abstract than even the busing thing, uh, and a hell of a lot more abstract than "[N*****, n*****]." (Perlstein 2012)

This very much parallels parts of what sociologist Eduardo Bonilla-Silva calls the ideology of Color-Blind Racism, which includes avoidance by White people of "direct racial language" (2002: 41), and favors "cultural rather than biological explanation of minorities' inferior standing in performance in labor and educational markets" (2002: 42). It especially precludes "saying things that sound or can be perceived as racist" (2002: 42).

In this chapter, we will closely examine the dogwhistling strategy. We will pay particular attention to differences between groups, and how the strategy allows for these divisions to be used in service of racist aims. I'll begin with some examples of how dogwhistles have been understood. Then I will move on to showing that we need to distinguish two very different ways that dogwhistles function. By the end of the chapter, we will see how dogwhistles can remain an effective strategy, even when what is going on becomes far more obvious. When this happens, dogwhistles function in a different way but may be no less effective for perpetuating racism. I will build on this in Chapter 3, which discusses the transition in our political discourse into increasingly explicit racist language.

1. Usage of Dogwhistle

First, a little pre-history. The first use of dogwhistle as a political term seems to have been by Richard Morin in a 1988 *Washington Post* article about opinion polling, and it's quite different from the usage popular today:

> Here's another example where respondents respond to something in a question that the pollster hadn't expected. Gallup and the prestigious National Opinion Research Center have both asked a question about happiness that began the same way but that in the NORC version ended, "Would you say that you are very happy, are pretty happy, or are you not too happy?" and in the Gallup version ended, "Are you very happy, are you fairly happy, or are you not too happy." The only language difference: the word "pretty" in the NORC question and the word "fairly" in the Gallup version. The results, however, differed significantly: About 15 percent more people were "very happy" when the alternative was being merely "fairly happy." Maybe they were really that happy, or maybe the pollsters offered them unacceptable choices. Anyway, researchers call this the "Dogwhistle Effect": Respondents hear something in the question that researchers do not. (Morin 1988)

It is apparent that this usage has nothing to do with racism or taboos against racism, or communicating in a deliberately manipulative manner. But it does include the idea of something going on communicatively that is not apparent. In particular, it includes the idea of one group hearing something that another group is unaware of. These ideas—of hidden effects and of different messages for different groups—form some of the foundations for the way "dogwhistle" has come to be used.

In sections 1.1 and 1.2, I'll move on to the ways the term is now used. Crucially, the term is now used in two very different ways, to pick out two different phenomena, which work very differently. At the same time, however, nearly all writers take themselves to be discussing a unitary phenomenon—despite describing just one of the ways that dogwhistles work. In sections 1.1 and 1.2, I will describe the two different ways that dogwhistles are understood. Each strand of thought, we will see, involves different definitions and different paradigm cases.

1.1 Dogwhistle as Code

Here are some representative passages which give a good picture of one of the two strands of thought about dogwhistles. (Theorists do sometimes call these by other names. Here I am only concerned with uses of the *term* "dogwhistle.")

- Language columnist and conservative speech-writer William Safire describes dogwhistles as messages "that seem innocent to a general audience but resonate with a specific public attuned to receive them" (2008: 190).
- Here's Merriam-Webster, echoing this in 2017: "a coded message communicated through words or phrases commonly understood by a particular group of people, but not by others."[1]
- Dictionary.com takes a similar line: "a political strategy, statement, slogan, etc., that conveys a controversial, secondary message understood only by those who support the message."[2]
- Urban Dictionary is also in agreement: "A dogwhistle is a type of strategy of communication that sends a message that the general population will take a certain meaning from, but a certain group that is 'in the know' will take away the secret, intended message. Often involves code words."[3]
- According to linguist Kimberly Witten, in one of the earlier academic discussions of dogwhistles, "A dogwhistle is when a person or group

sends a message containing a second interpretation that is meant to be understood by a select target person or group" (2014: 1).

- Political psychologist Ian Haney López writes in his *Dogwhistle Politics*: "In general, using a dogwhistle simply means speaking in code to a target audience. Politicians routinely do this, seeking to surreptitiously communicate support to small groups of impassioned voters whose commitments are not broadly embraced by the body politic" (2014: 4).

- Linguists Robert Henderson and Elin McCready suggest: "Dogwhistles can be defined as terms that send one message to an outgroup while at the same time sending a second (often taboo, controversial, or inflammatory) message to an ingroup" (2018: 231).

- Philosopher Anna Quaranto writes: A dogwhistle requires "a pair of practices, one shared by all competent speakers and the other known only to some" (2022: 329).

We find a nice clear example of this sort of dogwhistle in Ian Haney López's discussion of one of George Wallace's campaigns. Wallace, mentioned in Chapter 1 as well, was an old-school southern Democrat, meaning a supporter of segregation. Although he had not initially run on racism, after losing to someone who did, Wallace became an arch-segregationist. Initially, he did so by infamously declaring "segregation forever." This earned him national fame but also national ridicule. After this, Wallace discovered the power of "states' rights" as a dogwhistle:

"States' rights" was a paper-thin abstraction from the days before the Civil War when it had meant the right of Southern states to continue slavery. Then, as a rejoinder to the demand for integration, it meant the right of Southern states to continue laws mandating racial segregation.

(López 2014: 16)

But this was not the only dogwhistle that Wallace pioneered. And the dogwhistles that he used functioned as the sorts of codes described above. Here is a contemporary of his describing it, quoted by López:

He can use all the other issues—law and order, running your own schools, protecting property rights—and never mention race. But people will know he's telling them 'a [n*****'s] trying to get your job, trying to move into your neighborhood. What Wallace is doing is talking to them in a kind of shorthand, a kind of code.   (2014: 17)

This kind of dogwhistle is the one that fits the sorts of definitions most commonly given in both popular and academic discussion, where a dogwhistle is a kind of coded utterance which transmits a message to a select group that would be unacceptable to the broader audience. The select group knows the code, and happily receives the message; while the broader audience does not realize what is happening, and takes the message to have a more innocent meaning. In the case of racial dogwhistles (the most-discussed kind of dogwhistles), the coded messages are transmitted between those who are comfortable with their racism, having rejected the Norm of Racial Equality.

1.2 Willie Horton Ad as Paradigm

Now we turn to the second strand of thought, not generally distinguished clearly enough from the first one. On this line of thought, the Willie Horton ad used by George H. W. Bush against Michael Dukakis in 1988 is the paradigm case of a dogwhistle. We see this in discussions with titles like "George H. W. Bush's 'Willie Horton' ad will always be the reference point for dogwhistle racism" (Withers 2018) or "George H. W. Bush's Willie Horton ad remains flashpoint in dog-whistle politics" (Onley 2018). Strangely, many of these discussions then move to a definition like those we've seen in section 1.1, characterizing a dogwhistle as a coded message for a welcoming subgroup of the audience. But that is in fact very, very different from the way that the Willie Horton ad functioned.

The Horton ad has been deeply studied by Tali Mendelberg (2001), and her research is well known and usually cited prominently in discussions of the ad (even when these discussions are at odds with what Mendelberg says). The ad was designed by Lee Atwater, who initially denied any intent to play on racism, but then later admitted to having done so. Although popularly the ad is described as a "dogwhistle," it is often described in political psychology as an exercise in "implicit messaging." Because of the Norm of Racial Equality, Mendelberg argues, savvy operatives like Atwater knew that they could not be explicit about race. They wanted to find a way to reach and get the votes of racially resentful White people who nonetheless endorsed the Norm of Racial Equality. The idea was to make race salient to these people, without their awareness, so that they would bring it to bear on their voting decisions. The Willie Horton advertisement did this by never mentioning or using any racial terms. Instead it linked Bush's opponent, Michael Dukakis, to a prison furlough program[4] that led to the furlough of an incarcerated man, William Horton,[5] who was convicted of rape and murder committed during that furlough.[6] Crucially, the main visual for the ad was a photo of Horton, a Black man scowling at the camera. In order to be able to disavow responsibility for the ad, it was initially presented as a small, local campaign produced by an independent group. The plan, which worked beautifully, was that the incendiary ad would be played over and over again on the news. It was, as an example of crime as an issue in the campaign, and an example of negative campaigning—but race was not discussed. Although this was not the only factor that brought about Dukakis's defeat, it was a crucial element in turning his large lead into a deficit, over the course of just a few months.

Both voting intentions and levels of racial resentment were studied throughout the campaign. Mendelberg drew on these data, and learned that exposure to the ad did *not* increase White Americans' levels of racial resentment. However, it brought about an increased *correlation* between their level of racial resentment and their intention to vote for Bush. Racially resentful voters became more likely to vote for Bush as they were more exposed to the ad.

And then, the really interesting thing happened. Jesse Jackson spoke out against the ad, drawing attention to its racism. This received a great deal of media coverage, but very disrespectful coverage. Although interviews with Jackson were played on the news regularly, Jackson's claims were treated largely dismissively by mainstream media. Once the discussion of Jackson's views began, however, the correlation that had previously been present began to fall away, and the racially resentful voters began to pull back from their intention to vote for Bush. Indeed, Mendelberg believes that if the election had been held two weeks later, Dukakis would have won. Her analysis of this has become central to the way that the Willie Horton dogwhistle is understood. According to Mendelberg, the kind of messaging used in this ad raises racial attitudes to salience outside of consciousness, bringing them to bear on the issue at hand. Because of the Norm of Racial Equality, it is vital that this remain outside of consciousness. As soon as the issue of racism is openly raised, self-monitoring begins and the dogwhistle cannot function in the same way. That, according to her, is what happened when Jackson spoke up—even though his comments were treated in a dismissive, disrespectful way.

This picture of a dogwhistle, then, does not make any use of the idea that there is a coded message directed carefully at an approving group and concealed equally carefully from a disapproving group. It does not look anything at all like the definitions of dogwhistle that we saw in section 1.1. Instead, we have an obvious message that can pass as non-racial, at least to quite a lot of White people. (Using the distinctions from the last chapter: the anti-racist group that is good at recognizing racism will recognize it, but that won't keep the dogwhistle from functioning.) And yet, it activates the racial attitudes of those very same White people who fail to perceive it as racist. So the people who are targeted as recipients of the dogwhistle are the people who are oblivious to it. Because what the dogwhistle is doing is unwelcome to them, if they are even somewhat aware of what is happening, the dogwhistle fails. (This seems to be the understanding of dogwhistle at work in Stanley and Beaver's *Politics of Language*, where they write that "the practice of dog-whistling has clear *purposes*—to marshal unconscious racist biases towards political goals" (forthcoming: 62). The focus on unconscious biases means this statement of purpose is at odds with the secret code understanding of dogwhistles.)

As we have noted, the general characterization of dogwhistles that Ian Haney López gives in *Dogwhistle Politics* (2014), quoted above, is incompatible with this second kind of dogwhistle. Nonetheless, Haney López shows awareness in the very same book that this is not how all dogwhistles work. He in fact highlights that racial dogwhistles are often not meant to be consciously understood by their audience:

> [A] final important difference between routine coded political speech and racial dog whistling lies in what the target audience hears. To be sure, some voters clearly perceive a message of racial resentment and react positively to it; *politician W is with us and against those minorities*, they say to themselves. But many others would be repulsed by such a message, just as they would reject any politician who openly used racial epithets. For these voters, the cloaked language hides—even from themselves—the racial character of the overture.   (Haney López 2014: 5)

Haney López attempts to reconcile this difference by treating racial dogwhistles as a special subcategory of dogwhistles. But this is at odds with the overall definition he gives of dogwhistles as "seeking to surreptitiously communicate support to small groups of impassioned voters" (Haney López 2014: 4). Dogwhistles like the Willie Horton ad are not just a special variety of surreptitious communication to impassioned voters—perhaps with an additional feature. They work entirely differently: there's no desire to communicate with one group while concealing from another, there's no small group of impassioned supporters that one is trying to reach, and there's no coded message. Moreover, it is also mistaken to assume, as Haney López does, that racial dogwhistles must mostly be directed at people who would reject the more conscious dogwhistles like those that I have called Overt Codes. We will shortly see quite a few dogwhistles that are meant precisely for racists who are comfortable receiving such overt racial code dogwhistles. For example, White supremacist groups on the Internet have developed clearly articulated codes to communicate with each other while going undetected by nonmembers.

In his more recent book, *Merge Left* (Haney López 2019a), Haney López begins to move toward a model more like that which I develop below. On this model, dogwhistles are still understood as using code. But Haney López describes two versions of this code:

> (a) As in a secret handshake, sometimes the code hides the underlying message from the general audience but allows it to be clearly understood by intended supporters.

> (b) More often, like a used car fraud, the code aims to stoke fear and resentment among intended supporters while hiding from that same group that the route appeal rests on socially unacceptable stereotypes.
>
> (2019a: 41–2)

I think it is still quite misleading to describe both of these as a code. The second kind of "code" is one that the recipient is meant not to understand at all, but nonetheless to be affected by without their awareness. This is the kind required to make sense of the Willie Horton ad. But this kind of thing is nothing at all like a code. Codes are meant to be decoded, in full consciousness. The model I develop below (based on Saul 2018, 2019b) draws a distinction similar to that which he draws with his (a) and (b), but abandons the idea that this is a kind of code.[7]

Although the term "dogwhistle" is a recent one, the idea finds an important precursor in the work of Susan Stebbing, one of the founders of the journal *Analysis*, who turned her attention in the 1930s to public outreach about political manipulation through language, as she watched in horror what was happening in the world. One of many devices she identified was what she called "witch-words," which she says that cunning politicians may use to cast "a spell upon their hearers, appealing to their emotions in such a way as to destroy their judgment" (Stebbing 1961: 63). Her focus is on the emotions summoned up, rather than on associations with racial or other attitudes, but we will see that there are nonetheless some striking parallels

2. A Bifurcated Model

Because there actually are two very different ways that dogwhistles function, I argue that we should understand them on a bifurcated model.[8] The two different kinds of dogwhistles are united in several ways: they offer means of playing upon voters' racial resentments without being overly obvious; they allow for concealment of violations of the Norm of Racial Equality; and they are modes of communication whose success depends upon their being fully understood by *at most* a subset of the audience. Nonetheless, their methods for achieving these aims are very different. I call the two kinds of dogwhistles "Overt Code dogwhistles" and "Covert Effect dogwhistles."[9]

2.1 Overt Code Dogwhistles

Overt Code racist dogwhistles are the sort most naturally thought of as a kind of coded communication. These are used to communicate with voters who don't accept the Norm of Racial Equality, and who are happy to hear an overtly racist message. (This is the group of people I described in Chapter 1 as rejecting the Norm of Racial Equality.) They are *overt* because they are meant to be explicitly understood by those at whom they are directed, but they function like a *code* in that they are not meant to be understood by others. The reason that a politician selects an Overt Code dogwhistle rather than an explicitly racist statement is to communicate clearly with a sub-group of supporters who hold norm-defying views, while avoiding recognition of what they are doing by other voters who might be troubled by it (those who accept the Norm of Racial Equality). When a dogwhistle of this sort is used, it generally seems perfectly innocent to the voters at whom it is not directed, unless they are in the know about its meaning.[10] This sort of dogwhistle is sometimes spoken of as involving an ingroup who are the intended audience and an outgroup who are intended not to understand. In its primary form, it is intentional, but we will see (as we work through examples) that unintentional uses of these dogwhistles are crucial for understanding how they work in the world.

2.1.1 Historical Case: "States' Rights"s

A classic example of an Overt Code dogwhistle is the phrase "states' rights."s Although both meanings of the phrase are now fairly widely known, this used to be quite a clear case of an Overt Code dogwhistle. We have already touched on this example, but we will now look at it in more detail.

According to the US constitution, states have the ability to set their own laws on certain matters. One who thinks this is important might describe themself as a supporter of states' rights. This is not just a cover for racism but a position which does have things to be said in its favor. States' rights in this sense were arguably quite important to the progress of the marriage equality movement. As more and more states legalized same-sex marriage, stereotypes were broken down and minds were changed by all the photos of newly married happy couples.[11] This could not have happened if states did not have the ability to set their own laws on marriage.

However, the phrase "states' rights" also has some extremely important racist historical resonances. "States' rights" was a rallying cry of the southern states in the Civil War, which insisted that they should be allowed to continue with the practice of slavery. As we have already noted, the notion of states' rights was also used in defense of segregation during the Civil Rights era. This strong historical association with racism has meant that praising states' rights is very often a way of signaling one's support for racism.

Until fairly recently, many White northerners were unaware of the racist usage of the term "states' rights." This allowed the phrase to be used as a dogwhistle: it sounded innocuous to northern Whites who would be disturbed by an open expression of racism, but it signaled to racist southern Whites (who are of course just a subgroup of southern Whites) that the user of the phrase was one of them. (Importantly, this division of groups who recognize and don't recognize the dogwhistle is, of course, a little oversimplified. Among southern Whites there may have been some who were oblivious and among northern Whites there undoubtedly were plenty who did understand what was going on.[12])

The traditional use of the "states' rights" dogwhistle is as a way of transmitting messages to the people who oppose the Norm of Racial Equality. When this dogwhistle was originally developed, the norm was only emerging, and was widely held in some regions of the country but not in others. The idea was that the racist message transmitted to the norm-rejecting group would go unnoticed by others. As time went on, there came to be somewhat broader awareness of the racist message.[13] However, uncertainty remains about whether any particular usage of the phrase "states' rights" is meant to transmit a racist message or simply a statement about constitutional structure. This uncertainty allows some people to become convinced that maybe there isn't a racist message after all. When the strong supporters of anti-racism norms call attention to the racist message, they will sometimes be well received; but sometimes, it will seem like an overreaction to an ambiguous or innocuous message. This reaction to the criticism can be used to discredit anti-racists, and to foment division. We will see that this sort of dynamic is vital to understanding what has been happening to our political discourse.

2.1.2 Deliberate White Supremacist Codes
In our discussion of the history of dogwhistles, we saw deliberate strategizing by politicians to gain the support of disparate groups of voters. But this sort of deliberate strategizing is not confined to politicians. It is also a key part of what goes on in White supremacist organizations.

Sociologists Blee and Simi write that

> [The white supremacist movement] is organized through a deliberately created common culture that sustains a shared ideology of beliefs and goals grounded in an extreme differentiation between in-groups (whites/white supremacists) and out-groups (nonwhites/enemies).[14]

There is a very explicit commitment to the use of coded communication that is understood by insiders but not by outsiders:

> [The white supremacist movement] circulates and relies upon an insider mode of communicating that we term "double-speak"—language intended to deceive and to convey multiple meanings. Double-speak is a method of conveying white supremacist beliefs and intentions to those within the WSM culture while sending an innocuous meaning to outsiders.[15]

Blee and Simi discuss examples such as

> the circulation of images that refer to pre-Christian Nordic religions, such as Thor's hammer, that are intended to signal an innocuous reference to ancient spiritual traditions to outsiders. Cultural insiders, however, will recognize such images as associated with sectors of white supremacism that adopt traditions of ancient Aryan spirituality.[16]

They note that this practice is an old one, citing as an example

> the 1920s Ku Klux Klan's use of 3-K names, such as Kwik Kustom Kleaners, to signal to insiders an establishment owned by a Klansman while allowing the storekeeper to claim that the name was an innocent alliteration rather than a reference to the Klan.[17]

White supremacists have also developed code words for communicating with each other on social media. As social media companies became increasingly concerned about hate speech on their platforms, hate groups sought ways to evade detection and have the conversations that they wanted to have. This led to the development and propagation of specific coded language, with terms like "Skittles" and "Skype" used as names for racial groups (Katrowitz 2016). These terms have the added benefit of being unlikely targets of banning—since major corporations consider it important to use them. Words like these, very clearly, function to transmit messages between those who reject the Norm of Racial Equality, in such a way that the messages will go unnoticed by those who accept this norm.[18]

Another deliberate creation of a dogwhistle was the use of triple parentheses online to indicate that a person being discussed was Jewish.

Example: (((Jenny Saul)))[19]

This was a way of marking the people discussed as Jewish, using a method that would not be picked up by search engines looking for hate speech. These generally ignore punctuation marks altogether. So this code was meant to be like the product name code that we have just discussed. However, it quickly became known to Jewish people online, who engaged in an act of reclamation by putting the triple parentheses around their own names. In yet another phase of the life of this dogwhistle, non-Jewish anti-racist activists began to enclose their own names in triple parentheses, as a gesture of solidarity. This practice became quite widespread. Indeed, it was through this practice that I first learned of the triple parentheses—I saw a friend doing this. Googling, I found an article explaining the anti-Jewish use of the triple parentheses. Puzzled and concerned, I asked my friend what they were doing. That is when I learned about the anti-racist activist use. This example shows how quickly codes like this can change on the Internet, as well as the confusion that can be generated when they do so.

2.1.3 Name as Dogwhistle: Soros

Another interesting twist is the way that certain names have come to function as overt dogwhistles. Chief among these, perhaps, is "George Soros." Soros's name is widely used as an anti-Jewish dogwhistle. Representative Matt Gaetz, for example, suggested that Soros might be behind the "migrant caravan" often mentioned by Republican campaigners, and Donald Trump suggested Soros was behind protests against the nomination of Supreme Court Justice Brett Kavanaugh. It's very important that these suggestions are specifically of Soros as a shadowy figure pulling the strings behind large groups of people—this fits well into the long history of anti-Jewish conspiracy theories:

> Soros's Jewish heritage is well known—his experiences in the Holocaust formed his identity as a philanthropist, in a decades-long effort to beat back a revanchist right. And his name has become a synonym for a well-worn anti-Jewish canard: the idea that Jews are malevolent fomenters of social dissent, agitators slyly funding and masterminding protest, seeking to undermine a white, Christian social order. It is a canard that resonates not just in European history, where the deadly consequences of anti-Jewish conspiracies are well-known, but throughout American history, and its renewed form draws on a long tradition of American anti-Semitism.   (Lavin 2018)

Importantly, this plays into the increasingly popular Great Replacement conspiracy theory, which holds that Jews (or sometimes other elites) are replacing White people with people of color. This theory has become increasingly mainstream among Republicans, in part due to Fox News personality Tucker Carlson's frequent discussions of it (Rose 2022).

It is very clear to those who are explicitly anti-Jewish what is going on. After Trump mentioned Soros's name, anonymous racists on the internet rejoiced, exclaiming in all-caps: "TRUMP NAMED THE IMMIGRATION JEW" (Lavin 2018). However, others may see this just as the mention of a well-known billionaire (Farber 2020). This is clearly a case of anti-norm people seeing "Soros" as dogwhistling anti-Jewish sentiments, and specifically Great Replacement Theory. But that's not all that's going on. Trump and his more mainstream supporters retain deniability, able to insist that they are just speculating about the actions of a well-connected, rich, politically active person. The deniability gained by using dogwhistles like this one allows these people to feel more comfortable going along with Trump, and less likely to suffer repercussions for doing so: they can always insist that they had no idea "Soros" was a dogwhistle. Meanwhile, some will be unaware of the dogwhistle, or at least unsure about it. And once more, the outrage of those who endorse the Norm of Racial Equality, and recognize and criticize the dogwhistle, can be usefully claimed to be an overreaction—which fuels division.

Both 'Soros' and 'Skittles', you might be thinking, are very likely to be used by people who have no idea about the dogwhistle meaning. Somebody might simply want to eat Skittles, or George Soros might actually have done some things that they want to discuss. In short, speakers may unintentionally use dogwhistle terms. Uttering these terms can advertently convey messages that they do not intend. In fact, as we will see, unintentional uses are very important to the functioning of dogwhistles.

2.1.4 Unawareness: "Bad Hombres"

For those who see a dogwhistle clearly, understanding both meanings, it may be hard to believe that others genuinely miss what is happening. That seems, however, to be the case, as indicated by this remarkable anecdote:

> When Trump supporter Helen Beristain's husband—an undocumented Mexican immigrant—was deported last month, she was shocked, according to a recent interview by *Washington Post* reporter Peter Holley.
>
> Beristain claimed that she thought Trump would hold true to his promise of only going after "bad hombres," not her husband.
>
> While reading this, I thought, "This is so freaking ridiculous." This white woman really voted for someone whose virulent racism and xenophobia was an inherent part of his campaign—and then really thought her brown, immigrant spouse wouldn't be affected by it?....
>
> It seemed so obvious to me (and thousands of others I saw discussing it via social media), that despite not explicitly spelling it out, Trump was speaking about Mexicans and other Latinxs in his speeches about "drug lords" and "bad hombres."
>
> What I didn't realize until further research was that he was using an old political tactic called dog-whistle politics.   (Loubriel 2017)

This anecdote illustrates how phrases like "bad hombres" may very clearly be identified as a dogwhistle about Mexicans to some audiences, while others do not recognize this at all. In many cases, it can be hard to take it seriously when someone insists that they did not hear the racist meaning of a dogwhistle. It is often quite plausible to doubt the honesty of their report. But this is a case in which that explanation is really not so plausible. Beristain had a genuine deeply felt interest in making sure that her Mexican husband wasn't deported, yet she voted for Trump. She seems to have genuinely failed to understand what was going on in Trump's rhetoric. This is exactly what we would predict for a well-functioning Overt Code dogwhistle. (We would also predict that others would hear the code loud and clear, including both those who agree with the sentiment expressed and some who disagree with it. The author of the quoted piece clearly falls into the latter camp.)

2.2 Covert Effect Dogwhistles

I have already noted that Ian Haney López's definition of "dogwhistle" cannot do justice to the two very distinct types of dogwhistles that there are (Overt Code and Covert Effect). Although I disagree with his theorizing of the difference, I think he beautifully explains the importance of understanding that these work very differently:

> Relying solely on a secret handshake conception of dog whistling pushes critics in one of two very different directions: some critics assume almost all Republican voters understand the secret handshake of white supremacy, making that party seem a nest of racist vipers. Other critics start from the assumption that most Republican voters are not closet white supremacists, and therefore conclude that they must not receive the secret message, implying that racial dog whistling reaches few people and does little work... On the contrary... [t]oday, dogwhistling overwhelmingly works by... hiding the racist nature of the messages from the intended audience itself. (Haney López 2019a: 39)

The Willie Horton ad, we have already seen, functions in a very different way from the secret handshake conception—the Overt Code dogwhistles. It works by activating racial attitudes in its intended audience, outside their awareness, just like the second kind of dogwhistling Haney López describes above. This is how a Covert Effect dogwhistle works.

Now I turn to the way that particular words may serve as dogwhistles of the Covert Effect kind. (Again, Haney López discusses some of these, though I think his definition struggles to accommodate them.) Experimental studies (e.g. Mendelberg 2001; White 2007) have shown that particular terms may function in much the same way that the Willie Horton ad does, by raising racial attitudes to salience without the awareness of those whose attitudes are affected. They can be very effective at causing people to act on these racial attitudes. According to this research, a dogwhistle like this has a far better chance of playing on their racial resentments than a more overt appeal does (for those who accept the Norm of Racial Equality). I will call these "Covert Effect dogwhistle terms."

To see how this works, let's look at an illustrative example, this one from White (2007). He asked subjects to read a supposed news article about proposed spending cuts to food stamps and Medicaid, containing a congressman's criticism of these cuts. The congressman describes the cuts as harming "inner-city Americans" in one version, harming "African-Americans" in another version, and harming "Americans" in yet another. Control subjects read an article on an unrelated topic. After this, subjects answered an array of questions covering many different topics, including an increase to welfare spending, as well as questions designed to gauge their racial attitudes. The experiment found that the term "inner city" functioned very much like the Willie Horton ad, raising White subjects' racial attitudes to salience so that they played an important role in determining responses to the welfare spending increase question. This could be seen in the correlation between racial attitudes and responses to the welfare spending question for the group who had seen the 'inner-city; version. Importantly, making the racial reference the subject of explicit comment (as Jesse Jackson did) kept this from happening: racial attitudes for subjects who read the version containing 'African-American' were not correlated with responses to the question about welfare spending. Nor were racial attitudes correlated with this in the control group.[20]

The way that Covert Effect dogwhistles work means that the best way to test for them is via careful empirical study. Here is what psychologists look for:

- If a Covert Effect dogwhistle term is present, racial attitudes will be raised to salience without the subjects' awareness, and brought to bear on whatever question is under consideration. This will be seen by a correlation between racial resentment levels and responses.
- If an explicitly racial term is present, however, the subjects will be aware that race is under consideration and they will not allow racial attitudes to affect their decision-making. This will be seen by a lack of correlation between racial resentment levels and responses.
- If neither is present, the expectation is that there will be no correlation between racial attitudes and responses, just as in the explicit condition.

Because of the way that a Covert Effect dogwhistle works, we cannot be sure that a term works in this way until it is carefully studied: after all, it works by raising attitudes to salience *outside of consciousness*. There are, as we have seen, experimental tests that can show whether this is happening. That's how we know, for example, that 'inner city' worked like this, in the experiment. But without these tests, claims that a term functions in this way are always at least somewhat speculative—introspection is not a good guide. (It may also be somewhat speculative to assume, after some time, that one of these terms *still* functions in this way. In fact, I would not be surprised at all to learn that 'inner city' no longer works this way. It seems likely to me that it is by now far too widely seen as a term to substitute for 'African-American' or 'Black.')

A Covert Effect dogwhistle can also be understood in terms of the various groups discussed in previous sections. Importantly, when the dogwhistle is working as intended, none of the groups will be aware of it. It is meant to function outside of consciousness. However, the group that it works on is actually quite a specific one: those who accept the Norm of Racial Equality but nonetheless harbor high levels of racial resentment.[21] These are the people who are uncomfortable about the racial resentment. (Those who reject the Norm of Racial Equality don't need dogwhistles—they are fine with an explicitly racist appeal.)[22] Things can change, though, when people begin to discuss the racism of a Covert Effect dogwhistle, as happened with the Willie Horton ad. The ad became less and less effective as people heard Jackson's comments on it, because this caused them to engage in self-monitoring. At the same time, though, divisions between groups were heightened by the accusation that Jackson was unreasonably making accusations of racism. This may have helped to set the scene for some of the more explicit racism that we will begin to discuss in Chapter 3.

It is very important that Covert Effect dogwhistles be treated separately from Overt Code dogwhistles when considering how they function. The two kinds of dogwhistles work in fundamentally different ways. Overt Code dogwhistles depend on a division of the audience into those meant to understand their message and those meant to not understand their message. Those who are meant to understand are meant to do so in full consciousness. Covert Effect dogwhistles are not at all like this. Although in fact not everyone is affected by them in the same way, this is not essential to their functioning. What is essential to their intended functioning is that those who are affected by them in the intended way are not aware that this is happening. In short, Overt Code dogwhistles work like a secret code. Covert Effect dogwhistles do not. And being aware of this is important: if one takes the threat of dogwhistles to be only that of secret communication among explicit racists, one will miss the ways that Covert Effect dogwhistles can unconsciously influence so many more.

2.3 Definitions

At this point, it may be useful to pause and remind the reader of the main distinction I have drawn between two kinds of dogwhistles, and to state general definitions of them. Each needs to be defined differently for intentional and unintentional versions.[23]

Overt Code dogwhistles:[24]

- Intentional: a term or speech act with (at least) two plausible interpretations, such that one of these violates some widespread norm, and is meant to be understood primarily by those who are comfortable with this norm violation; and one appears innocent, and is meant to be understood primarily by those who would not want to see the norm being violated.
- Unintentional: a term or speech act with (at least) two plausible interpretations, one of which violates some widespread norm, and one of which doesn't violate that norm, which is used by someone unaware of the norm-violating interpretation.

Covert Effect dogwhistles:

- Intentional: a communicative act[25] meant to raise particular attitudes to salience without the audience's awareness, where the attitudes being raised to salience violate some widespread norm.
- Unintentional: a communicative act of unintentionally raising to salience attitudes that violate some widespread norm. Often this will be through unwitting use of a term that has these effects.

3. Non-Linguistic Dogwhistles

In keeping with the philosophical literature on dogwhistles, my focus here has been on the linguistic side of dogwhistles. Even so, I have actually not been able to avoid discussing images. After all, the Willie Horton ad's racial content comes entirely from the image shown of Willie Horton. There is no racialized terminology in this ad. In fact, images are crucial to properly understanding dogwhistles. They are common means by which dogwhistling takes place, and they feature prominently in paradigmatic cases like the Willie Horton ad. But they are also especially important to one of the most important sites for political discourse today: the Internet, and particularly social media. I have explored visual dogwhistles in more depth elsewhere (Drainville and Saul, forthcoming), but my goal here is simply to call attention to their existence and the fact that they can be either Overt Code or Covert Effect dogwhistles. After this, I turn briefly to another sort of non-linguistic dogwhistle.

3.1 Visual Overt Code Dogwhistles

For an example of a visual Overt Code dogwhistle, consider the Hawaiian shirts worn by the Boogaloo Bois (Delgado 2020). The Boogaloo Bois are a militia group that attends protests hoping to foment violence. They are partly, but not uniformly, White supremacist and neo-Nazi. (There seems to be a wing of the group that is libertarian and opposed to police violence against Black people (Delgado 2020; Newhouse and Gunesch 2020).) According to the Boogaloo Bois, a civil war is to be encouraged. In order to avoid social media restrictions on the use of their name, they make heavy use of words which resemble the word "Boogaloo," including "big igloo" and "big luau," the latter giving rise to the Hawaiian shirts.

> As a symbol for the movement, the shirts stem from the term "Big Luau" and the association of Luaus with pig roasts, which is appealing to Boogaloo Bois as they often call police "pigs."
> (Newhouse and Gunesch 2020)

The Hawaiian shirts function as a visual dogwhistle. This is very much an Overt Code dogwhistle, meant to be consciously understood by a small group but missed by the larger group. To those in the know, they are indicators that the wearer is a member of the Boogaloo Bois. This is presumably helpful to the Boogaloo Bois, who might want to find each other at protests. To those who do not recognize the symbol, the wearer of a Hawaiian shirt is simply making an ordinary fashion statement. The indication of membership in the Boogaloo Bois is only available to those who know the code. (One can easily imagine an unintentional version of this dogwhistle, in which an unfortunate ordinary lover of Hawaiian shirts is mistaken for a Boogaloo Boi.)

Another fine example of visual dogwhistles comes from the Twitter feed of Pete Evans, an Australian celebrity chef turned far-right conspiracy theorist.

> On Sunday evening, Pete Evans posted a cartoon to his millions of followers on Facebook and Instagram. The cartoon features a caterpillar wearing a Make America Great Again hat speaking to a butterfly featuring the Black Sun symbol—also known as the sonnenrad or sunwheel. It's an ancient symbol appropriated by the Nazis, and now associated with Neo-Nazis according to the Anti-Defamation League, an anti-hate organisation. In recent times, it featured on the Christchurch terrorist's rucksack and manifesto.   (Wilson 2020)

This symbol, the Black Sun, is a visual dogwhistle. It might, of course, be used unintentionally. However, in this case the following took place soon after the posting.

> When a commenter on Evans' Facebook page asked about it, he confirmed he knew the symbol.
>
> "The symbol on the butterfly is a representation of the Black sun lol," one person wrote.
>
> "I was waiting for someone to see that," Evans' account replied.
>
> Later, Evans responded to another user on Instagram saying that he sees "the caterpillar as colourful and at peace whereas the butterfly embodies darkness and perhaps shadow…Or you can look at it as something completely different."   (Wilson 2020)

These responses, especially when taken together, seem like a pretty clear acknowledgement that the dogwhistle was intentional. Afterwards, Evans attempted to deny any knowledge of the symbolism. But the denials have not been very successful: the incident seems to have led to many advertisers and brands distancing themselves from Evans.

Our final example of a visual dogwhistle is also a culinary dogwhistle.[26] Hitler's favorite food was supposedly egg dumplings and green salad. In Austria, it has become common for restaurants sympathetic to the far right to advertise this food as their special on Hitler's birthday. Neo-Nazis deliberately eat this food on Hitler's birthday, and post images of it on social media. These are clearly visual Overt Code dogwhistles, signaling support for Nazism. A police officer in Austria was even sentenced to prison for posting such an image, which was judged to violate a law against promoting Nazism (Roche 2021).

3.2 Visual Covert Effect Dogwhistles

A good example of a covert visual dogwhistle can be found in the manipulation of images to darken Barack Obama's skin, something that Hillary Clinton's campaign was (inconclusively) accused of doing in 2008. The effect of this sort of manipulation has been experimentally studied, as discussed by Drainville and Saul (forthcoming):

> Messing et al. (2016) conducted a careful study of the effects of digitally darkening Barack Obama's skin tone. In their research, participants first viewed an image of Obama with either lightened or darkened skin and then completed a standard task of negative stereotype activation (completing words related to negative stereotypes about Black people). They found that those who had seen the darker Obama showed greater activation of negative stereotypes about Black people.

What this study reveals is that the darkening of skin tone and images seems to function as a Covert Effect dogwhistle, activating negative racial stereotypes, almost certainly without the viewer's awareness. It is raising negative features to salience outside the audience's consciousness. (This can occur either intentionally or unintentionally. Color reproduction is a very tricky matter, so in some cases darkening of skin color will not be deliberate.)

3.3 Location/Date Dogwhistles

In the lead-up to Donald Trump's arrest for hush money payments regarding an affair with an adult film star, Trump declared his intention to hold a rally. The rally was held in Waco, Texas during the 30th anniversary of the deadly raid on the Branch Davidian compound by government forces. This raid has assumed immense importance on the far right as an instance of government overreach, one seen as providing justification for extreme and violent actions against the US government, including—crucially—the Oklahoma City bombing in 1995, which was itself on the anniversary of the

Waco raid. As a result, holding an event on this date in this location serves as an Overt Code dogwhistle—even without using words or images that serve as dogwhistles. Here, for example, are two experts on extremist speech being interviewed about this topic:

> "Waco has a sense of grievance among people that I know he's (Trump's) got to be trying to tap into," Beirich said. "He's being unjustly accused, like the Branch Davidians were unjustly accused—and the deep state is out to get them all."
>
> Megan Squire, deputy director for data analytics at the Southern Poverty Law Center, scoffed at the idea that Trump would be holding a rally in Waco for anything other than the city's symbolic resonance among the far right.
>
> "Give me a break! There's no reason to go to Waco, Texas, other than one thing—in April," Squire said. "I can't even fathom what that's about other than just a complete dog whistle"   (Carless 2023)

One of the experts interviewed (very much in the minority) counted himself as uncertain about the Trump campaign's *intentions*—arguing that Waco actually makes sense as an important city for a Republican to visit because it's one of few Republican cities in the large Republican state. This expert was waiting to see if Trump said anything that referenced the raid, in order to make inferences about intentions. Importantly, however, Kathleen Belew (Rachel Maddow Show, 28 August 2023) notes that whatever the intention, the action will still serve for White supremacists as a reference to Oklahoma City, and all the violence that entails.

> Waco, to many people, may simply signify the Branch Davidian siege and the sort of general anti-Federal Government sentiment that people take from that. But to White Power activists Waco is a direct reference to the Oklahoma City bombing. It is a call to further violence. So, you know, we can have a discussion about whether or not they meant it this way. But there is plenty of information, plenty of historical precedent, plenty of expert analysis that can tell us what this movement will perceive, and all signs point to increasing acts of violence.

Whether intentional or not, a rally on this date, in Waco, by someone railing against government overreach, *will* act as a dogwhistle. And indeed we saw this, with far-right figures like Laura Loomer tweeting that it was "very symbolic".[27]

3.4 Protean Dogwhistles

Protean dogwhistles (Saul 2019a) are especially shifty ones, named for the Greek mythological figure Proteus who was so difficult to catch due to his shape-shifting. These are communicative devices which may dogwhistle different things to different audiences. There probably are Overt Code Protean dogwhistles, but the Covert Effect ones will be my focus. We will take as our example the anti-immigration rhetoric of the pro-Brexit Leave campaign in the United Kingdom.

The extremely successful Leave campaign had as its goal persuading British voters that the UK should leave the European Union. There is no doubt at all that much of the rhetoric of this campaign was overtly anti-immigration. Typical ads showed maps with arrows and population figures, suggesting that entire countries were about to join the EU and then move to the UK. Others showed images of overcrowding, or queues at borders. What was often left unsaid was *which* immigrant groups were at stake. And this mattered, because there were actually several prejudices clearly at work in the British public (along with other concerns, but those aren't our topic). Some were racist in a way readily recognizable to North Americans—prejudiced against people with darker skin. We do see evidence that some ads were designed to play on this prejudice: the infamous "Breaking Point" ad depicted a huge queue of people massed at what was (falsely) suggested to be the UK border. All of these people were dark-skinned, because the one light-skinned person had been carefully covered by a vote-reminder graphic (Drainville 2016). But other ads were less clear—is an ad about Turkey's imminent membership in the EU (another false claim) about skin color or religion? Is scare-mongering about immigrants taking jobs about foreigners in general, dark-skinned people, or eastern Europeans? How these ads worked was left up to the audience. And there were audiences with all these prejudices. (North American readers might be surprised to learn of the role that prejudice against eastern Europeans played in the Brexit campaign, but this prejudice is a powerful one in the UK. Indeed, it was the main subject of the *Sun*'s triumphant headline the morning after the referendum vote: "Where the Brex Was Won: Streets Full of Polish Shops, Kids Not Speaking English, but Union Jacks Now Flying High Again"). My contention is that anti-immigration messages in the Brexit campaign may have served as Protean dogwhistles, bringing various prejudices to bear, depending on the audience.

4. Why Unintentional Dogwhistles Matter

As we have worked through examples, we have seen dogwhistles used both intentionally and unintentionally. The fact that dogwhistles can be used unintentionally follows from their nature. Moreover, it's absolutely crucial to their accomplishing what they do in the world. And this is a point that Susan Stebbing called attention to beautifully in her early discussion of "witch-words." Stebbing notes that others have assumed witch-words to always be "cunningly chosen." But, she argues, this not always the case:

> But not all "witch-words" are cunningly chosen; they may be used honestly although stupidly. Certain words have been used so frequently with a strong emotional significance that we are likely to use them in this way without realizing that our thinking is dominated by the emotional meaning that has been associated with these words. Similarly we react to them emotionally when used by other people.   (Stebbing 1961: 33)

Again, Stebbing's focus is solely on emotional associations, but I think her basic point generalizes. In this section, I look at the importance of unintentional use of dogwhistles in a bit more detail.

First let's take the case of Overt Code dogwhistles. If somebody is only aware of the innocent meaning, and uses the term, the dogwhistle meaning will still be present to be picked up on by those in the know. For example, someone might think that triple parentheses are just a trendy new thing to do on the Internet and start using them, without realizing that others will take their message to be an anti-Jewish one.

It is hard to see this as anything but an unintentional dogwhistle. This dynamic is, if anything, even more widespread in the case of Covert Effect dogwhistles. Every news broadcaster who repeated the Willie Horton ad without realizing what was really going on will have been an unintentional dogwhistler. And these people are crucial to the spread of the dogwhistle—indeed, elsewhere I have called their utterances *amplifier dogwhistles* (Saul 2018).

The fact that people can unintentionally use dogwhistles is absolutely crucial to understanding their functioning. Those who create dogwhistles in order to manipulate political discourse count on the fact that some of the people, indeed many of the people, who use them, will do so unintentionally. There are at least two reasons that this is important. First, unintentional use of dogwhistles spreads the ideas that the dogwhistler wants to introduce to the public discourse. This allows these ideas to travel more widely than they otherwise would, with potentially widespread and long-lasting affects on how issues are seen and discussed. A very clear example of this is the way that "government spending" has become a racial dogwhistle. Valentino et al. (2002) found that an advertisement using no overtly racial language, but phrases like "government spending," was enough to activate racial attitudes in the same way as a more often-discussed dogwhistle racial term like "inner city." If it is not possible to discuss whether government spending is wasteful or not without activating racial attitudes, then it is clear that whole topics have been successfully racialized in ways that are very useful to those who benefit from bringing racial resentments to bear on these topics. This racialization is very far from obvious to most people; they will not be aware of the fact that they are introducing dogwhistles into the discussion, or of the ways that racial attitudes are shaping that discussion. It is worth noting that there is probably a large number of other terms which also do this, of which we are still unaware.

Second, the fact that people can unintentionally use dogwhistles lends deniability[28] to those who use them intentionally. A nefarious creator of dogwhistles can claim, with varying degrees of plausibility, that they had no idea there was another meaning to what they said. Any plausibility that this has is the result of the fact that it is genuinely possible for people to make these utterances while having no idea of the more nefarious meaning. When asked whether there might be "a tinge of racism" in the Willie Horton ad, Lee Atwater replied:

> Absolutely not. Absolutely not. I don't even think many people in the South know what race Willie Horton is. I think that's totally irrelevant.
>
> (Forbes 2008)

This denial is ludicrous to us now, but it had plausibility—for some—at the time. Because it is possible for people to view or replay that ad without seeing the racial content, there is some modicum of plausibility to Lee Atwater claiming that was the case for him. Even where it is not very plausible, deniability can have damaging effects.[29] As Elisabeth Camp writes:

> The key feature of denial...is that it trades on the gap between what is in fact mutually obvious to the speaker and hearer, on the one hand, and what both parties are prepared to *acknowledge* as mutually obvious, on the other.   (2018: 48)

This sort of move is "annoying" (Camp 2018: 49) and difficult to respond to because it is so uncooperative, and at odds with how conversation *should* proceed. Plausible deniability introduces many complications and difficulties into our public discourse, which we will grapple with throughout this book.

5. Application: The Pinker Controversy

The distinctions I have developed help us to make sense of a recent high-profile controversy about dogwhistling—a dispute that I take to be partly grounded in flawed understandings of "dogwhistle." This case is an especially interesting one, because of the fact that both sides of the controversy are being argued by professional linguists. In 2020, a large group of professional linguists signed an open letter to the Linguistic Society of America calling for the group to distance itself from linguist and psychologist Steven Pinker in various ways. The letter provided several reasons for proposing this course of action, involving utterances by Pinker related to race and gender. One of these reasons (the only one that we will discuss) was his use of dogwhistles:

> On June 14th 2020, Dr. Pinker uses the dogwhistle "urban crime/ violence"…A *dogwhistle* is a deniable speech act "that sends one message to an outgroup while at the same time sending a second (often taboo, controversial, or inflammatory) message to an ingroup", according to recent and notable semantic/pragmatic work by linguistic researchers Robert Henderson & Elin McCready…"Urban", as a *dogwhistle*, signals covert and, crucially, **deniable** support of views that essentialize Black people as lesser-than, and, often, as criminals. Its parallel "inner-city", is in fact one of the prototypical examples used as an illustration of the phenomenon by Henderson & McCready.[30]

Many came to Pinker's defense, including linguists like Barbara Partee:

> I thought something was a dogwhistle when a politician was using it to appeal in a sort of covert or coded way to a base he didn't want to publicly acknowledge, e.g. to appeal to racists. This is Pinker talking to his friends and colleagues and all of us…I cannot find anything to censure in the use of the terms "urban crime" and "urban violence" in that context. The piece that Pinker links to here is arguing that it's important to use all the

resources of the community to prevent violence. I don't see anything
objectionable in that tweet. Maybe there's something more pernicious in
the one I didn't find.   (Partee 2020)

In this quotation, it seems that Partee is taking all dogwhistles to function
like intentional Overt Code dogwhistles. She assumes that a dogwhistle is
meant to reach a subgroup of supporters with coded language, and that
this needs to be intentional. Moreover, she finds it implausible that Pinker
would be doing this deliberately. But it's absolutely crucial to how dogwhistles work that they are often used unintentionally.[31] Indeed, this is
inherent in the very idea of a dogwhistle *term*: if the word itself is the
dogwhistle, then it doesn't stop being a dogwhistle when used by someone
who doesn't mean it to be. This means that Partee's response misses its
mark. What Pinker was trying to do is just not relevant to whether he
used a dogwhistle term or not. It also means conceding that a term is a
dogwhistle is not at all decisive with respect to blame. I would have
expected defenders to maintain that his usage was unintentional, rather
than that it was not a dogwhistle term.

A further defense of Pinker comes from linguist Jason Merchant, as
quoted in Partee's post:

"Urban" appears to be a usual terminological choice in work in sociology,
political science, law, and criminology. To cite only one example that's
close at hand (because I happened to have read it last year), my sociologist
colleague Robert Vargas, in his award-winning book, *Wounded City:
Violent Turf Wars in a Chicago Barrio*(OUP 2016), uses both "inner-city
violence" and "urban violence" (twice) on p. 5 alone (and many times
throughout the book)…So there is no real evidence for the idea that
Pinker is using "urban violence" and "urban crime" as dogwhistles: if he is,
so are the fields I mentioned above.   (Partee 2020)

Again, this is a perfectly good argument that Pinker might not have been
using the dogwhistle term intentionally. But it does nothing to establish that
the term is not a dogwhistle. Whether "urban" is an Overt Code dogwhistle
is dependent on whether it is sometimes intentionally used as a code to
communicate among racists. It could be used in this way, even if it is also
used by those who have no such intention.

The original letter-writers, and Henderson and McCready (2018)—the
authors they reference—do not seem to require *intention* for a term to

function as a dogwhistle. Henderson and McCready are much more focused on the audience interpretation process. This means they have room to say that a dogwhistle term might be used unintentionally.

However, I am less convinced than they are that theirs is a plausible picture of how "urban" works as a dogwhistle. The coded messages of an Overt Code dogwhistle are a very appealing way to understand the use of "88," or "states' rights." But it's far from clear that this is how "urban" works: it could very well work instead by activating racial attitudes without audience awareness, as a Covert Effect dogwhistle. Whether "urban" is a Covert Effect dogwhistle depends on how it affects listeners. If it has the effect of raising these racial attitudes to salience without listeners' awareness, then it has this effect, even if it is a common term in an academic discipline. (In fact, an Overt Code dogwhistle could also be a common term in an academic discipline—"heritage" is plausibly an Overt Code dogwhistle, and there is a field of "Heritage Studies.") The fact that Covert Effect dogwhistles may easily be unknown to their users means that one can well imagine an entire discipline of well-meaning people using the terms without awareness. I would expect, for example, that terms like "government spending" are widely used in academic discussions by people who have no idea of their dogwhistle effects. Citing a term's widespread academic use, then, as Merchant does, does not show it not to be a dogwhistle.[32]

The observation that the term "urban" is widely used in these academic fields is not, then, relevant to the question of whether it is a dogwhistle term or not. However, it is relevant to other questions. Pinker may or may not have been aware that "urban" has a dogwhistle use, but even with this awareness he may have thought it was acceptable to follow normal usage in these fields of academia. He may even, like his colleagues Partee and Merchant, have believed that this usage in academia showed the term to not be a dogwhistle. On the other hand, given both his background as a linguist and his long involvement with political issues, one might argue that he *should* have been aware of the dogwhistle usage, and of the importance of dogwhistle effects.

The issue of Pinker's culpability for using a dogwhistle term is a tricky one, on which I will not take a stand—it depends a great deal on Pinker's state of mind, which I don't have access to. I will also not take any stand on the legitimacy of the demands in the original Pinker letter. To settle the issue would require substantial work not just on culpability for use of dogwhistle terms, but also on all the other claims made in the letter, and on issues of academic freedom.

My interest here is not in individual assessments of culpability, but rather in understanding the way that certain manipulative linguistic devices may distort a political discourse in immensely damaging ways. Use of the term "urban" very likely does this, whether or not its user intends it to. And this case study shows how very difficult it currently is to discuss these issues accurately, even among professional linguists. It also shows the importance of fully recognizing the very different ways that Overt Code and Covert Effect dogwhistles work.

Because of the very significant effects that dogwhistles have when they are used, whether or not this usage is deliberate, I think that in many ways we should be equally concerned about intentional and unintentional uses of dogwhistles. Of course, those who are trying to decide how to feel about a friend or member of their profession—or, for that matter, whom to vote for—will be interested in issues of individual culpability. But when it comes to broader issues, it is more important to consider the effects on our political discourse. And in a discussion like that around Pinker's comments, it is important to *separate* the issue of whether a term is a dogwhistle from the issue of culpability. Different evidence will bear on these issues.

6. Application: Canadian Conservative Party slogan

Another fascinating case study comes from a slogan adopted by the Conservative Party of Canada in 2021: "Canada's Recovery Plan will secure the future for you, your children and their children."[33]

Fairly quickly, some Canadians noticed a striking resemblance between this and one of the most famous White supremacist slogans worldwide, created by The Order's David Lane: "We must secure the existence of our people and a future for White children" (Smith 2021). This slogan is known as "The 14 Words," and because of this the number 14 has become an Overt Code dogwhistle enabling the user to signal support for White supremacy. Blee and Simi use this as one of their key examples of White supremacist codes:

> An example is the use of "14" to reference the "14 words" of David Lane, a member of a white supremacist terrorist group, The Order, that was responsible for the 1984 murder of Denver talk show host Alan Berg and a $3.6 million robbery of an armored car. Lane's "14 Words" ("We must

secure the existence of our people and a future for White children") have penetrated widely throughout the WSM culture, initially through the circulation of Lane's writings and now by circulation through social media and other WSM communication venues.[34]

Some even noticed[35] that the tweet also contained 88 characters. This is significant as well, since in White supremacist circles "88" functions as code for "Heil Hitler" (since "H" is the eighth letter of the alphabet). All of these together represent either a carefully constructed dogwhistle or a truly remarkable coincidence. It is very hard to see how it could happen by chance that a political party picks a slogan that resembles "The 14 Words," stated in 14 words, and uses 88 characters.[36]

Nonetheless, the dogwhistle never got much mainstream attention, and deniability was fully maintained. The idea that the Conservative Party of Canada was dogwhistling to White supremacists was never taken seriously. Even one of those who noticed this and remarked on it, Justin Ling,[37] tweeted "and I genuinely don't believe the party is trying to wink at neo-Nazis...it's peculiar that the message contains 14 words and 88 characters." David Fisman, a prominent epidemiologist, *did* sound the alarm on his Twitter feed, but seems to have received only mockery from the media for doing so. Here is a typical example, written in a tone of snarky sarcasm by Chris Selley in the *National Post*:

> The most astonishing thing about Twitter is how many intelligent, respectable people you'll see effectively yelling "watch this!" and then cannonballing off the deep end. Dr. David Fisman, a highly regarded epidemiologist at the University of Toronto's Dalla Lana School of Public Health and perhaps the most prominent independent medical voice in Ontario media for the duration of the pandemic, is only the latest.
>
> On Sunday, Fisman encountered the following perfectly anodyne claim from the Conservative Party of Canada: "Canada's Recovery Plan will secure the future for you, your children, and your grandchildren."
>
> He concluded it was an obvious "dogwhistle" to neo-Nazis.
>
> The sentence is 14 words long, you see, and three of the words are "secure," "future" and "children."
>
> The "14 Words" is a white supremacist slogan coined by the American neo-Nazi terrorist David Lane: "We must secure the existence of our people and a future for white children."
>
> "So creepy," Fisman intoned.   (Selley 2021)

This utterance, then, never received mainstream attention as a potential racist dogwhistle.

Some of those who ridiculed Fisman's claims seemed to find it ludicrous to suppose that one would use a different (though in this case overlapping) collection of 14 words to signal a message about Lane's 14 words. But this is a very explicit strategy among White supremacists. Blee and Simi cite discussions among White supremacists about the need to use 14 words but not "the specific" 14 words.[38] To those who are aware of this, there is nothing at all implausible about signaling White supremacy with the 14 words chosen as the Conservative Party slogan.

A further reason for the dismissal of Fisman's claims was that the Conservative Party seemed to have made a decision to run an apparently moderate and inclusive campaign, leaving the more openly racist end of the electorate for the People's Party of Canada. Indeed, as Selley noted, the slogan was announced with a photo of the party leader greeting a voter of color. (We will come back to this case in Chapter 3, because the photo functions as a figleaf, providing additional deniability.) To think that this is conclusive evidence against the presence of a dogwhistle, however, is to fundamentally misunderstand dogwhistles. Dogwhistles can easily be used to allow a moderate-seeming party to also get the support of White supremacists, without the awareness of the more moderate voters.

We cannot know *for certain* at this point that this was a deliberate racist dogwhistle; nor, if it was, can we know who was responsible for this—was it a decision from the top, or was it from a low-level person who did not inform their superiors what they were doing? All this, of course, could change if insider testimony comes out. Nonetheless, it seems very likely that it was intended as a dogwhistle: simply echoing the slogan on its own might be a coincidence. Writing a slogan with 14 words might be a coincidence. So might writing a slogan with 88 characters. But doing all of these at once? That seems highly unlikely.

It is important to also look at how the slogan was received by one other group: those who might be expected to pick up on and delight in a White supremacist dogwhistle. And here the evidence is clear. David Fisman writes, "What was interesting to me was that while I was being derided by Jonathan Kay et al., US White supremacist twitter accounts were sliding into the conversation to say "wow...check out Canada, this is so great."[39] White supremacists, then, clearly saw the dogwhistle as Fisman did. The difference was that for them it was a very welcome message.

7. Knowing whether Something Is a Dogwhistle

As we have seen, it is in the very nature of dogwhistles (of any kind) to be non-obvious—at least to many, and sometimes to all. This can make it hard to find and discuss clear examples. It may well not be apparent what kind of dogwhistle a term or an utterance is, or even whether or not it is a dogwhistle. Although this is sometimes given as a reason for doubting the existence of dogwhistles, or the distinctions between the different kinds, it should be neither. It is in fact precisely what a proper understanding of dogwhistles would predict.

How, then, should one go about finding out whether a term is a dogwhistle? The methods are different for the different kinds of dogwhistle. To establish that a term is a Covert Effect dogwhistle, the only really reliable method is psychological studies like those discussed in this chapter. These dogwhistles are not meant to be available to introspection by anyone, and when they become available to introspection they are probably not working in the intended way. Their existence needs to be established through psychological tests which have been shown to give insight into our less conscious mental processes.

Very different methods are needed to establish that a term is an Overt Code dogwhistle. Sometimes, we can learn about this because the code has been formally established, like the "Skittles" code for White supremacists online mentioned earlier. If we find a website which explains the code words, and then find people using the code, we can be pretty sure what we are dealing with. Alternatively, an informant from the relevant linguistic community might give us this information. For example, a former White supremacist might explain the way that the term "heritage" functions in their erstwhile community. Given the nature of the Internet, we might also learn such things from someone who has no intention of being an informant. Think, for example, of the anti-Jewish bigot mentioned earlier, gleefully tweeting "he named the immigration Jew!" when Trump mentioned George Soros. Because Overt Code dogwhistles are available to introspection for the group that they were meant for, reports of this sort are an excellent way to find out whether a term functions in this manner. But we do not always have this sort of evidence available.

The difficulty in discerning whether a dogwhistle is of one kind or another should not make us doubt the distinction. Although there are particular terms that we may not know how to classify because we don't yet have the empirical evidence, it is clear that the two dogwhistle types function very differently, and it is also clear that there are dogwhistles of each type. A clear example of each is perhaps helpful for making this point.

A very clear paradigm case of an Overt Code dogwhistle is the use of codes like "88," used by White supremacists online to mean "Heil Hitler." There is no question that this functions by the Overt Code dogwhistle method. Messages are written online which seem innocuous to a larger group (and even to AIs looking for hate speech), but which transmit a norm-violating secret message to a smaller group. This example is especially clear since we even have statements of the code and how to use it.

For a very clear paradigm case of a Covert Effect dogwhistle, it is best to look to one that has been thoroughly studied in the psychological literature. Here a great paradigm case is "inner city" as it was used and understood in the early 2000s, when White (2007) studied it. At this time, White found that racial attitudes were activated and brought to bear on the issue at hand when the phrase "inner city" was used. But he also found that they were not activated if the phrase "African American" was used. This fits precisely with Mendelberg's (2001) predictions. The term functions as a Covert Effect dogwhistle, raising racial attitudes to salience outside of awareness, thereby bypassing the self-monitoring that might otherwise take place. If a more explicit term is used, self-monitoring happens, and due to concern about norm violation, racial attitudes are not brought to bear on the issue at hand. As already noted, I am somewhat uncertain about whether the term "inner city" still functions in this way. But because its earlier use was so well studied, it provides us a very clear paradigm case of a Covert Effect dogwhistle.

Many, many terms have been plausibly claimed to be dogwhistles. But without fully studying them, we cannot be sure of all the ways that they may function. Here are just a few:

- "Superpredator," a term infamously used by Hillary Clinton in the 1990s in discussions of "tough on crime" policies now widely acknowledged to be a part of what Michelle Alexander (2020) calls the *New Jim Crow*—policies that unjustly targeted Black people (Moorman 2020).
- "Heritage," a term frequently used in discussions of celebrating confederate history, seen as a celebration of racism by some and a mere interest in history by others.
- "Law and order," a phrase infamously employed by segregationists, by Richard Nixon, by Reagan and Clinton in the war on drugs, and by Trump. It is very clear that, as Vanessa Wills puts it, "The call for a

'return to law and order'...must be understood alongside the recollection that the law had been segregation and the order was racial hierarchy" (Wills 2016).

- "Radicalization" and "terrorist," which are on their face neutral terms referring to people who engage in certain sorts of activities; but are also very clearly used as anti-Islamic terms.
- "Taxpayer," which has recently been argued to be coded as White, male, and middle class (Walsh 2021).

To learn what kind of dogwhistle each of these is (and also to be sure that it is one), investigation is needed. And this may be a bit complicated. Even if, for example, we get clear evidence of "law and order" working as a Covert Effect dogwhistle, that does not rule out it also functioning as an Overt Code dogwhistle for some users and in some contexts. We'd learn that it did if we found a community of users deliberately using it to communicate with each other, without the awareness of a broader group.

8. Deniability, after Concealment Weakens

A dogwhistle is meant to function by concealing at least some of what is happening from at least some of the audience. In the case of a Covert Effect dogwhistle, the people whom that dogwhistle is meant to work on are not meant to be aware of the effect. In the case of an Overt Code dogwhistle, one subgroup is meant to get the message clearly while another subgroup misses the message entirely. But we live in a complicated and messy world, and in this world there are lots of groups of people who may receive or not receive the message in many ways. Moreover, the speed with which information travels on the Internet means that these sorts of concealment are harder to maintain than they used to be. Our question now is what this means for the functioning of dogwhistles. Once discussion of a dogwhistle's meaning is widespread, can it still be an effective dogwhistle? My answer will be that a dogwhistle in this state (which one might call a broken dogwhistle) can still be extremely useful, because it can still offer deniability to the speaker. Moreover, it may be especially helpful for fomenting division between groups.

To examine this issue, let's take a concrete example. One of the most studied dogwhistle terms, which we have already discussed quite a bit, is "inner city." It seems clear that this term functioned as a Covert Effect dogwhistle when it was studied in the early 2000s. However, its use as a dogwhistle is *now* extremely widely discussed on the Internet and in mainstream media. As a result, it is entirely possible that very few, if any, people are by now unaware of the term's dogwhistle use. Without empirical study, of course, we cannot know whether this is the case. But we can consider what would be true if it in fact turned out that the racial associations of the term "inner city" are no longer hidden. In order to explore this, let's consider what we should think if this *is* true.

Suppose it's the case, then, that everyone is in fact aware that "inner city" is a dogwhistle term. (This supposition is surely too strong, but it is illuminating to consider it nonetheless.) Importantly, everyone may know this without everyone being aware *that everyone knows*. Indeed, if this is true of our current time, then we have a situation in which there may be a widespread false belief that the racial associations of the term "inner city" are hidden from many people. And this matters.

Now consider a usage of the term "inner city," bearing in mind this supposition. Here are some infamous comments from then-congressman Paul Ryan:

> We have got this tailspin of culture, in our inner cities in particular, of men not working and just generations of men not even thinking about working or learning the value and the culture of work, and so there is a real culture problem here that has to be dealt with.   (Lowery 2014)

After the criticism that ensued, Ryan defended himself by denying that there was anything racial in the comments:

> This has nothing to do whatsoever with race...It never even occurred to me. This has nothing to do with race whatsoever. This isn't a race based comment; it's a breakdown of families, it's rural poverty in rural areas, and talking about where poverty exists—there are no jobs and we have a breakdown of the family. This has nothing to do with race.
>
> (Lowery 2014)

This denial is available to Ryan because of his use of the term "inner city" rather than a term like "Black" or "African-American." He could not even have tried this strategy if his utterance had used an explicitly racial term like this. The dogwhistle term "inner city" makes it possible for Ryan to make this move.

Is Ryan's use of the strategy convincing to anyone? I have been unable to find data on this topic. I cannot say whether Ryan convinced people that he wasn't thinking about race at all. Widespread awareness that "inner city" is a dogwhistle will surely have made it harder for him to do so. But the strategy may succeed even if Ryan does not *convince* them of this. For his purposes, it may well be sufficient just to raise some doubt about whether he was thinking about race. This doubt may be raised, even if people know that "inner city" is a widespread dogwhistle. Despite this knowledge, they may hold open the possibility that *Ryan* did not know this, or that Ryan was not using "inner city" in this way. Even universal knowledge that the term is a dogwhistle does not mean universal knowledge *that there is such universal knowledge,* so it does not rule out Ryan's use of this strategy, or even necessarily make it ineffective.

Moreover, the possibility of raising this doubt about whether a person was using the term as a dogwhistle is tremendously effective for further dividing the electorate. Those who criticize the dogwhistle can be accused of inappropriately policing innocent speech. They will in turn be angered that their criticisms of racial dogwhistles are not being taken seriously. Playing these two groups off against each other has played a crucial role, as we will see extensively in Chapter 3, in facilitating the rise of increasingly blatant racism.

Dogwhistles are extremely effective methods for injecting racial content into public discourse, while maintaining deniability. And this is a crucial thing to do to reach that large chunk of the US electorate who would like to think of themselves as non-racist, but who nonetheless harbor racial attitudes that may be harnessed to a savvy politician's cause if this is done in a deniable manner. We have spent a substantial amount of time discussing dogwhistles, because they are the best-known and best-studied method for doing this. However, I am far from convinced that dogwhistles are currently the most potent force for deniably injecting racial content into public discourse. Figleaves, which I turn to in Chapter 3, have the potential to do even more damage.

3

Figleaves for Racism

As I've already noted, seemingly well-established results from political psychology seemed to support the widespread view that there was almost no chance that a politician making openly racist utterances—widely noticed and remarked on as such—could succeed in winning the presidency. Predictions for the 2016 US presidential election reflected this. But, as we all now know, things didn't go that way. Despite extremely widespread mainstream recognition of Donald Trump's racism, and despite the very blatant expression of that racism, he won the electoral college and therefore the presidency.

Our question now is how it is that Trump was able to succeed despite the obvious racism of his utterances, and widespread condemnation of them as such. In particular, my focus here will be on what happened to the Norm of Racial Equality, discussed extensively in Chapters 1 and 2.

Broadly speaking, there seem to be three main possibilities.

- Possibility 1: The Norm of Racial Equality is simply dead. There is no longer a social stigma against being explicitly racist, and White Americans are totally comfortable with blatant expressions of racism from their politicians. This doesn't seem to be right, however. Throughout the presidential campaign, headlines and editorial boards across the mainstream media expressed outrage about Trump's racism. And even many of those who defended Trump felt the need to argue that he wasn't racist.
- Possibility 2: *2016 Trump voters* were totally comfortable with explicit racism. This might be because they had abandoned the Norm of Racial Equality, or it might be because they never actually accepted it. (After all, they were not a majority of the population—or even a majority of those who voted (Krieg 2016).) This also seems implausible, although it is clearly true of some of them. While it's certainly true that some of Trump supporters are absolutely explicit racists, this does not seem to be the case for all (or even most) of them. In a poll taken just before

the 2016 election, 87 percent of Trump supporters said that they believed him not to be racist (Haney López 2019a: 27). These people either genuinely believed Trump not to be racist, or they said this even though they did not believe it. Either way, the poll is at odds with the thought that Trump supporters are generally quite comfortable with identifying as racists or supporters of a racist. If we take the poll at face value, then it tells us simply that the Trump supporters have managed to believe Trump is not racist. But even if we don't, it tells us that Trump supporters are not comfortable saying that they support some-one they believe to be racist. This shows very clearly, then, that the Norm of Racial Equality still has some grip on these people.

- Possibility 3: Many of those who voted for Trump have found a way of seeing his utterances as not violating the Norm of Racial Equality. They managed to believe that supporting Trump did not mean sup-porting a racist. I will be arguing for this final option, and suggesting that the linguistic mechanism I call figleaves played an important role.

1. Introducing Racial Figleaves

A racial figleaf, as we will see, is an utterance that provides cover for another utterance that—without the figleaf—would be recognized as racist. If Donald Trump simply asserted that Mexicans are rapists, this would be very readily recognized as racism. Instead, he made a more convoluted utterance:

When Mexico sends its people, they're not sending their best. They're not sending you. They're not sending you. They're sending people that have lots of problems, and they're bringing those problems with us [sic]. They're bringing drugs. They're bringing crime. They're rapists. And some, I assume, are good people.   (Phillips 2017)

This utterance, of course, was still widely recognized as racist. However, some of the elements it contained allowed Trump supporters who worried that it was racist to reassure themselves and each other that it was not. Online discussions among Trump supporters about whether or not he was racist cited the fact that he was not talking about all Mexicans, but just the ones who were sent. And they cited the fact that he said that some, he assumed, were good people (Saul 2017). Both of the bits that they cited to reassure themselves and one another are what I call "figleaves." That is, they are additional utterances which help to block the inference to the claim that the speaker is racist. The rest of this chapter will be devoted to explaining how this kind of mechanism works.

Two keys to the success of figleaves are the immensely flawed White Folk Theory of Racism (Hill 2008) and the very thin Norm of Racial Equality (Mendelberg 2001), both discussed in Chapters 1 and 2. Figleaves, we will see, function in concert with the White Folk Theory of Racism. Together, these allow White people to avoid facing up to their own racism and the racism of those that they like or support. In short, the false White Folk Theory of Racism allows for a remarkable range of excuses for racist actions or utterances—excuses which may convince adherents to the folk theory that no racism was present. Figleaves weaponize this fact, using the deeply wrong folk theory in order to provide excuses for what would otherwise be seen as clearly racist utterances. Crucially for our purposes, they also allow racism to run rampant in our political discourse.

1.1 Rough Definition

I'll start with a rough definition of a figleaf, one which is intuitive and good enough for most purposes. Unsurprisingly, there are tricky cases which serve to motivate a number of revisions to this definition. I'll discuss these cases, and the revisions needed, in section 2 of this chapter. Those who are less interested in the technicalities should be able to skip it without any loss.

In order to motivate a rough definition, let's begin with a look at two infamous utterances from Donald Trump. Along with what many take to be shockingly obvious racism, each of these utterances contains some other interesting bits, which I have underlined below.

(1) When Mexico sends its people, they're not sending their best. They're not sending you. They're not sending you. They're sending people that have lots of problems, and they're bringing those problems with us [sic]. They're bringing drugs. They're bringing crime. They're rapists. And some, I assume, are good people. (Phillips 2017)

(2) Donald J. Trump is calling for a total and complete shutdown of Muslims entering the United States until our country's representatives can figure out what the hell is going on. (Johnson 2015)

Most of the media attention to these utterances, both rightly and unsurprisingly, has focused on their racism: (1) calls Mexicans rapists, and (2) calls for banning Muslims from entering the US. These are shockingly explicit instances of racist speech, and it was absolutely right to focus on that. However, there's also something else going on in both of these, and that's the presence of figleaves.

In (1), there are at least two important kinds of figleaves. The first is the focus not on all Mexicans, but on just the Mexicans who are sent. A person who understands racism as requiring hostility toward all members of a group can take this as an indication that the speaker isn't racist after all. If Trump's focus is on the Mexicans *who are sent*, then he is not making a claim about all Mexicans.[1] This fact allows one who subscribes to the folk theory to reassure themself that Trump is not racist. In case this is not enough, however, there is also an additional figleaf in the statement that Trump assumes some of the Mexicans to be good people. This extremely weak praise nonetheless serves as a further indicator that Trump is not criticizing all Mexicans, and it reassures in much the same way as the first sort of figleaf does.

It is vital to note that this does not work in the same way for everyone. Some see the racism very clearly and are extremely happy with it. Others see the racism very clearly and are horrified. But there is a group in the middle, who can be persuaded either that there is no racism here or that it's not such a bad instance of racism that they need to worry about it. This middle group is the group that the figleaves are for. They are reassured by the presence of the figleaves. Some of them may be reassured enough to support Trump, while others may simply be reassured enough not to feel outraged, and not to reject him quite yet. All of these people are useful to those who want to make Trump and his racist message acceptable.

In (2), the obvious racism of a ban on Muslims is tempered by the qualifier suggesting that it will only be in place while US officials figure out what is going on. This qualifier works as a figleaf for those who believe that a racist is one who condemns a group based on their biology or other essential features. They might worry about a ban on Muslims. But a ban based on biological features would not be a temporary one, until we figure out what is going on. It would be permanent. Because the figleaf is included, then, adherents to the White Folk Theory of Racism can once more comfort themselves by believing that there was no racism indicated by the utterance.

Again, the figleaf is just for those who need the reassurance that it provides, and who can be convinced by the figleaf not to worry (or not to worry too much) about the racism of the utterance. Those who are eager to hear a message of racism do not need the figleaf, and they are likely to ignore it. Those who recognize Trump's message as racist or Islamophobic are generally not reassured by the figleaf. But the figleaf reaches at least some of those whom it is meant to reach, and it does important work by reassuring them.

These examples lead us to a simple rough definition of "racial figleaf."

A racial figleaf is a bit of speech which (for some portion of the audience) blocks the conclusion that either (a) some other bit of speech, R, is racist; or (b) the person who uttered R is racist.

To see how this works, consider Trump's announcement of his intended Muslim ban. On its own, "a total and complete shutdown of Muslims entering the United States" (R) would be extremely widely seen as explicit racism. Accompanied by the figleaf, it (R) is still widely seen as explicit racism. However, for some of the audience the figleaf works. For some, it provides reassurance that the announcement was not an instance of racism, and that Trump was not racist. For others, it does not lead to the belief that Trump is *not* racist. Yet it is nonetheless quite powerful: it introduces just enough doubt about the claim that Trump is racist to keep them from inferring to that conclusion. Because the conclusion that someone is racist is such an undesirable one to draw, all that is needed for many people is a little bit of doubt. To function as a figleaf, an utterance needs to block this sort of conclusion for some of the audience, but it does not need to do so for the whole of the audience. (A would-be figleaf that does not block such a conclusion for anyone is merely an attempted figleaf.)[2]

1.2 Examples

In this section, I will offer a partial list of kinds of racial figleaves, with the goal of giving some idea of the breadth of utterances that can fulfill this function. The list is not intended to be comprehensive.[3] At the outset, though, it is worth calling attention to two broad types of figleaves. A synchronic figleaf takes place at the same time as the utterance or partial utterance that it provides cover for. A diachronic figleaf takes place at a different time, often afterwards when the racism of a previous utterance is criticized.

1.2.1 Racism Denial

An infamously common sort of figleaf is to simply assert that one is not racist, often in conjunction with an utterance that would otherwise be recognized as clearly racist: as in *I'm not racist, but R.* This figleaf is so widely known that it is the subject of jokes and Tumblr blogs, and many of us begin to. flinch in expectation of a racist comment as soon as we hear "I'm not racist but…" Eduardo Bonilla-Silva cites this sort of move as one of "the most common verbal strategies used by whites in post-civil rights race talk" (2002: 46) in order to "talk nasty about blacks" (2002: 41). It is also discussed by van Dijk (1993) as a kind of linguistic test for the phrase that comes after it. According to van Dijk, if it is appropriate to introduce a phrase with "I'm not a racist but," then that is an indicator that the phrase is probably overtly racist. Hill (2008: 120) uses this as a test for *covert* racism, suggesting that if something is racially problematic but fails this test, that is an indication that it is covertly racist.[4] Despite being widely seen as a phrase that accompanies racist utterances, it *remains* a common accompaniment to racist utterances, and thus a common synchronic figleaf.

It is also a popular diachronic figleaf, often used in response to criticism. Here are just a few examples of this from Donald Trump, in response to allegations of racism:

"I'm not a racist. I am the least racist person you have ever interviewed, that I can tell you" (Shear 2018)

"No. 1, I am the least anti-Semitic person that you've ever seen in your entire life. No. 2, racism, the least racist person" (Snyder 2017)

"I am the least racist person in this room" (Nagourney 2016)

"I'm the least racist person anybody is going to meet"[5]

Obviously, not everyone is equally convinced by this sort of figleaf. Most readers of this book, probably, will not be the slightest bit convinced by this sort of declaration. But readers of this book are not the intended audience. The intended audience is people who are moveable and persuadable by this sort of utterance. And because the White Folk Theory of Racism is widely held, there will be many such people. This is, after all, a theory which allows for almost any utterance to be excused as resulting from the (misleading) head rather than the (genuine) heart. According to this theory, it is only the most blatant, obvious, and monstrous who need to be considered racists. There is ample room, then, on this theory for the thought that a person who sincerely declares their non-racism cannot be a racist, and any evidence to the contrary can be dismissed as not really indicating the person's heart.

1.2.2 Friendship Assertion

One of the most clichéd and well-known ways of attempting to cover for racism is to assert that one has close friends from the relevant racial group. In its classic form this is rendered as "some of my best friends are Black." But it has many variants. For example, Eduardo Bonilla-Silva reported that 20 different interviewees (out of 124) used some variant of the phrase, "to signify that they could not possibly be 'racist' " (2002: 47).[6]

This can be used as a synchronic figleaf as in "some of my best friends are Black but R," where R is an utterance that would otherwise be easily recognized as racist. The reason this figleaf succeeds, when it does, is again due to the acceptance of flawed theories of how racism works. If one accepts the widespread false belief that racists will be hostile to all members of the racial group against which they are prejudiced, then having a friend from that group would actually seem like evidence that one is not racist. Acceptance of this deeply problematic folk theory of racism, then, is crucial to the working of this figleaf. Most of the readers of this book, who I presume to be people interested in racist and manipulative language, will not be moved by this figleaf, but others are. And it is still very widely used.

Here are two examples, just from Donald Trump. Both of these are what I called diachronic figleaves—figleaves which occur at a different time from the utterance for which they provide some cover. In the case of both of these, the utterances were made in response to criticism of previous utterances which had led to accusations of racism:

> After weeks of criticism over his attempts to reach out to African-American voters, Donald Trump on Thursday professed to have "so many African-American friends" who are "living the good life."
>
> "I have so many African-American friends that are doing great. They are making good money. They are living the good life. They've got the American dream going," the Republican nominee said Thursday on Fox News' "The O'Reilly Factor." (Lima 2016)

Here is another example:

> "I have great African-American friendships. I have just amazing relationships, and so many positive things have happened." (Scott 2015)

The remarkable vagueness of these examples does a bit to undermine their plausibility, but for those who accept them and also the flawed folk theory, they may provide reassurance that Trump is not racist. Alternatively, it may not be necessary to provide such a positive reassurance. Raising a doubt about his racism might be sufficient, and that is surely easier to do.

This figleaf, like the racism denial figleaf, is widely known and widely mocked. It will definitely not succeed with everyone. However, it will succeed with some. The subjects interviewed by Bonilla-Silva may have been reassuring themselves of their own lack of racism as they mentioned their Black friendships (as well as attempting to convince Bonilla-Silva). And people like this are probably also reassured by the Black friendships of others. Again, knowledge of the White Folk Theory of Racism explains why people would find this reassuring. One who adheres to this theory will think that friendship with a Black person shows that someone cannot possibly be racist in their heart. On this theory, a racist is a monstrous person who would never form such a friendship. Those who hold this theory, then, will be genuinely reassured by seeing such friendships or hearing about them. Obviously, others will not be; and the use of the figleaf will, for these people, not provide reassurance. But this group is not whom the figleaf is meant for.

1.2.3 "It's a Joke"

As Blee and Simi, researchers on White supremacist movements, have noted:

> the tactic of joking can be used as a form of double-speak to deny culpability. This is a broad cultural practice, although more pronounced in particular subcultures such as white supremacism, in which the claim that "I was only joking" becomes a defense against possible challenge.[7]

What they are describing is the use of an extremely popular figleaf. The claim that one is joking provides a ready and all-purpose defense against any accusations of racist rhetoric. This technique has long been known and used, and it was even quite deliberately adopted by the early Ku Klux Klan:

> Descriptions of attacks by men in hoods, who had titles like "dragon," "ghoul," and "wizard," were often seen by white Americans as tall tales and ghost stories. Newspapers that supported the KKK played up those aspects of the group and mocked their opponents for supposedly taking the KKK too seriously, said Elaine Frantz, a historian at Kent State University...Pro-KKK newspaper editors would often "talk jokingly

about what the Klan has done," said Frantz, "in order to be deniable." (Driesbach 2021)

White supremacist groups to this day deliberately employ this technique, and teach it to their members. Here is an instruction from a style guide written by Andrew Anglin, founder of *The Daily Stormer*.

> Generally, when using racial slurs, it should come across as half-joking—like a racist joke that everyone laughs at because it's true. This follows the generally light tone of the site. It should not come across as genuine raging vitriol. That is a turnoff to the overwhelming majority of people.[8]

A further reason that sites like the *Daily Stormer* use humor is that it can help newcomers[9] to feel more comfortable with racist content:

> Far-right communities online have, for several years now, been using humor specifically as a recruitment tool for young, disillusioned people and particularly young, disillusioned men. In fact, a really popular neo-Nazi website, a couple of years ago its style guide got leaked. The founder of that website explicitly wrote that humor is a recruitment tool because it gives the far-right extremists plausible deniability about their extremist beliefs. (Wood 2019)

The current success of the technique is also facilitated by the large regions of Internet culture which are devoted to offensive speech presented as jokes.[10] This is particularly, but not exclusively common in the so-called "manosphere" of disgruntled, largely White men who feel rejected by and disconnected from mainstream culture. Their own subculture, formed online, gives a crucial role to such speech:

> When Trump announced his candidacy on June 16, 2015 from the lobby of his office, his speech condemning Mexicans as "rapists" was considered an offensive publicity stunt. However, it turned out that the politics of offensive publicity stunts aligned in an uncanny way with the vast group of netizens waiting for someone who spoke to their lived experience of racist jokes, screen performances, and garbage ads. (Beran 2019: 150)

The assertion that one is joking can work as a figleaf only because the White Folk Theory of Racism focuses its attention exclusively on the conscious beliefs and intentions of the speaker. According to this theory it is only speakers that can be racist, and, as we've seen, this is only if they are racist in their hearts—a very rare phenomenon, only achieved by truly monstrous individuals. This is also a manifestation of what Jane Hill calls personalist ideology, whereby all that merits consideration is the state of mind of the person speaking—rather than the meanings of the words (2008: 95–6).

To close this section, let's consider an especially egregious use of this fig-leaf (combined with another) from a website discussed by Blee and Simi.[11] This website offers a printable target of a caricature of a Black person, headed "Official Running N***** Target." It comes with instructions on how to print it at the right size for shooting practice and asserts that "most felons are n******." But then it says "we are strong against violence, and do not support violent or illegal behavior. This page is for laughs only." Here we get not one, but two figleaves: the first is an assertion of anti-violence on a page that obviously promotes violence. And the second is, once again, that all-purpose humor figleaf.

1.2.4 "People Are Saying"

Another wonderfully useful figleaf is to insist that one is merely reporting what others have said. This allows one to draw attention to certain sentiments and ideas, without taking responsibility for them. All that this requires is the assertion that something has been said by others, with no further details. Once more, this draws upon personalist ideology: if intention is all that matters, one can avoid accountability by insisting that one is only quoting others.[12] Donald Trump often uses this form of the technique—and we will see more on this in Chapter 5.

One form of this figleaf has been very much facilitated by Internet communication. It is extremely easy to retweet someone else's utterance as a way of disseminating the ideas contained in it. There is no clear convention about whether doing this counts as endorsing these ideas, as Regina Rini (2017) has noted.[13] And it is almost always possible to insist after the fact that no endorsement was intended. Here's an example from Trump:

In January, Trump retweeted a photoshopped image of Jeb Bush from a user with the handle WhiteGenocideTM. In response to the backlash he received for retweeting a white supremacist, Trump simply shrugged: "I don't know about retweeting. You retweet somebody, and they turn out to be white supremacists. I know nothing about these groups that are supporting me." (Mercieca 2016)

But there's absolutely nothing new about this technique. One of the most famous racist speeches in British history is Conservative MP Enoch Powell's "Rivers of Blood" speech in 1968. Powell carefully used this technique, with many of the most blatantly racist portions of the speech actually being reports of what others had said. His use of the technique is somewhat more sophisticated than Trump's, involving anecdotes which at least appear to be about specific individuals:

> A week or two ago I fell into conversation with a constituent, a middle-aged, quite ordinary working man employed in one of our nationalised industries. After a sentence or two about the weather, he suddenly said: "If I had the money to go, I wouldn't stay in this country." I made some deprecatory reply to the effect that even this government wouldn't last forever; but he took no notice, and continued: "I have three children, all of them been through grammar school and two of them married now, with family. I shan't be satisfied till I have seen them all settled overseas. In this country in 15 or 20 years' time the black man will have the whip hand over the white man."
>
> I can already hear the chorus of execration. How dare I say such a horrible thing? How dare I stir up trouble and inflame feelings by repeating such a conversation?
>
> The answer is that I do not have the right not to do so. Here is a decent, ordinary fellow Englishman, who in broad daylight in my own town says to me, his Member of Parliament, that his country will not be worth living in for his children.[14]

Powell uses this anecdote to disavow all responsibility for the racist sentiments expressed. Indeed, he insists that he has no choice but to bring the sentiments to our attention. The figleaf provides tremendously useful cover, by distancing the speaker from responsibility for the racism expressed, while introducing it into the discussion. In so doing, the expression of these sentiments can gradually become normalized.

1.2.5 Criticize Someone Else's Racism

One of the very first figleaves that I noticed was Donald Trump's discussion of Supreme Court Justice Antonin Scalia's comments about affirmative action. Scalia had suggested that affirmative action was actually bad for Black people, as it resulted in them being admitted to institutions which they found too difficult. Trump criticized this:

"I thought it was very tough to the African-American community, actually," Trump said. "I don't like what he said. No, I don't like what he said."..."I heard him," Trump continued, "I was like, 'Let me read it again' because I actually saw it in print, and I'm going—I read a lot of stuff—and I'm going, 'Whoa!'" (Jerde 2015)

This criticism of someone else's racism can be a very powerful diachronic figleaf, to be pulled out and pointed to as needed.

Donald Trump is by no means the only one to use this technique. Ian Haney López offers a nice set of observations about the many times that the Republican Party makes use of it, "publicly posturing against racism" (2019: 27), in order to achieve deniability:[15]

The right obfuscates its basic racial strategy by issuing impassioned denunciations of blatant racism. It does so against right-wing extremists as well as the occasional Republican who strays too far into audible range, as when the house GOP leaders stripped Iowa representative Stephen King of committee seats after he defended the terms "white supremacist" and "white nationalist". Party officials often also condemn racism from Democrats, thereby polishing their credentials as anti-racists while also fostering the both-sides sense that the two parties are equally susceptible to occasional eruptions of racism. (2019: 27)

Again, we can see why this is so effective by thinking about the White Folk Theory of Racism, and in particular the image of the racist as a monster who is truly comfortable with racism and would never criticize the racism of others. If one holds this view of racism and racists, then any criticism of someone else's racism proves that one is not a racist.

1.2.6 Snowflake/Cancel Culture/Political Correctness/Wokeism

Recall that a figleaf is a bit of speech that blocks the inference from something that a person has said to the claim that the person or utterance is racist. An excellent way to block this inference is to accuse anyone who makes it of being unreasonable. This makes the inference unattractive, reducing the likelihood that one will make it. It also changes the topic from the racist utterance to the question of whether or not pointing this out is unreasonable. The strategy has a long history and it comes in many guises. Just in the last few decades the accusation has moved from one of being "politically correct" to one of being "a snowflake" to one of "cancel culture" to "wokeism." On the right side of the political spectrum, all of these terms suggest unreasonable-ness and overreaction, with the risk of excessive restrictions on speech. As Janet McIntosh notes, there is also often a suggestion of class prejudice and contempt for those who use the wrong terminology (2020: 9).

The use of these ideas in defense of racism is sometimes mistaken for a dogwhistle.[16] This seems to be because it has become so common for those who express racism to also make these claims. What is really going on, though, is that they are employed as figleaves in order to discredit anyone who criticizes racism, and to distract by shifting the attention onto those people. This makes it a highly effective diachronic figleaf, which can dis-credit criticism both after the fact and in advance:

> "I think the big problem this country has is being politically correct," Trump tells the moderator, Fox News' Megyn Kelly. "I've been challenged by so many people and I don't, frankly, have time for total political cor-rectness. And to be honest with you, this country doesn't have time, either." (Chow 2016)

It can also be deployed synchronically:

> At a rally a year ago in South Carolina, he called for a "total and complete shutdown of Muslims entering the United States." He told a cheering crowd that his statement on the subject was "very, very salient, very important and probably not politically correct." (Chow 2016)

In the above instance, Trump is mentioning political correctness at the same time as discussing his prior call for a Muslim ban. Mentioning politi-cal correctness signals that he realizes people might object to what he say-ing, but due to the negative associations with the phrase "politically correct," he's discrediting anyone who might make those criticisms.

1.2.7 Racism Accusation

It has become very common to parry an accusation of racism with the claim that the person making the accusation is the real racist. This goes well with a deeply flawed color-blind understanding of racism (Bonilla-Silva 2002, 2018) on which any reference to race is evidence of racism. (It also conven-iently designates such things as affirmative action, or even tracking of racial disparities, as racist.)

Importantly, however, this also functions beautifully as a figleaf. A figleaf blocks the inference from a racist utterance to the conclusion that the speaker or that utterance is racist. Accusing a person who points out racism of being a racist is an extremely effective diachronic figleaf. For many audience members, it will block the inference to the claim that the original speaker was racist. There are several ways that this can happen. One is that it serves as a distraction, switching attention to the person who made the racism accusation rather than the person who made the racist utterance. The other is that it makes the utterance unappealing. If people who name and criticize racism are the real racists, as this figleaf suggests, then concluding that something is racist is extremely undesirable: it makes one a racist. Given the currency of the color-blind racism view among the White population, this figleaf works well.

This figleaf has quite a history. Haney López discusses its use by George Wallace in 1968. At this time, Wallace was using dogwhistle language referencing "law and order" and "states' rights." As always, some people recognized and criticized the dogwhistles as racist:

> In turn, Wallace was saying to his crowds, "you know who the biggest bigots in the world are? They're the ones who call others bigots"
>
> (Haney López 2019a: 33)

Haney López notes that this confirmed "the sense among many of [Wallace's] supporters that they, and not minorities, were the actual victims of racial discrimination" (2019a: 34). It also served as a figleaf for some, by redirecting their critical attention to the people who criticized Wallace for racism. This kept them from inferring to Wallace's racism, and it made inferring racism an unattractive move.

Trump, and Republicans more generally, continue to make regular use of this figleaf. Derek Anderson describes this pattern well:

> Trump's second line of defense is, somewhat ironically, to redeploy the word "racist" against his adversaries in order to defame and demonize them. He tweets: "The 'Squad' is a very Racist group of troublemakers who are young, inexperienced, and not very smart." In another tweet about a month later, Trump wrote, "The Amazon Washington Post did a story that I brought racist attacks against the 'Squad.' No, they brought racist attacks against our Nation."   (2021: 9)

Anderson considers this usage of "racist" to be an instance of what he calls "linguistic hijacking":

> They are hijacking the word "racist," using it against people of color. Patterns of linguistic hijacking perpetrated by dominant agents spread misinformation and false belief about systems of oppression and function to preserve the status quo against movements that seek to create a more just society.   (2021: 12)

In addition to the uses that Anderson describes, this sort of linguistic hijacking also allows for a very effective figleaf—making people hesitate to agree with those who point out racism, and changing the topic to those people rather than the one whose racism should be at issue.

1.2.8 That's Not a Race!

In Chapter 1, we discussed the fact that prejudice against members of nationalities or religious groups is not always seen as racism. We also saw that many scholars and ordinary people do in fact take such prejudice to be racism. Indeed, Donald Trump's remarks about Muslims and Mexicans are often seen as paradigmatic cases of racist utterances, even though they are about a religious group and a nationality, respectively. It is not surprising, then, that a common defense against racism is to insist that one is talking about a group like a nationality or religion, and to maintain that this group is not a possible target of racism.

Anya Topolski, in her rich and fascinating discussion of the relationship (both historical and present day) between race and religion, discusses the use of this maneuver, which I would characterize as a diachronic figleaf:

> Marine Le Pen and Geert Wilders [far-right European politicians] . . . rarely miss an opportunity to claim that they are not racists precisely because their critique of Muslims has nothing to do with race—for them it's about religious or cultural differences that are unassimilable (and thus naturalized, as biological race was for Jews by way of anti-Semitism). A common argument voiced in response to claims about the rise of Islamophobia is a denial that it is a form of racism.   (2018: 74)

Although there may be genuinely good reasons for distinguishing racism from other prejudices, these distinctions also have immense utility as a figleaf which allows one to dodge criticism for bigoted sentiments.

1.3 The Danger of Figleaves

To really appreciate the danger of figleaves, it will be helpful to briefly examine a popular picture of how our conversational permissibility standards evolve. This picture starts from the simple fact that in conversations we generally assume one another to be cooperative, at least in a minimal communicative sense (Grice 1975). Because of this, we have a tendency to absorb and take on board whatever is needed to make sense of what our interlocutors are saying. This is what is called accommodation (Lewis 1979). So, for example, suppose I mention that my cats woke me early because Daylight Savings Time ended. You may not have known before this utterance that I had cats, and you might even not have known that Daylight Savings Time has ended for me (perhaps it hasn't where you live). But in order to make sense of me as a cooperative conversational participant, you will probably accept these claims, perhaps even without noticing that you are doing so. After this, it is no longer permissible to ask me if I have any pets, or to ask whether Daylight Savings Time has ended yet. Conversational permissibility facts evolve quickly and fluidly through this sort of process of accommodation.

Some of those who study oppressive language have built on this understanding to construct a powerful story of how racist, sexist, and other oppressive norms may be introduced or perpetuated through processes of conversational accommodation. According to this story, if somebody makes a racist or sexist comment, and nobody objects, the other conversational participants will make whatever racist and sexist assumptions are necessary in order to make sense of that conversational contribution (McGowan 2009, 2012, 2019; Langton 2012, 2018; Maitra 2012). Mary Kate McGowan (2012) gives the example of someone who makes a blatantly racist comment on a bus. When no one on the bus speaks up to protest, she argues, the norms for that context shift so that racist speech becomes permissible. This picture offers a compelling reason for placing great importance on speaking up in the face of racist utterances. But on its own, it is not actually a fully plausible picture of how the norms change.

The problem is that norms don't really change this smoothly in response to a *blatantly* racist utterance. If people in the conversation accept the Norm of Racial Equality, then they won't smoothly assimilate the blatantly racist utterance and think that it's become permissible to make racist utterances now. The fact that no one speaks up will not make them feel that this is acceptable. In fact, silence is a common response to a norm-violating utterance that makes people intensely uncomfortable (Saul 2017, Klieber 2023). There are some audiences who would happily accept and assimilate the blatantly racist utterance. But those are the people who already rejected the Norm of Racial Equality. Making these people *comfortable* with a racist utterance is not actually any kind of change: they already were comfortable with it.

To actually change what people find acceptable with regard to racist utterances, a different approach is needed. People who accept the Norm of Racial Equality need to become convinced that an utterance which they would otherwise have found problematic is actually not one to worry about. And this is a task for which figleaves are ideally suited. Consider a speaker who makes an utterance R, that would otherwise have been easily recognized as racist, but who accompanies it with an effective figleaf. Those who accept that figleaf will become convinced that R is the sort of thing that a non-racist might say. R—which would otherwise have been seen as blatantly racist—now becomes acceptable to some of the people who worry about the Norm of Racial Equality. This, then, is a powerful mechanism for changing standards of acceptable utterances. As a result, it is a highly effective means of rendering racist utterances far more socially acceptable than they previously were. This allows the blatantly racist utterances to spread far and wide, with far-reaching consequences for political discourse.

To take a vivid example, consider again Donald Trump's campaign tweet declaring his intention to ban Muslims from entering the United States, accompanied by a figleaf. He called for:

"a total and complete shutdown of Muslims entering the United States until our country's representatives can figure out what is going on."

(Johnson 2015)

Now think about the people on whom this figleaf works. These people might have worried about calling for a complete and total ban on Muslim entry to the United States, but Trump allayed that worry by saying that it was only temporary. They concluded that the ban wasn't really racist, and Trump wasn't really racist for proposing such a ban. Now take a moment to reflect on what this means: it means that these people came to believe that calling for a ban on Muslims was not racist, and also that calling for such a ban was the sort of thing a non-racist might do. The once-shocking ban was mentioned over and over, accompanied by the figleaf, and ceased to even be shocking. Figleaves can help changes like this to happen. If figleaves have the power to convince people that things like Muslim bans are not racist, then they are quite clearly extremely dangerous. Because figleaves facilitate much more open expression of racism, they have the ability to shift people's understanding of what counts as racism. And this is where their special danger lies.

If we were seeking an example of how standards of acceptable discourse have shifted, we could hardly do better than a comparison between what happened to Representative Steve King and what happened to Representative Marjorie Taylor Greene. In 2019 King's fellow Republicans removed him from all of his congressional committee assignments due to his comments musing over what could be wrong with "White supremacy" and "White nationalism." By 2021, Marjorie Taylor Greene could suggest that the Rothschilds (classic target of anti-Jewish conspiracy theories) used lasers to set forest fires (Chait 2021); that George Soros, who is Jewish, is a Nazi (Fox 2021); that Hillary Clinton is involved in pedophilia and human sacrifice (Chait 2021); and the Great Replacement Theory that Jews are plotting to replace White people with immigrants (Chait 2021)—all with overwhelming continued support from Republicans in Congress. (She was eventually removed from her committee assignments, by the Democratic majority, but in 2023 was welcomed back by the incoming Republican majority.)

And of course there is the fact that Trump has, over and over, made the sorts of utterances that would be expected to end a career. Each time, these did not have nearly the negative effect that was expected. Part of this, it seems likely, is due to the shifting of norms facilitated by figleaves. Figleaves made it possible to make utterances like these and politically survive. Repetition of these utterances, and the figleaves, allowed for habituation and normalization to the point where what would once have shocked came to seem normal.

2. Tough Cases, and Refining the Definition

Our first refinement of the definition will simply be to add a little bit more explicitness about the relativity to audiences (addition in italics):

A racial figleaf F *for an audience A* with respect to an utterance R is a bit of speech which blocks A from concluding that either (a) R is racist; or (b) the person who uttered R is racist.

This will allow us to acknowledge that something may be a figleaf for one audience, A; while being merely an attempted figleaf for another audience, B. It also helps us to see the extent to which the working of a figleaf is dependent upon a particular audience's assumptions, including their understanding of racism (in many cases, these assumptions include the White Folk Theory of Racism, as discussed earlier). Racial figleaves, as we have already noted, often depend for their functioning on deeply flawed understandings of racism.

2.1 Counterexamples

Both the rough definition of "figleaf" with which we began, and this refined definition, are susceptible to some very convincing counterexamples.

2.1.1 The Language Learner

Consider the case of somebody who is just learning English, who mistakenly utters a racial slur, as a result of a purely linguistic error. When this person learns of their error, they apologize in horror, and explain that they had made a linguistic error. Now consider the question of whether this apology and explanation count as a figleaf. One who hears this apology will not change their mind about the slur being a racist bit of speech (clause (a)), but they are very likely to change their mind about whether the speaker is racist (clause (b)). This apology and explanation, then, seem to block the inference from the utterance to the claim that the speaker is racist. It counts, then, as a figleaf. But this seems wrong. It doesn't seem to be providing any sort of manipulative cover for a problematic utterance, but rather explaining how a terrible mistake came to be made, and genuinely apologizing for it.

2.1.2 The Anti-racist Speaker

Now turn to the case of an anti-racist speaker, giving a talk in favor of prison abolition. One sentence of this talk states some statistics about relative percentages of Black and White men who are incarcerated. On its own, that sentence might seem like a racist utterance—one that reinforces stereotypes of Black criminality. In context, however, this seems wrong. But consider now the question of whether the rest of the speech meets the definition of figleaf, with respect to the audience that would have found the sentence racist on its own. That audience, having heard the whole of the speech, will not conclude that either the speaker or the speech is racist. And this is because of all the sentences other than the one about relative incarceration rates. Those sentences, then, do seem to be a figleaf for the incarceration rate sentence, relative to this audience. Those sentences, after all, are the reason that the audience doesn't take the speaker or the sentence about incarceration rates to be racist. Again, this seems clearly wrong.

2.2 Revising the Definition

A first attempt at discerning why these verdicts seem wrong is that the speakers in question simply do not seem racist. And, in the second case, the full utterance in question does not seem racist. A figleaf seems like it should actually be *covering for racism* and in these cases there does not seem to be racism to cover for. The utterance that is considered to be a figleaf, moreover, seems not to be covering for *anything* but rather to be revealing the true facts of the situation. This suggests I need to build in the idea that figleaves are covering up the truth. Here's a first attempt at doing this (changes in italics):

A racial figleaf F for an audience A and utterance R is a bit of speech which blocks A from *correctly* concluding that either (a) R (the bit of speech) is racist; or (b) the person who uttered R is racist.

Does this definition deliver the correct verdict in our problem cases? Unfortunately, it's not so clear that it does. Let's start with our language learner. We are hoping to get the result that the explanation is not a figleaf. In order to do this, it needs to be the case that our language learner is not racist—otherwise the explanation would be serving as a figleaf for their racism. But this seems like a lot to require, especially when we consider that there are theories on which a person counts as racist if they harbor some implicit racism, which arguably most (perhaps all) of us do.

Consider again our language learner, using a racist term without the awareness that they are doing so. But now imagine that they also harbor some degree of implicit bias, as many believe that most of us do. The fact that the speaker might harbor some implicit racism, totally unrelated to their linguistic error, does not seem like enough to make it correct to conclude that the explanation of their linguistic error is a figleaf. Similar considerations hold for our anti-racist speaker. Even though the speaker is working hard to fight racism, it may well be that they still harbor some.

Once again, this seems irrelevant to the issue of whether the rest of their speech serves as a figleaf for one line that could be taken out of context and understood as racist. And this problem is not dependent on a theory of racism which includes subtle or implicit racism. Even if the speakers actually harbored quite explicit racial hatred, the putative figleaves simply don't seem to be connected in the right way to the utterances for which they supposedly serve as figleaves.

Here, then, is another definition, which allows for more of a focus on the connection between F, the figleaf, and R, the racist utterance (changes in italics):

A racial figleaf F for an audience A and utterance R is a bit of speech which blocks A from *correctly* concluding that either (a) R (the bit of speech) is racist; or (b) R *indicates that* the person who uttered R is racist.

This definition fares much better with our problem cases. Since it's obviously not the case that our language learner's utterance indicates that they are racist (remember, it's just a genuine linguistic error), the explanation does not block the audience from *correctly concluding* that the utterance indicates that they are racist. Likewise for the anti-racist speaker: it is clearly incorrect to suggest that the incarceration rate sentence indicates the speaker's racism, even if it might have done so for a different speaker in a different context. Once more, then, a figleaf is correctly ruled out. Interestingly, this does not seem to depend on what definition of "racism" one holds. There is no plausible definition of racism on which a language learner's linguistic error leads to the result that they are racist; similarly, there is no plausible definition of racism on which a single sentence of an anti-racist talk, ripped misleadingly from its context, indicates that the speaker is racist.

2.3 Knowing whether Something Is a Figleaf

It might seem reasonable to conclude from what I have said so far that use of a phrase that is a racial figleaf is a sign, possibly even an infallible one, that a speaker or utterance is racist. However, I think this is deeply mistaken. It is perfectly possible to use a phrase that is typically a racial figleaf, without being racist, or to pair it with an expression that is not an expression of racism. This is true even of the best-known and most maligned figleaves. We can imagine, for example, a very nervous and misguided speaker saying something like this:

- I'm not a racist, but I don't agree with Obama's use of drones.

This nervous speaker is so worried about being taken to be a racist when they criticize a Black President that they attempt to prevent this. Unfortunately, the device that they choose to try to prevent this is one which for many people is a signal that a racist utterance is on its way. (For others, of course, it might provide some reassurance that they are not racist.) Importantly, there's nothing racist about criticizing Obama's use of drones. And we can well imagine a non-racist speaker making this criticism. It may be harder to imagine such a person pairing it with the phrase "I'm not a racist, but…"; however, if they come from a community where this sort of phrasing is common and they are not very knowledgeable about racial discourse, they might well say something like this. This lack of knowledge is in all likelihood not accidental, but results both from racial segregation and from well-established practices and traditions of White ignorance (Mills 2007). But none of that shows that this particular speaker is racist or saying something racist. In a case like that which I have described, the racism is structural—about patterns and traditions—rather than individual.

How does one know, then, whether a phrase like this is an attempted figleaf, trying to cover for racism, or just a misguided utterance? The answer is that there is no simple way to tell. The only way to know is through a real understanding of the person, the context, and what has been said. This may be easy to come by, as it would be if "I'm not a racist, but" is paired with something blatantly racist. Or it may be much more difficult to figure out. But it is not something we can read off the linguistic form of an utterance. Figleaves are important to understand, because they help to cover for and normalize expressions of racism. But they do not provide a shortcut for identifying racist utterances or people.

2.4 Caring whether Something Is a Figleaf

A further question, and quite a compelling one, is whether we should care at all about whether an apparent figleaf is really a figleaf or not. This amounts, in significant part, to the question of whether we should care whether individuals are personally racist or not—since an utterance is only a figleaf if it is providing cover for another utterance that would be a correct indicator of racism. I think this is an excellent and difficult question. I will answer in a perhaps unsatisfying way: sometimes we should care about this, but often we shouldn't.

I'll start with a bit about why and when we should care. Sometimes we really do need to know whether someone is expressing their own racism, or simply saying something that sounds racist. We need to know this if the person in question is someone close to us, or someone that we're considering getting close to. It may affect whether or not we want to get close to them or continue the relationship. It can let us know what sorts of potentially difficult conversations we need to have with such a person (Emerick 2016). But this is not the only time that we need to know this sort of thing. It also matters when we're making a decision about, for example, whom to vote for or whom to trust. Ideally, the people we are considering voting or trusting would not say things that sound even somewhat racist. But the world we live in is far from ideal. That being the case, it is more than reasonable to prefer to elect or trust those who are speaking clumsily rather than those who are expressing their personal racism while trying to seek some bit of cover.

For other purposes, however, whether or not a problematic utterance is actually expressing a person's individual racism doesn't matter at all. If racist utterances are made, and passed on, and spread far and wide through the Internet, accompanied by figleaves to facilitate their spread, enormous damage is done regardless of what's in the heads of those doing the spreading. The ubiquity of the racist utterances habituates the community to these expressions of racism. The stereotypes and hate become more likely to be adopted and shared by members of the community. The targets of the racism are exposed to harmful and abusive treatment. The standards of what is normal to express shift to accommodate these utterances, a shift greatly facilitated by the figleaves. And this shift can be a devastatingly dangerous one, as well documented by Lynne Tirrell's work on genocidal speech (Tirrell 2012, 2017). In terms of spreading and inciting hateful and discriminatory views and behavior, then, it is utterly irrelevant what is going on in the minds of those making or sharing racist utterances. In this very important sense, we should not care whether a person is actually expressing racism or not—and therefore, whether an utterance is a real or merely apparent figleaf.

2.5 What Figleaves Need to Do

It is important to emphasize that the effectiveness of a figleaf does not depend on its audience becoming convinced that the relevant utterance or person is *not racist*, or even that the relevant utterance is *not an indicator of racism*. A figleaf does not have such strong success conditions as these. In order to succeed, all a figleaf needs to do is *raise some doubt*—how much doubt is needed will depend on the context. For example, consider a politician who makes a racist-sounding comment just before an election. They already have loyal voters who have been committed to them for some time, but some of these voters feel hesitant in light of this utterance. The politician issues a statement about all the Black friends that they have. The voters who had already planned to vote for this person really want to do so, and are seeking a permission structure for this. Without the figleaf, they might find it morally unacceptable to vote for this person. But the figleaf gives them just enough of an excuse to think that they can't be quite sure what that racist comment was really about. With this in hand, they can vote for the politician. This very small amount of doubt, then, is sufficient in this situation.

One key reason that this doubt can be generated so easily is that White people will often distance themselves from any obligation to understand racism, using as an excuse the fact that they are not Black. Bonilla-Silva writes:

> One such move that appeared frequently among white college students...was the phrase "I'm not black, so I don't know". After respondents interjected this phrase they proceeded with statements that indicated they have strong views on the racial issue in question.   (2018: 82)

This move is both a figleaf in its own right and an important assistant for figleaves. We will focus on the latter here. The acceptability of not really knowing what's racist means that it's easy to back away from a condemnation of someone's racism. The voter we imagined, who wants to support the politician who made a racist utterance, can easily use the figleaf as an excuse for saying that she doesn't really know what to think anymore. If not really understanding how racism works is acceptable to many White people, and it seems that it is, then such people can be quite reassured by just their own uncertainties—which are easy to generate.

3. Possible Extensions

3.1 Figleaves for Non-utterances, Possible Revision

Because my focus is on the increasing legitimation of explicitly racist utterances, I have been focused on figleaves for a racist *utterances*. However, there is no reason that the concept needs to be confined in this way. One moderate extension would be to instead focus on racist behavior more generally. Here's a revision that would accomplish this:

A racial figleaf F, for an audience A and *bit of behavior* R, is a bit of speech which blocks A from correctly concluding that either (a) R is racist; or (b) R indicates that the person who did R is racist.

This sort of extension would easily include cases such as figleaves for politicians who wore Blackface in their younger days, apparently a disturbingly common pastime for politicians from across the spectrum, including Ralph Northam in Virginia and Justin Trudeau in Canada. But the clearest example I have found of using such a figleaf for such a behavior comes from UK Tory member of parliament Sir Desmond Swayne. In the course of defending Trudeau's use of Blackface, Swayne admitted to his own such use at a party in the past. Responding to criticism of this, he employed not one but two figleaves (bold face mine, to highlight these):

> A Conservative MP has stoked controversy after saying that **"people have lost their sense of proportion and sense of humour"** over wearing Blackface. Sir Desmond Swayne said he saw nothing offensive in painting his face Black, while insisting there **"is not a racist bone in my body"**. The former international development minister was widely criticised last September after admitting he had dressed up as soul singer James Brown for a fancy dress party. (Lovett 2021)

Conceptually, this sort of extension makes great good sense. Racial figleaves are a device used to cover for communicative acts that might otherwise be taken to indicate to indicate racism. I can see no good reason to limit the scope of this concept to *linguistic* communicative acts.

3.2 Third-Party Figleaves

So far, we have been assuming that figleaves are additional bits of speech from the same speaker who utters the bit of speech that would otherwise be seen as racist/an indicator of racism. However, diachronic figleaves in particular seem like they could easily be uttered by another speaker.[17] Our definition of "figleaf" does not actually say anything about who must utter the figleaf:

A racial figleaf F for an audience A and utterance R is a bit of speech which blocks A from correctly concluding that either (a) R (the bit of speech) is racist; or (b) R indicates that the person who uttered R is racist.

Indeed, we would expect to see many cases where a friend or supporter of the person who makes a racist utterance defends them with an utterance that serves as a figleaf. And we do.

Here's an example from the case of Ralph Northam, mentioned above for his Blackface photos from his younger days. People who knew him leapt to his defense, citing the fact that he had friendships with Black people (Eligon 2019):

> "He is the last person on earth that would be racist," one of Mr. Northam's white childhood friends, Harry Mears, told me when I visited Onancock recently. "We have just as many black friends together as we do white friends."

Although our focus has been on people giving figleaves for their own utterances, it is worth noting that this utterance by Harry Mears *does* fit the definition of figleaf, if it is successful. If it does the work it is intended to do, it blocks the audience from inferring to the belief that Northam is racist.

3.3 Collections of Utterances as Figleaves

So far, I have discussed figleaves as single utterances or parts of utterances. However, there is no good reason to limit the concept in this way. There may well be cases in which collections of utterances serve, together, as a figleaf. A nice example of this comes with the collections of chaotic and contradictory utterances that we get from figures like Boris Johnson and Donald Trump. These collections of utterances are frequently pointed to as reasons for not taking anything they say too seriously, and thereby absolving them from responsibility for any problematic utterances. The problematic utterances, it is claimed, do not really indicate their beliefs. And the evidence for this is the chaotic nature of their utterances more generally. (For more on this, see Saul (2019b).)[18]

3.4 Human Figleaves, Possible Revision

Anyone who pays attention to the news, and watches with enough cynicism, will have noticed a certain phenomenon: the woman defense attorney speaking for the serial sexual harasser; the Black politician put forward as spokesperson by a party accused of racism; the truly remarkable number of speakers of color at the 2020 Republican convention, given the demographic makeup of the party (Saul 2020). These people, it is very natural to say, function as *human figleaves*. Because of their own demographic category, their utterances, and sometimes their mere presence, serve to allay doubts about a person, action, or utterance that might otherwise seem racist or sexist.

Here's a first attempt at defining this notion, from my previous work (Saul 2021), with respect to racism:

A **human figleaf** is a person who makes an utterance R that would otherwise be seen as racist. The fact that R is uttered by a person belonging to the social category that they do blocks at least some of the audience from inferring that R is racist.

But this version is limited—for one thing, it is only a synchronic version, and we know that sometimes such people are pulled in after the fact (or before the fact) to provide cover for a racist utterance. We also know that they may sometimes be covering for an *action* not an utterance. And, finally, sometimes a human figleaf need not speak at all—their supportive presence is sufficient. So here is a possible expansion, with respect to racism:

A **human figleaf H** is a person who provides deniability for an action or utterance R that would otherwise be seen as racist. This deniability is provided by the fact that H is known to be from the demographic category targeted by R; and the fact that H is taken to be in some way expressing their support for the person(s) who engaged/s in action or utterance R.

This feels, I think, like a very natural extension of the concept of a figleaf. And it is a useful one, covering an extremely common and often noted phenomenon. We could easily see how a person who accepts the White Folk Theory of Racism would be reassured by the presence of a human figleaf, and moved to doubt that something which would otherwise have worried them is racist. After all, the White Folk Theory holds that a racist is a monstrous individual who consciously and explicitly holds extremely negative attitudes about all members of the racial group in question. It is very unlikely that a member of that racial group would be willing to offer their support for such a monstrous individual. Thus, their utterance or even mere presence is seen as providing evidence the person or group who did something which seems racist is not, after all, racist.

We see a great example of a human figleaf in action in the Conservative Party of Canada example from Chapter 2. Moreover, this example illustrates how a figleaf can work in concert with a dogwhistle. Recall that in this case, the Conservative Party of Canada adopted a slogan with notable similarities to a very famous White supremacist slogan known as "The 14 Words." They expressed the slogan in 14 words. Use of 14-word sayings and the number 14 are both known White supremacist dogwhistles, as observed by Blee and Simi.[19] All of this was publicly noted. However, the claims that the party was dogwhistling to White supremacists were resoundingly and mockingly dismissed. A key reason for this was that the slogan was rolled out with a photo of the party leader greeting a person of color. This fact was cited as conclusive evidence that the slogan could not be a racist dogwhistle. Now, however, we have the tools to recognize that this was a highly effective case of dogwhistle accompanied by a human figleaf for maximum deniability. (It was also a visual figleaf, since the figleaf came in the form of a photo.)

It's worth pausing to briefly distinguish this figleaf from a related but more standard figleaf. We have already noted that a popular figleaf is the assertion that one has friends from the group in question. Closely related to this is the actual pointing out or drawing attention to those friends. Here is a famous example from Trump:

"Oh, look at my African American over here," Trump responded with a smile, pointing at Cheadle as some people in the crowd cheered. "Look at him. Are you the greatest?"   (Blake 2020)

This utterance is an instance of the friendship/supporter assertion figleaf for anti-Black racism—it is an utterance that asserts one's friendship with a person of the targeted race. But it is also, in addition, attempting to enlist the person (Cheadle, in this case) as a human figleaf.

3.5 Figleaves in Thought

Although my primary focus has been on figleaves as utterances, it is not difficult to see how there may be a correlate in thought. Figleaves, when used in thought, can block inferences to the conclusion that one is oneself racist. Self-knowledge is never easy, particularly when it comes to something as socially unacceptable as racism. Figleaves can make this harder. Take, for example, the case of someone who says or does something that they then realize appears to be racist. This is a disconcerting thought. For some people, it will be reassuring to remember that they have a Black friend, that really they were only joking, or that they're not really racist in their heart and that's what matters. Calling up such thoughts may provide total reassurance that they are not racist, or they may simply provide enough doubt that the disconcerted person can move on to thinking about something else. Either way, the figleaf has functioned in thought as a way of blocking the conclusion that the person was racist. Again, we can see how this fits well with the White Folk Theory of Racism—a theory on which people can easily say and do things which sound racist, while not really being racist; and a theory on which any evidence that one is not a monster is evidence that one is not racist.

4. Figleaves and Dogwhistles: Their Relationship

4.1 Are Figleaves a Kind of Dogwhistle?

Figleaves and dogwhistles serve some of the same purposes. They both allow speakers to get away with injecting racist views and sentiments into political discourse, without falling foul of the Norm of Racial Equality. They both provide deniability for expression of racist sentiments. Indeed, Haney López (2019a) discusses many examples of figleaves, but considers them to be dogwhistles. For example, he discusses the way that Republicans on the right engage in condemnation of particularly extreme instances of racism, and then use this to defend themselves against charges of racism:

> Part of dog whistling involves publicly posturing against racism. Sometimes…[t]he right [issues] impassioned denunciation of blatant racism.   (Haney López 2019a: 27)

Or consider this example, also a diachronic figleaf in our terms:

> Other times, dog whistle politics defends itself by denying that its coded assaults refer to race at all…"This has nothing to do with race. I've never

said anything about race. This has nothing to do with race or anything else." (Haney López 2019a: 27)

Haney López also discusses Trump's many utterances of the claim "I'm the least racist person," also classifying these racism denial figleaves as dogwhistles.

Given the commonality of purpose described above, it is of course possible to treat dogwhistles and figleaves as members of a common category, as Haney López does. However, I think this feeds confusion about how the two phenomena work. Here is Haney López's official definition of dogwhistle politics, in the version of his view which has been updated for the Trump era (2019: 41–2):

The strategy of mobilizing electoral support by:

1. Stoking widely condemned social hostilities.
2. Through the use of code.
   (a) As in a secret handshake, sometimes the code hides the underlying message from the general audience but allows it to be clearly understood by intended supporters.
   (b) More often, like a used-car fraud, the code aims to stoke fear and resentment among intended supporters while hiding from that same group that the root appeal rests on socially unacceptable stereotypes.

The two forms of code, (a) and (b), map nicely onto what I have called Overt Code and Covert Effect dogwhistles. It is, however, somewhat strained to call the latter a code, since successful transmission of a coded message is usually thought to involve it being decoded by its intended audience. Such decoding would be a disaster for a dogwhistle of this kind (b). Although this is somewhat problematic, we can (perhaps) see how the word "code" could be stretched to cover this kind of case. This would involve a substantial broadening of what counts as a code, but there is no reason that technical terminology needs to adhere to the standard meanings of words.

It is not clear at all, though, how figleaves can fit into dogwhistle politics on this definition. Consider Donald Trump's declaration of his lack of racism. Haney López gives us two options for how a dogwhistle functions. Is this a case of Haney López's (a)—a message designed to be understood by a small group but not by larger one? Clearly not: everyone is meant to understand it the same way, as a declaration of non-racism. What about (b)? Does

this utterance "[aim] to stoke fear and resentment among intended supporters while hiding from that same group that the root appeal rests on socially
unacceptable stereotypes"? No, the declaration of non-racism is not aiming
to stoke fear and resentment, and in fact it does not rest on socially unacceptable stereotypes. Moreover, both (a) and (b) are meant to be ways of
"stoking widely condemned social hostilities." This is not what the declaration of non-racism is doing.

Alternatively, one might suppose that it is the figleaf plus the racist utterance which together make up the dogwhistle, as understood by Haney
López. This would make sense of how the utterance can be seen as aiming
to stoke fear and resentment while hiding the appeal to racism. It might,
then, fit fairly well with option 2(b), if we put aside concerns about the use
of the word "code." However, this only makes sense for synchronic figleaves.
Consider, for example, a week in which Donald Trump has made four
openly racist utterances Monday–Thursday and been criticized for them. In
response he makes a declaration of how very unracist he is, on Friday. This
declaration is very clearly a diachronic figleaf in my terms. To understand it
as a dogwhistle in Haney López's terms, however, we would need to pair it
with a racist utterance and call that whole thing a dogwhistle—otherwise it
is not stoking racist hostilities. But there are at least two problems for doing
this. One is that it puts quite a strain on our notions of both utterance and
dogwhistle to consider as a single dogwhistle utterance a racist comment
made on one day and a declaration of non-racism made on a different day.
Further, it is unclear which racist utterance to pair with the figleaf and call
"the dogwhistle." Any choice we make would ignore important elements of
the whole. If we chose to call the whole series of racist utterances and the
figleaf a dogwhistle, this puts even more strain on our notions of dogwhistle
and utterance. It also means that somebody who has only heard two of the
racist utterances and the figleaf counts as not having heard the dogwhistle.
Treating figleaves and dogwhistles as separate phenomena seems to capture
the reality better.

4.2 How Figleaves and Dogwhistles Interact

Haney López is right, however, to see the sort of utterance I call a figleaf as
working hand in hand with dogwhistles, to facilitate the stoking of racial
hostility. There are at least two important ways that this takes place.

4.2.1 Figleaves for Failed Dogwhistles

Some of Donald Trump's utterances that seem blatantly racist may well have been intended as dogwhistles. Take, for example, his claim that four congresswomen of color should "go back and help fix the totally broken and crime infested places from which they came" (Rogers and Fandos 2019). Suggesting that people of color *go back to where they came from* is extremely blatant racism. However, it does not explicitly mention race, and it uses no slurs. In a different era, then, this might conceivably have been an effective Covert Effect dogwhistle—functioning to activate racial attitudes *without* audience awareness. It may even have been intended by Trump to work this way. Extensive familiarity with the "go back to where you came from" trope, however, means that this cannot be an effective Covert Effect dogwhistle. Nor does it work as an Overt Code dogwhistle—sending a concealed message to just one part of the audience. So if this was intended as a dogwhistle, it failed.

When a dogwhistle fails, another method is needed to achieve social acceptability in the face of the Norm of Racial Equality. This is one of many places where figleaves can be helpful. And, indeed, in the controversy that followed Trump responded with a diachronic racism denial figleaf: "I don't have a racist bone in my body" (Haltiwanger 2019). As with many figleaves, there was a large audience for whom this was utterly ineffective. But for others, it may have served as a helpful reassurance that Trump was really not racist after all.

4.2.2 Figleaves and Dogwhistles to Own the Libs

So far, we've been discussing how figleaves and dogwhistles can work together to cover up for racism. But Haney López (2019a) makes an extremely important point about the modern Republican party's, and in particular Donald Trump's, strategies regarding racist speech. Older strategies were focused on ways to play on voters' racism without being too obvious. Of course, there would always be some voters who realized what was going on—in particular, voters of color were not likely to be fooled. But having the racism of the utterance be noticed by some of the audience was no part of the strategy. The idea was to avoid this as far as possible. Haney López observes that this has changed:

> Trump made his racist narrative obvious to his critics and a constant focus of media storms. Rather than seeking to use dogwhistles to keep race

below the surface, Trump repeatedly stoked heated debates about his racial demagoguery...he no longer obscured his racial appeals from the engaged political center. Instead, Trump intentionally instigated accusations of racism, believing that such accusations helped him dominate the public's distracted attention.   (2019a: 32)

The use of dogwhistles and figleaves allows Trump to get away with saying things that he could not get away with without them. While many voters will at least worry about whether his comments are racist, a large number of these will be reassured by the figleaves and dogwhistles. Even if they do not become convinced that he is *not* racist, they may be left uncertain about whether he is racist. At the same time, what he is doing is very obvious to a large number of voters, including both some centrists and highly engaged anti-racists. These people justifiably respond with condemnation to Trump's displays of racism.

This dynamic helps Trump, in two ways. First, as remarked upon in the quote above, it secures an enormous amount of attention, and allows him to dominate news coverage. Equally important, though, is that Trump uses his opponents' condemnation of racism in order to energize his base and make them feel under attack—a key strategy for authoritarians the world over. As Jason Stanley notes, the sense of victimization is essential to the rise of fascist politics, and White victimhood is crucial to the rise of the racist right in the United States:

Fascist politics covers up the structural inequality by attempting to invert, misrepresent, and subvert the long, hard effort to address it...The experience of losing a once unquestioned, settled dignity—the dignity that comes with being white, not black—is easily captured by a language of white victimization.   (2018: 99–100)

A very clear instance occurred in reaction to Hillary Clinton's labelling of some of Trump's supporters as a "basket of deplorables" (Reilly 2016). Trump quickly seized this opportunity to exploit the utterance in order to enhance his followers' sense of victimization:

It's the oldest play in the Democratic playbook...When democratic policies fail, they are left with only this one tired argument: you're racist, you're racist, you're racist. They keep saying it. You're racist. It's a tired disgusting argument…She lies and she smears and *she paints decent Americans—you—as racists.* (Haney López 2019a: 33)

This kind of criticism enhanced the sense, already present among many White Americans, that they were under threat by elites who want to control what they can think and say, and who unjustly accuse them of racism. According to a study in 2018, 80 percent of all Americans felt that "political correctness" was a problem (Mounk 2018). Republicans, according to another study, also increasingly believe that discrimination against White people is a serious problem and that White people have been asked to make too many sacrifices (Sides, Tesler, and Vavreck 2018: 89). This set of background conditions allowed Trump to make extremely effective use of the racism accusation figleaf, in which one insists that the person raising the issue of racism must be the real racist.

The strategy, more generally, of attempting to provoke the left to expressions of anger is known on the Internet as "Owning the Libs": it's a deliberate strategy of attempting to infuriate those on the left and center-left. This tactic particularly focuses on seeking loud accusations of racism and sexism. It helps the White supremacist right to claim that its opponents "are overly sensitive, or are capable of being triggered, or hypocritical," according to Marshall Kosloft (Robertson 2021). In so doing, it provides ample opportunity for racism accusation figleaves, while at the same time generating considerable attention, *and* feeding the sense of White victimization. This strategy has been vital to the rise of explicit racism.

5. Conclusion

Over Chapters 2 and 3, we have seen how particular linguistic maneuvers have aided in the rise of blatant racism. The background, widely held White Folk Theory of Racism, set the stage for this by conceiving of racists as monstrous figures, and offering many ways that White people can convince themselves that those they support or want to support are neither racist nor saying racist things—or at least that they are not sure whether this is happening. Making use of the assumptions of this deeply flawed theory, dogwhistles and figleaves enable a wide variety of racist speech acts. Dogwhistles, in their Overt Code variety, allow explicit racists to communicate with each other while concealing this communication from many others. In their Covert Effect variety, dogwhistles allow those who would like to repudiate racism to be nonetheless influenced by it without their own awareness. Figleaves work together with these. They provide cover for dogwhistles that have been found out, and for other utterances that would be very obviously racist without them. In so doing, they render these utterances far more acceptable than they would otherwise be, allowing explicit expressions of racism to spread much more widely, and giving those who might otherwise be inclined to worry a permission structure to go on supporting those who make racist utterances.

But figleaves do much more than this. Because they are linked to *blatant* racist utterances, they can change the way that the blatant racist utterances are seen. (Dogwhistles cannot do that due to their much more stealthy nature.) This makes them an especially serious threat to our norms of discourse, and our standards of social acceptability. Through figleaves, a once-appalling sentiment or idea can become normalized and mainstream.

Dogwhistles and figleaves, working together and separately, also play an important role in dividing the populace and inflaming divisions. Because racist utterances have been given just enough cover, those who call them out and criticize them can be painted as judgmental extremists. Their (legitimate) criticisms can be used to stoke fear and resentment, enhancing the sorts of dynamics that feed authoritarianism. These linguistic devices, then, have played a crucial role in bringing our political discourse to the deeply flawed state in which we now find ourselves. In Part II, we will examine ways that parallel devices have enabled the spread of blatant falsehoods. First, however, we'll need to examine exactly what the change has been with regard to falsehood. That will be the subject of Chapter 4.

II
FALSEHOOD

4

The Rise of Blatant Falsehood

On 29 March 2017, I was passing, bleary-eyed and exhausted, through Amsterdam airport on my way from the United Kingdom to the United States, far too early in the morning. I was still reeling from the shocking developments in both of my countries. Donald Trump had been inaugurated in late January, with a crowd in attendance that was manifestly much smaller than his immediate predecessor Obama's, but which Trump repeatedly insisted was the largest in history (Palmeri 2017). That very morning, the United Kingdom had invoked Article 50, officially beginning the process to withdraw from the European Union after a campaign based on obvious lies both about the European Union itself, and about what withdrawal would mean (BBC 2017). As I rushed through, my eye was caught by newsstand after newsstand featuring *Time* magazine with a simple cover—black background, red letters, and a huge font: "Is Truth Dead?" (Pine 2017). Overwhelmed, confused, and frankly sleep deprived, I wanted to stop right there and shout "yes it clearly is!"; and a part of me wanted to just burst into tears on the floor of the airport. Something about the cover felt deeply and profoundly right.

And yet, I actually think the answer is clearly "no." Truth is very much not dead. We are not living in a post-truth era, and the idea of a post-truth era is not a helpful one. I understand the emotion behind that *Time* magazine cover, and I have felt it quite deeply. But I think the reality is more complex, and that it's vital to understand the complexity. There *have* been some extremely important recent changes, and these have led to manifest falsehoods gaining a currency and social acceptability in our political culture that does represent a large change from the past. This is something that we need to understand. But the changes that have taken place are in some communities and not in others. And they do not amount to the death of truth, a post-truth era, or any of the other sweeping terms that have been used to characterize the current epistemic situation.

In what follows, I will attempt to describe the ways that things have indeed changed. But I will also be explaining the ways that these changes have been misdescribed. Section 1 considers the question of whether political lying is new, and also the suggestion that we are living in a post-truth era, and examines more than one time that this claim has been made. Section 2 looks at the idea that our era is best characterized as one of bald-faced lies and bullshit. Section 3 considers various claims that have been made about the rise of conspiracy theorizing. In each section, we will see that some insist that nothing has actually changed, while others suggest that change has been sweeping and comprehensive. I will argue each time that the truth lies in the middle, rather than at either of these extremes. But I will also insist that the change which has taken place is very serious and very worrying—and that it will be well worth understanding linguistic devices that have facilitated it. That's what we will turn to in Chapter 5.

1. Lies and Post-truth

1.1 Lies That Are Not New

One line of thought has it that there actually isn't anything new happening—we have *always* had lies in politics, and what is happening now is no change at all.

1.1.1 Political Lies Are Not New

There is indeed nothing new about falsehood in political speech. Hannah Arendt famously noted this back in 1972:

> ... the deliberate falsehood and the outright lie used as legitimate means to achieve political ends, [has] been with us since the beginning of recorded history. Truthfulness has never been counted among the political virtues, and lies have always been regarded as justifiable tools in political dealings.
>
> (Arendt 1972)

Although Arendt made a point of noting that political lying had a very long history, she was in fact arguing that there *was* something new about the political lies of her time, those emerging from the Pentagon papers, revealing the lies that led to the Vietnam War and helped to keep it going. What she took to be new about these lies was that they were wartime lies, but they were being told not to the enemy—who was fully aware of all relevant facts—but to US civilians, including politicians.

Historians James Cortada and William Aspray (2019) have recently made a much more sweeping claim about the lies and falsehoods of our time. They insist that there really is *nothing* new happening. Instead, they argue that it is only historical ignorance that has fed the idea that something new is now taking place with respect to falsehood in US politics:

> After the election of Donald Trump as president, people in the United States and across large swaths of Europe, Latin America, and Asia engaged in the most intensive discussion in modern times about falsehoods pronounced by public officials. In the United States, shock and disbelief in the wide use of "fake news", "alternative facts", and other similar concepts such as misinformation, disinformation, rumors, and lies dominated both the media and private conversations. The shock was caused in part by the belief that pronouncements by President Trump and others, challenged by the mainstream "trusted" media, represented a new phenomenon in American life... However, an examination of the historical record exposes a very different reality, one in which lies and misrepresentation are far more widespread.   (Cortada and Aspray 2019: v)

Cortada and Aspray make their argument by presenting a series of case studies that illustrate various themes in the history of deception. These themes include an examination of the way that misinformation is used to accomplish goals, the use of different language in different time periods to do this, the kinds of organizations involved, and the role of institutions. Importantly, none of these involve the sort of shockingly strange claims that have gained prominence in the Trump era—claims which are very obviously false and pronounced as false by large segments of the public and the mainstream media. As we will, see, I think these do represent an important change.[1]

1.1.2 Racist Lies Are Not New

Part I of this book was concerned with racism in political discourse. Very obviously, much of this is about the propagation of falsehoods. Racist falsehoods, it will not surprise the reader to read, are nothing new. Moreover, many of these have been widely known to be untrue—their falsehood has been obvious to the well informed, and often also (though not always) to those propagating them.

Let's consider just one small case study.[2] It is well documented that, in the late nineteenth and early twentieth centuries, mainstream newspapers in the United States regularly published falsehoods about violence against Black people, both denying its existence and attempting to justify it with false claims about Black people's violent actions and plans. These claims were, obviously, known to be false by many Black people. And the truth was published in Black-owned newspapers, at great risk to the writers and publishers. As Brent Staples writes (2021):

> The white press in the South dictated how anti-Black atrocities were viewed all over the country by portraying even the most grotesque exercises of violence as necessary to protect a besieged white community. White news organizations elsewhere rubber-stamped this lie. The editors of small, struggling Black publications often risked their lives to refute what they rightly saw as white supremacist propaganda masquerading as news.

It is very important to realize that the lies published in the White newspapers were recognized as false, indeed obviously false, by Black newspapers and their readership. This is, however, importantly different from what is widely seen as happening in our current era. The racist lies described above were known to be false by a minority of citizens, many of them citizens who were oppressed, marginalized, and terrorized if they tried to spread their knowledge. Current concerns *include* this—indeed, disseminating knowledge of this sort is a key part of what Black Lives Matter has been about. But, as we will see, claims that "truth is dead" seem to be based on something else—the widespread circulation of falsehoods that are known to be false not just by an oppressed minority, but by the mainstream media. Widespread currency for false claims that are recognized as false—and clearly designated as such—*by the mainstream media* is, perhaps, new.

1.2   But Something Is New

I will be arguing, against Cortada and Aspray, that there has been a change. Strangely, I think the most convincing way to do this is to examine misguided claims of this sort of change from not too long ago. Although it may easily be forgotten now, in our recently post-Trump era, claims of post-truth eras were made both about the Bush era and the Obama era. Looking at the specifics of these claims, and contemplating what was shocking then, is quite an eye-opener now. The incidents taken to show that the American public had lost all interest in truth look from our current perspective rather quaint.

1.2.1 It's Not This: Misguided Claim of Post-truth

Many uses of the term "post-truth era" trace its start back to the G. W. Bush administration, and the war on Iraq that was waged supposedly for the sake of weapons of mass destruction in Iraq that did not actually exist (Boland 2018). The falsehoods underlying this war also gave rise to a sudden spike of interest in Harry Frankfurt's notion of bullshitting, formulated decades before but reissued as a book specifically because of its apparent relevance to the Bush regime (Frankfurt 2005). For Frankfurt, the bullshitter is someone with no interest in the truth or falsehood of what they assert. This, Frankfurt famously maintains, is what makes them more dangerous than a liar—who at least respects the truth enough to avoid it.

Others insist that the Bush administration was not so much bullshitting, as engaging in bald-faced lies—deliberately saying false things which they knew would not be believed. In particular, some hold that that the Bush administration's claims about weapons of mass destruction were bald-faced lies that nobody believed at the time. Here, for example, is Matt Taibbi (in 2018) on what was—according to him—obvious to us all back in 2003:

> The invasion was no mistake, and nobody above the age of eight believed the WMD story. Anyone who says otherwise is lying. We all knew what was going on.

According to Taibbi, the Bush administration's claims about weapons of mass destruction were nothing but bald-faced lies, believed by nobody—and not even expected to deceive anyone.

But both of these ideas are starkly at odds with the historical record. There is good evidence that the Bush administration went to considerable lengths to create a plausible deception about the justifications for war, and also that this deception was believed by many. They wanted to be believed, they worked to bring that about, and this effort was remarkably successful.

The Bush administration decided to go to war with Iraq for reasons other than those that they used to justify the war to the public, and even to top officials like General Colin Powell. Once the administration made this decision, however, it deliberately set about constructing plausible justifications and the appearance of evidence to support this decision. We see this very clearly in the immense effort put in to getting the right person to give the right speech to the United Nations (Draper 2020). Although Colin Powell was thought to be insufficiently supportive of the war effort, the administration knew that he had great personal credibility. They wanted someone with this credibility to present their case at the United Nations. In order to bring this about, they had to convince Colin Powell to do it. Powell thought the war was a bad idea, but he was a loyal member of the administration and willing to present the argument for war if he could be convinced that every element of it was true. He insisted on extensive meetings with George Tenet, the head of the Central Intelligence Agency (CIA), and with the agents responsible for the evidence Tenet was presenting.

Whenever Powell seemed concerned about a particular claim, Tenet's staff would usher in what seemed to be the proper analyst to affirm the source's validity. What Powell did not know was that there were other CIA officials not present in the conference room who seriously doubted much of the National Intelligence Estimate's contents (Draper 2020).

These are not the actions of an administration that was simply bullshitting and totally uninterested in truth and falsehood. Nor are these the actions of an administration that was happy to simply engage in bald-faced lying, without any concern for convincing its audience. Moreover, all this was notably successful, and not just with Powell. The WMD story that Taibbi said no one above the age of eight believed was, according to a poll by Fairleigh Dickinson University, still believed by 51 percent of Republicans in 2015; 42 percent of Americans overall believed that US troops discovered such weapons (Breitman 2015).

Why, then, did people think that this administration was especially uninterested in even the appearance of truthfulness? I think there are at least two elements to this. First, they did not feel the need to persuade everyone, but only *enough* people. (This, I will be arguing, is also a crucial part of today's dynamic.) Understanding this properly requires distinguishing between two different groups in the audience. One group was reachable by the Bush administration's deceptions. They came to believe, at least for a time, that there were weapons of mass destruction which justified the push for war. It was at this group that the deceptions were directed. Another group was simply not reachable by the deceptions: this group had paid attention to weapons inspectors like Hans Blix, did not trust the Bush administration, and was firmly convinced that there was no case for war. Many marched in protests against the war. While it would be wrong to say that the Bush administration was *simply* engaging in bald-faced lying, it probably is true that they engaged in bald-faced lying with respect to the anti-Bush segment of the audience. The administration knew that they would not convince their committed opponents.

The second reason for particular suspicion about the Bush administration's attitude toward truth was an infamous quotation, attributed to an unnamed source who is often said to actually be Karl Rove:

The aide said that guys like me were "in what we call the reality-based community," which he defined as people who "believe that solutions emerge from your judicious study of discernible reality." I nodded and murmured something about enlightenment principles and empiricism. He cut me off. "That's not the way the world really works anymore," he continued. "We're an empire now, and when we act, we create our own reality. And while you're studying that reality—judiciously, as you will—we'll act again, creating other new realities, which you can study too, and that's how things will sort out. We're history's actors . . . and you, all of you, will be left to just study what we do."   (Suskind 2004)

This quite clearly indicates a lack of interest in adapting policies to the world, and a highly authoritarian point of view on which the world is to be remade in line with the administration's preferences. The disdainful use of the phrase "reality-based community" might on its own suggest a rejection of the idea that there *is* a reality. But in full context, this is not quite right: instead, it indicates a willingness to wield power to change reality. It is an assertion of power. Nowhere in this quotation can one find the idea that the speaker is perfectly happy to be seen as uttering falsehoods, or not caring about whether they are believed. Moreover, the quotation is committed to the existence of a reality out there to be studied—as a distraction while the administration sets about changing it. But the very idea of *changing* reality presupposes that there is a reality there to be changed. It is mistaken, then, to read the quotation as opposed to the ideas of truth or reality.

1.2.2 Not This Either: Another Misguided Claim of Post-truth
Here's Jason Stanley in 2012, midway through Obama's presidency:

The public's trust in public speech, whether by politicians or in the media, has disintegrated, and to such a degree that it has undermined the possibility of straightforward communication in the public sphere. The expectation is that any statement made either by a politician or by a media outlet is a false ideological distortion. As a result, no one blames politicians for making false statements or statements that obviously contradict that politician's beliefs.   (Stanley 2012)

According to Stanley, it was already the case back in 2012 that nobody expected politicians to speak truthfully.

Why did Stanley argue that Americans no longer expected politicians to say true things? Let's look at his examples. These included Paul Ryan criticizing Obama for funneling money out of Medicare, when he himself had long argued for funneling money out of Medicare, and Mitt Romney criticizing Obama for weakening work requirements on welfare, when what Obama had actually done was to consider "issuing waivers to states concerning worker participation targets" (Stanley 2012). Neither of these claims is in any way ridiculous. It was perfectly possible that Obama might take money out of Medicare, depending on what that meant and on what he wanted to do with that money, and Ryan's hypocrisy has no bearing on how likely it is that Obama might do this. (It was also very likely unknown to most voters.) It was also quite possible that Obama might weaken work requirements on welfare. And certainly it was not generally understood that he had considered "issuing waivers to states concerning worker participation targets," a highly technical matter that would not be well understood by ordinary voters.

In short, these falsehoods would be obvious only to an exceptionally well-informed voter. It is deeply puzzling to suppose that these give rise to the sort of skepticism Stanley suggests—a *general* feeling that if politicians might lie about *this* then we could not expect any truth from them. This feeling might have been strongly held by people like Stanley, who were highly informed about the relevant issues. But it is unlikely to have been widespread.

1.2.3 But This *Does* Seems Different

The easiest way to see that there is indeed something importantly different going on now is to remind ourselves of the sorts of falsehoods the above authors were discussing when they made the very broad claims that they did. So let's take stock. The Bush administration lied about weapons of mass destruction in order to start a war in Iraq. Many people clearly did disbelieve the lies it, and they had good reason to do so: weapons inspectors had repeatedly reported that there were no weapons of mass destruction. However, Bush and his inner circle went out of their way to provide apparent justifications for their claims, to produce apparent evidence, and to procure the most credible spokesperson they could find, Colin Powell—and many believed these claims. Now turn to Stanley's discussion. Ryan and Romney made claims about Obama's policies that were overblown, and they criticized him for things that they themselves supported. These facts could be found reasonably easily, by consulting political fact checkers on the Internet. But they were not widely and publicly dismissed as shocking falsehoods on mainstream media, nor were they transparently ridiculous or at odds with mainstream understandings of the world.

It's time now to compare these sorts of falsehoods with the ones that have gained so much attention in the Trump era. Here are just a few examples:

- Trump's inauguration crowd was bigger than Obama's, a claim that is readily seen to be false from photographs that are in extremely widespread circulation.
- COVID-19 is a hoax and hospitals were never actually very full.
- Wearing a face mask dangerously restricts one's oxygen supply, even though doctors and nurses do this all day long while performing surgery.
- Injecting bleach might be a good cure for COVID-19.
- The QAnon conspiracy theory, which holds (among many other things) that major celebrities and Democratic Party officials hold satanic rites in which they harvest adrenochrome from kidnapped children, sometimes in the basement of a Washington DC pizza parlor.
- Trump won Georgia and Pennsylvania by landslides in 2020, even though even the Republican election officials in these states say that Biden won.
- Bill Gates is using COVID-19 vaccines to spy on vaccinated people.
- The Great Replacement Theory, which holds that elites (sometimes specified as Jews) are plotting to replace White people with people of color.

It is very important to see how these claims are different from the ones that had previously led commentators to argue that we are living in a post-truth era. The claims Stanley discussed were perfectly plausible sorts of claims. It was entirely possible that Obama might take money from Medicare budgets, and entirely possible that this might be at odds with Paul Ryan's policies. One could easily learn that these claims were false, but that would require some checking on the Internet. Similarly, Obama might have agreed to loosen work requirements on welfare. He hadn't done so, and again this fact could be relatively easily learned, but it was not simply obvious that the claim was false. The Bush administration claims were indeed believed by many to be false, but they were also believed by many to be true. Infamously, even the *New York Times* featured them in such a way as to lend a great deal of credibility (Okrent 2004).

The Trump-era claims are nothing like these. Reputable news organizations have been admirably clear about their absolute falsehood, often refraining from the usual representation of two sides to every story, and running footers noting their falsehood in real time. Many of the claims themselves have an obvious air of ridiculousness about them that is lacking from the claims commented on by Stanley and Taibbi. Injecting bleach to treat Covid? Hillary Clinton kidnapping children and draining substances from their bodies in the basement of a pizza parlor? So many election officials, including the Republicans, falsely insisting that Biden won the election? Face masks, a garment standardly worn for many hours while performing surgery, cutting off one's oxygen? Bill Gates, with easy access to the phones and computers of millions, deciding to monitor people through vaccines? Others show a remarkable resilience even in the light of clear counter-evidence. It was by no means impossible that Trump would have a larger inauguration crowd than Obama did, but it is genuinely startling that people continue to insist on this even when looking at the two photographs. These claims really are of a different sort. The previous ones, despite the hype, were not so obviously false at all. These, on the other hand, really do represent some sort of a shift.

1.2.4 Post-truth Era?

I have just been arguing that previous attributions of a post-truth era were inaccurate and overblown. A crucial part of my argument involved comparing that era to our own. This might lead one to believe that I take us to now be living in a post-truth era. However, I don't think that this is a useful description. Joshua Habgood-Coote (2019) has argued, very convincingly, that the idea of a "post-truth era" suffers from two important problems.[3] First, there's a high degree of imprecision. Does it refer to a problem with journalistic standards, a neglect of critical thinking, a lack of respect for truth among the populace, or with a proliferation of bullshit and falsehood from politicians? These are all real problems, but they are different problems, which may call for different conceptualizations and different solutions. Running them together under the name "post-truth" obscures this.

Moreover, the name "post-truth" suggests that there was in the past some sort of a golden age of truth from which we have fallen, and that all we need to do is to restore our epistemic systems to their former excellent functioning. Habgood-Coote rightly argues that this deeply misrepresents our former state of affairs. Political lies are nothing new, as we have seen. Moreover, our epistemic systems have traditionally been skewed sharply in favor of perspectives other than those of people of color, poor people, colonized people, and oppressed people more generally. Falsehoods that derive from and hold in place systems of oppression have traditionally flourished, while truths that might undermine these systems have been suppressed. The phrase "post-truth" suggests that this was a desirable state of affairs which we should return to. Habgood-Coote calls this the "return to norms" narrative and argues that we should resist this line of thought.

> The connection between 'post-truth' and the return to norms narrative is indicative of a propagandistic usage of 'post-truth'. I don't know what the intentions of these authors are, but I think that it is plausible that they see themselves part of a defence of established institutions against a rising tide of populism that aims to wind back the clock to before the supposed crisis. The effect of these contributions is to establish a reactionary ideology that aims to defend established institutions and practices, irrespective of the problems with those practices and institutions.   (2019: 1056)

The idea of post-truth also seems overblown when understood as the claim that people have in general ceased to expect truth from their politicians or to care about whether their politicians' utterances are true. Throughout the 2020 election, news organizations carefully tracked the truth and falsehood of claims made by both Biden and Trump, and each side eagerly leapt on what it took to be falsehoods from the other. Ted Cruz was nicknamed "Lyin' Ted" by Donald Trump, and Trump used this nickname over and over (Cillizza 2016). It did not look at all like an election in which people no longer expect truth from their politicians, though it did look a lot like an election in which people assumed that the politicians they disliked would lie. Importantly, though, this was treated as a further reason to dislike those politicians, rather than a predictable and uninteresting fact that nobody cares about.

For all these reasons, then, I do not think we should use the phrase "post-truth era." Therefore, we need some other way to characterize what is new now.

2. Is It the Bald-Faced Lies and Bullshit?

Another very appealing characterization of what has changed during the present time is one that characterizes it as an era of bullshit and/or bald-faced lies.[4] In this section, we will see that the truth is more complex than this because the public is deeply divided, and I'll suggest a different characterization is in order. However, I will return to bald-faced lying and bullshit in Chapter 6—not as a general characterization of our era, but instead with respect to a very particular subgroup.

2.1 Bald-Faced Lies and Bullshit

It is common to describe Donald Trump as a bald-faced liar, one who knowingly asserts falsehoods that they are perfectly aware will not be believed, and who cannot therefore be described as intending to deceive (Sorensen 2007). This certainly appears to be something that Trump does frequently. A classic example would be Trump's claim, already mentioned, that more people attended his inauguration ceremony than Barack Obama's, even though the photographic evidence makes it blindingly obvious that this is false.

It is also very appealing to describe Donald Trump as a bullshitter,[5] famously defined by Harry Frankfurt (2005) as someone with no concern at all for the truth of their utterances. (Frankfurt views such a person as a greater enemy of the truth than a liar is, because a liar at least takes an interest in the truth in order to conceal it.) Peter Pomerantsev puts this idea well, with reference to both Trump and Putin: "there is nothing new about politicians lying, but what seems novel is their acting as if they don't care whether what they say is true or false" (2019: 119). Quassim Cassam (2021) discusses an exceptionally clear case of Trump's bullshitting, in which Donald Trump made false claims about the US trade deficit with Canada, to Canadian Prime Minister Justin Trudeau. He followed this up shortly after by saying to reporters that he actually had no idea whether it was true or not.

There are many additional examples of what appear to be bald-faced lies or bullshitting from Trump and his associates. Here are just two.

- In 2019 Trump gave a press briefing about the path of an impending hurricane, insisting that it was likely to hit Alabama and backing this up with a map on which the likely path of the hurricane had been very obviously altered with a sharpie (Cillizza 2016). Because the alteration was so obvious, this is a plausible case of a bald-faced lie or bald-faced bullshitting.
- During a briefing on COVID-19, Trump floated the idea that bleach might somehow be put into the body in a way that would create a cure

for the disease. Because Trump was suggesting this quite dangerous technique without apparent concern for the truth of his suggestions, this is a very plausible case of bullshitting (BBC 2020).

"And then I see the disinfectant where it knocks it out in a minute. One minute. And is there a way we can do something like that, by injection inside or almost a cleaning? So it'd be interesting to check that."

Pointing to his head, Mr Trump went on: "I'm not a doctor. But I'm, like, a person that has a good you-know-what."

Indeed, it seems possible to describe Trump as a bald-faced bullshitter (Meibauer 2016; Kenyon and Saul 2022): one with no concern for the truth, who knows that he will not be believed. This is a rare and not often discussed breed. Indeed, Frankfurt rules this out in his discussion, noting that bullshitters aim to deceive about what they're up to (2005: 54). However, Trump does not seem to share this aim, as evidenced by the Trudeau example in which he happily and openly told reporters he had no idea whether what he was saying was true or not. There is a compelling case to be made that Trump has shown Frankfurt to be wrong in overlooking the possibility of a bald-faced bullshitter.[6] It was hard to imagine, when Frankfurt wrote, that someone could meet with success by openly displaying such a lack of interest in truth. But Trump, one might argue, proved this wrong.

Simply characterizing these utterances as bald-faced bullshit, however, leaves out something very important. It assumes a unitary audience, all recognizing that the claims are bullshit. But this is not realistic. As we have seen with dogwhistles and figleaves, exploiting division among audience members is a powerful strategy for sowing division. And this holds true also when it comes to lies and bullshit.

To me and the likely readership of this book, the utterances just discussed are very obvious bald-faced lies and bullshit. But this is—counterintuitively—precisely what makes them function so well as devices for dividing the public. We, and the mainstream media, call out the obvious falsehoods—often with shock and indignation. This gives Trump a perfect opportunity to rail against the liberals and—even more important—the mainstream media. Railing against the mainstream media is a vital part of what Trump does, especially at his rallies. Calling reliable news sources "fake news" is a crowd favorite. It is very important for him to have his base focused on the news media, and those who support his political opponents, in this sort of adversarial way. The obviousness of the falsehoods *helps*. The outrage of the mainstream media, and the public who trust the mainstream media, is a crucial part of how all this works. Creating both divisions and distrust in the media is a crucial part of Trump's strategy. Moreover, there's nothing surprising about this to those who study authoritarian leaders. It's a long-standing strategy for fascist leaders and those who emulate them: this very much aids in the narrative of the press as the enemy. (I will discuss all this much more in Chapter 6.)

But this is not all that is going on. For each of these utterances, there's another audience that actually finds it credible. It's absolutely true that Justin Trudeau cannot possibly believe Trump's lies about the trade deficit with Canada. It's also true that Trudeau was one of Trump's intended audiences: it is entirely plausible that Trump was aiming to get a hostile reaction from Trudeau, so frequently maligned as a "socialist." But Trump also had another intended audience, his base. Trump's base find him trustworthy, and indeed far more so than the Canadian leader. They've been trained to also distrust the mainstream media. To them, this encounter was one in which Trump bravely spoke the truth to a foreign leader, and the "fake news" media tried to lie about it.

Trump's claims about Covid and bleach seem transparently unsupported and dangerous to us. But in the hours after he made these claims, there was a dramatic rise in calls to poison control centers about ingesting bleach (Reimann 2020). Clearly, some believed these claims, and believed them strongly enough to endanger themselves. However, downplaying the risks of Covid and discouraging vaccination has also been a prominent thread of Republican discourse. And we see the effects of these, with partisan affiliation the strongest predictor of vaccination and Republican counties showing substantially lower vaccination rates than Democratic ones (Kates, Tolbert, and Rouw 2022).

Similarly for Trump's claims about the size of his inauguration crowd. It might seem impossible that people could believe this, since it is not simply a matter of accepting his testimony: there is photographic evidence, which seems to be in stark contradiction to that testimony. But we actually have quite strong experimental evidence telling us that Trump supporters will in fact insist, while looking at the photos, that Trump's crowd is bigger than Obama's (Schaffner and Luks 2018). Some may do this because they accept explanations that have been given for why a larger crowd may in fact falsely appear to be smaller, like this one from Sean Spicer:

...photographs of the inaugural proceedings were intentionally framed in a way, in one particular tweet, to minimize the enormous support that had gathered on the National Mall. This was the first time in our nation's history that floor coverings have been used to protect the grass on the Mall. That had the effect of highlighting any areas where people were not standing, while in years past the grass eliminated this visual. This was also the first time that fencing and magnetometers went as far back on the Mall, preventing hundreds of thousands of people from being able to access the Mall as quickly as they had in inaugurations past.   (Politico Staff 2017)

These explanations are not terribly convincing, so accepting them is likely a case of motivated reasoning, in which (roughly speaking) people manage to construct justifications for the beliefs that they want to maintain.[7] But that does not mean that these people fail to believe what Trump and Spicer are saying.

In short, some people *do* genuinely and fervently believe the listed Trump-era claims. Their obvious implausibility does not mean, surprisingly, that they are "not believed by anyone above the age of eight." This is one of the startling and important facts that needs to be understood about our era. These claims are completely unbelievable bald-faced lies, I would wager, to all readers of this book. However, the public is now famously polarized, into much-discussed echo chambers (Nguyen 2020). (We will discuss these more in Chapter 6.) For those who get their news from Breitbart, Fox, and Newsmax, these claims are not so implausible. And for those who get their news from Q Drops, and conspiracists on social media more generally, they will seem extremely plausible. To fully understand what is happening, it is essential not to treat the audience for these claims as a monolith. What is a bald-faced lie to one group is a deceptive lie that inspires belief to another.

Once more, we come back to the very great range of people that there are and their diverse reactions to political lies. As Mathiesen and Fallis note:

Politicians typically address very large audiences. Thus, it is not surprising if some of these people are quite credulous. As Jonathan Swift reminds us… "as the vilest writer has his readers, so the greatest liar has his believers" (Swift 2004 [1710], p. 195). Thus, even if a politician says something that is extremely implausible, or that can easily be shown to be false, some people will believe.   (2016)

No simple classification, then, can be made of these claims as bald-faced lies or bullshit.

In this section, we have begun to understand some of what is special about Donald Trump's and his followers' relationship to truth-telling. It is not, as some have held, that they are bald-faced liars who never expect *anyone* to believe them. Or that they are simply bullshitters who never think about the truth. Rather, they exploit divisions among the audience. This allows them to be deceptive liars for some, bald-faced liars for others—and even, at times, bald-faced bullshitters.

It's worth noting that some of the obvious falsehoods discussed in this section take the form of conspiracy theories. This topic is important enough that it merits its own discussion.

3. Conspiracy Theorizing

A notable candidate for what is so different now is the rise of conspiracy theories.[8] Worries about conspiracy theories have become increasingly acute with the rise of QAnon and Covid-related conspiracy theories, and the invasion of the US Capitol on January 6, 2021, by Trump-supporting conspiracy theorists. Importantly, however, there is nothing new about conspiracy theories or even about widespread belief in them. Conspiracy theories about Jewish people have played central roles in widespread anti-Jewish prejudice for centuries. More recently, in 2018 the belief in some sort of Kennedy assassination theory was at almost 60 percent among Americans (Uscinski 2018).

So is there something new here? In this section, I will begin with a flawed theory of what is new about current conspiracy theorizing, moving on to a claim that there has been no rise in conspiracy theorizing. In this latter case, it will turn out that it's important to distinguish multiple things which might be meant by a "rise in conspiracy theorizing." On the construal relevant to this book, there has been a rise in conspiracy theorizing. I will conclude with some thoughts regarding what *is* new about current conspiracy theorizing.

First, however, it's important to do some stage-setting. Some conspiracies have clearly happened: the murder of Julius Caesar, the Watergate break-in and cover-up, the Iran-Contra scandal, to name just a few. Theories describing these conspiracies are in some sense conspiracy theories, but clearly we should all believe in these theories. Thoughts like this have motivated some philosophers to argue that conspiracy theories should not be viewed as problematic, and some have even suggested that "conspiracy theorising is essential to the functioning of any democracy" (Basham and Dentith 2016: 13). Yet nonetheless psychologists and sociologists have investigated conspiracy theories in a way which seems to presume that they are epistemically unsound. It seems likely that these groups are focused on different paradigm cases of conspiracy theories. Cassam (2019) usefully distinguishes between the two kinds of conspiracy theories by designating the epistemically problematic kind in capitals as Conspiracy Theories.[9] He gives many paradigmatic features of these theories, but my focus here will be simply on the *wildly implausible* ones—the ones based around claims widely known to be blatantly false. Unless otherwise indicated, these are what I mean by "conspiracy theorizing." In addition, I will often be particularly focused on those that pose serious dangers.

3.1 New Conspiracism?

There has recently been a high-profile argument made that a new form of conspiracy theorizing has taken hold, which is responsible for the state of affairs in which we find ourselves today.

Russell Muirhead and Nancy Rosenblum (2019) suggest that conspiratorial thinking has recently undergone a change. According to them, what they called the New Conspiracism is "conspiracy without the theory" (2019: 19). Like older conspiratorial thinking, this new version of conspiratorial thinking maintains that the surface appearance around us is deceptive, and that something bad is going on that is not readily apparent. But there are also important differences.

Muirhead and Rosenblum maintain that New Conspiracy Theories do not serve the same sort of explanatory function that old ones did. Older conspiracies were posited as explanations for shocking or puzzling events, such as the assassination of a President or the attacks on September 11, 2001. But the newer conspiracy theories, they say, do not work like this. According to them, there's generally no shocking event in need of explanation. They write:

> In contrast, the new conspiracy system sometimes seems to arise out of thin air, as with the claim that Hillary Clinton and her campaign chairman, John Podesta, ran a child molestation operation from the basement of a pizza parlour in Washington DC.   (Muirhead and Rosenblum 2019: 25)

They also note that older conspiracy theories involved researching lots of bits of evidence (albeit often faulty) that might support the theories. New Conspiracy Theories, according to them, involve simply repeated assertion rather than provision of evidence:

The New Conspiracists posit odious designs but not the how or the why, or even the who. They do not marshal evidence, however implausible; there is no documentation of a long train of abuses all tending the same way. They do not make use of what Keeley calls a conspiracist's "chief tool", errant data.   (Muirhead and Rosenblum 2019: 25)

3.2 Against New Conspiracism

This picture, however, is not actually true to the detailed workings of the theories that they call "New Conspiracy Theories."

3.2.1 Pizzagate

The Pizzagate conspiracy is a paradigm case of New Conspiracism, crucially involving the claim that top Democratic officials like Hillary Clinton are performing satanic rituals to drain children of adrenochrome in the basement of Comet Ping Pong, a DC pizza parlor. It had its origins in some genuinely strange emails, which were released as part of the Russian influence campaign in the 2016 election. Because these emails, from the accounts of Hillary Clinton and close allies of hers, were released at a key moment in the election, they were scrutinized for material that could be damaging. And some strange things were indeed found. Take this one, from performance artist Maria Abramović to Tony Podesta, brother of Clinton's adviser John Podesta, to whom it was forwarded:

> "I am so looking forward to the Spirit Cooking dinner at my place. Do you think you will be able to let me know if your brother is joining?"   (Lee 2016)

It makes sense that a strange phrase like "spirit cooking" would attract the attention of people seeking to harm Clinton's campaign. And here's what spirit cooking turns out to be:

> The act of spirit cooking involves Abramović using pig's blood as a way of connecting with the spiritual world, to cook up thoughts rather than food. A video of the practice shows her writing various statements with the blood, such as "with a sharp knife cut deeply into your middle finger eat the pain".   (Lee 2016)

This sounds pretty disturbing, and it's not at all surprising that one might wonder why a Clinton campaign operative (John Podesta) would be involved with it. In fact, John's connection was that his brother Tony knew Abramović due to his involvement in the art world, and the dinner was actually an ordinary one:

Abramović spoke about the reaction today to Artnews. "I'm outraged, because this is taken completely out of my context," she said. "It was just a normal dinner. It was actually just a normal menu, which I call spirit cooking. There was no blood, no anything else. We just call things funny names, that's all." (Lee 2016)

But the phrase "spirit cooking" *is* a strange one, and the description of spirit cooking from Abramović's performance art does sound rather disturbing. This is just the sort of thing in need of explanation that might well seed an old-style conspiracy theory.

As this conspiracy was built up, rather quickly, it included a lot of emails involving the Podestas and Italian food. One of the key emails was this one, to John Podesta:

The realtor found a handkerchief (I think it has a map that seems pizza-related. Is it yorus? [*sic*] They can send it if you want. I know you're busy, so feel free not to respond if it's not yours or you don't want it.

Again, this email is at least mildly strange. It's odd to describe a handkerchief as pizza-related, and odd for it to have a map. It's not terrible or deeply incriminating, but it's strange enough to form a part of a conspiracy narrative. The conspiracy was helped along by some of the theorists finding pages online which claimed that pizza-related vocabulary is used as code for child pornography and pedophilia on the internet (Aisch, Huang, and Kang 2016). Whether or not that code actually existed, the discussion of this point involves online research leading to the discovery of claims which suggest a new interpretation of emails about pizza. This is a far cry from Muirhead and Rosenblum's view, on which New Conspiracies involve simply repeated assertions rather than research and the marshalling of evidence.

From this beginning, the Pizzagate conspiracy was born. It involved the claim that the Podestas and Clinton, and other prominent Democratic officials, were running a pedophilia ring from the basement of a Washington DC pizza parlor. This led a gunman to show up at the pizza parlor in an attempt to rescue the children. This conspiracy was one of those that became a part of the much larger QAnon conspiracy theory that has risen to national and indeed global prominence (Rothschild 2021). QAnon is supposedly an anonymous highly-placed intelligence official posting cryptic messages on the Internet about a secret operation to round up a global network of Democratic and celebrity pedophiles, including those who supposedly made use of the DC pizza parlor. There are many branches to this vast conspiracy theory. I want to turn now, however, to another high-profile strand, also strikingly implausible.

3.2.2 Wayfair

Wayfair is a furniture company, which sells products online. The Wayfair conspiracy theory holds that Wayfair is actually selling trafficked children, using codes involving cabinets that allow the children to be purchased over the Internet. The names of the cabinets correspond to the names of children who have been reported as missing. According to the conspiracy, purchasing a cabinet allows one to purchase a missing child. So far, this seems to fit Muirhead and Rosenblum's story well. Surely these claims are so strikingly ridiculous that no evidence could be marshalled for them. And it is hard to see what startling event could be in need of an explanation like this.

In fact, however, even the Wayfair theory does not ultimately fit their picture well. This is because there *was* a startling and strange event in need of explanation. The cabinets were appearing online with prices so high that it was totally reasonable to see them as puzzling and in need of explanation: ordinary storage cabinets were being sold for $13,000, and a pillow was being sold for $9999 (Associated Press 2020). Wayfair explained some of these prices as errors and others as standard for industrial usage, but these explanations happened only after the fact. Moreover, it doesn't take a conspiracist to find it puzzling that industrial use of an ordinary cabinet could be so expensive. So there was a deeply puzzling fact in need of explanation. The explanation given was not simply asserted. Conspiracists did research, examining lists of names of missing children and matching them to the names given to the cabinets. Whether or not we think this research was sound, or that the explanation was good, it is clearly wrong to characterize it as simply assertion, and to say that there was nothing in need of explanation.

3.2.3 America's Frontline Doctors

Characterizing present-day conspiracy theories as evidence-free is not just an error but a dangerous one.[10] It means that we might fail to properly recognize a conspiracy theory which does make use of evidence and argumentation in order to offer an explanation. Let's take as an example some of the conspiracies put forward by America's Frontline Doctors (AFD):[11]

America's Frontline Doctors [are] a handful of conspiracy-minded physicians that include luminaries such as Dr. Stella Immanuel who alleges that alien DNA is being used in medical treatments and that researchers are working on a vaccine to prevent people from becoming religious. She also believes in a conspiracy by the "Illuminati" to destroy the world with abortion, gay marriage, and of all things, children's toys. As far as gynecological diseases go, they can be caused by having sex with witches and demons that appear in dreams.   (Schwarcz 2021)

This certainly sounds like the sort of group that is likely to put forward evidence-free assertions of conspiracies, very much the New Conspiracism. But, as it turns out, this assumption would lead us into error. If we go to the organization's website, we find a very professional-looking site,[12] with links to what appear to be respectable research and documents called "white papers".[13] These are filled with charts, figures, and footnotes.[14]

Much of the material at the AFD website is devoted to Hydroxychloroquine (HCQ), an arthritis medication. This medication was not effective against COVID-19, but the idea that it was nevertheless became a prominent part of the QAnon conspiracy theory. It was, according to QAnon, a miracle drug whose efficacy was being hidden by a conspiracy including Big Pharma and the mainstream media (Rothschild 2021: 128). The AFD website was substantially devoted to arguing for the use of HCQ, offering paid appointments with doctors who would prescribe it, and also selling the drug (Bendix 2021). Some of the "white papers" appear to provide quite compelling evidence of a link between HCQ availability and lower death rates,[15] as shown in the graph.

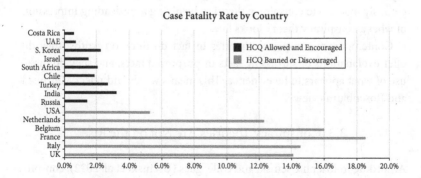

Case Fatality Rate by Country

These claims, then, feed into a conspiracy theory which holds that the truth about HCQ and COVID-19 are being suppressed. According to this theory, the disease is easily treatable, neither masks nor vaccines are needed, and doctors who attempt to reveal these truths are persecuted.

There are many reasons to be dubious about an inference from the chart shown here to the belief that HCQ is an effective treatment for COVID-19: the chart is apparently from June 2020, quite early in the pandemic; case fatality rates are strongly affected by testing rates; and case fatality rates are also strongly affected by country-specific issues such as when COVID-19 arrived, adoption of prevention methods, and availability of healthcare. Moreover, it is difficult to find out much about this chart's reliability, as the link in the footnote goes nowhere. I think it's safe to say, given what is known about HCQ's effectiveness and about the expertise and reliability of AFD, that something is deeply wrong with either this chart or the inference from it to the conclusion that HCQ is effective. But to figure out what exactly is wrong will take a bit of work.

This situation is very different from what would be predicted by Muirhead and Rosenblum. According to them, we should be finding mere assertion and repetition, without any argumentation. One who adopts their picture of what conspiracy theories look like today would look at the website from AFD and conclude that it is definitely not a conspiracy theory. They could reassure themself that conspiracy theories today are things asserted without argumentation, without evidence, and without any effort to explain observed facts. The presence of purported authorities, white papers, charts, evidence, and footnotes is enough to show that this isn't the sort of unreliable information we should be worried about in our current age. The AFD website looks like something that should be taken seriously. And this is why Muirhead and Rosenblum's characterization of current conspiracy theorizing is so problematic. It actually lends credibility to some of the most dangerously inaccurate conspiracy theories, by giving a misleading impression of what a conspiracy theory looks like.

Contemporary conspiracy theories in fact do draw on truths, they do offer explanations of surprising facts or purported facts, and they do make use of what appears to be evidence. This means we should reject Muirhead and Rosenblum's view.

3.3 Conspiracy Theories Are Not on the Rise

According to Joseph Uscinski and colleagues (Uscinski et al. 2022), conspiracy theories are not on the rise. They argue for this via data showing that belief in conspiracy theories, including but *not* limited to wildly implausible and dangerous ones, is not increasing in the United States. In what follows, I will grant Uscinski et al.'s claims regarding what their data show about belief in conspiracy theories. However, I will also argue that there is another reasonable understanding of the claim "conspiracy theorizing is on the rise" which seems to be true.

Uscinski et al. support their claim by examining data about belief in a wide variety of specific conspiracy theories, over time. Their finding is that while some conspiracy theories do show an increase in support, even more show a decrease. Further, they look specifically at COVID-19 conspiracy theories, arguing that these are not on the rise because their level of support remained relatively constant from 2020 to 2021. Finally, they examine support for QAnon, finding that the number of people explicitly declaring support for QAnon remained flat during the pandemic years 20–21. Moreover, this number was small: 5–6 percent. Given that 80 percent of Americans once believed in a Kennedy assassination conspiracy, this number suggests, they think, that concern over QAnon may be overblown (Enders and Uscinski 2020).

However, there do appear to be shockingly high levels of belief *in key elements of QAnon.* A poll in December 2020 found that 17 percent of Americans believed it to be true that "a group of Satan-worshipping elites who run a child sex ring are trying to control our politics and media" (Rose 2020). Another finding from the study is, if anything, even more remarkable: 37 percent of Americans said they didn't know whether this claim was true or not. That's a startling result for such a stunningly implausible claim. And it means that a solid majority of Americans, 54 percent, felt they couldn't rule it out. One might object that these responses do not involve a view *named* as QAnon, and that's true. But the view in question is in fact at the core of QAnon, and is not otherwise widely held.[16] Whether or not respondents know its name, there's good reason to think QAnon is what they're discussing.[17]

Quite obviously, levels of belief in QAnon and in COVID-19 conspiracy theories *have* risen, in the sense that they are higher than they were in 2015, before either the birth of COVID-19 or the beginning of Q's posts. But of course this is in some sense an unfair point—surely that's not what is meant by people claiming a rise in conspiracy theories. And that's right. However, I would urge closer attention to what's meant. My suggestion is that what's meant—by at least some—is *a rise in public prominence of dangerous and wildly implausible conspiracy theories.* Certainly, this is what my own focus is.

To see this, start by considering the classic example of a widely-held conspiracy theory, and one that's been widely believed for a long time—that regarding the Kennedy assassination. This is generally tested by asking whether respondents believe more than one person was involved in the assassination. There is nothing wildly implausible about the thought that more than one person might have been involved in this assassination: the idea that there were, say, two people, doesn't require a huge shift in what one knows about the world. Moreover, believing this does not seem to lead people into dangerous behaviors. Compare it to the belief that Satan-worshipping elites are running a child sex ring (considered a live option by 54 percent of Americans, and accepted by 17 percent); or the Great Replacement Theory that elites are plotting to replace the White population with people of color (accepted by 54 percent of Republicans in May 2022 (Romano 2022)). Both of these beliefs are wildly implausible and have led to violent crimes. My suggestion here is that one thing people mean when they talk about a rise in conspiracy theorizing is a rise specifically in wildly implausible and dangerous conspiracy theorizing. And this certainly does seem to be the case. Importantly, these belief levels are nowhere near as high as the 80 percent who once believed in a Kennedy assassination conspiracy theory. But that's to be expected—there really is nothing strange or implausible about more than one person having been involved in the assassination of a President. The levels of belief in wildly implausible and dangerous conspiracy theories is still shockingly high, given what these theories say and the behaviors that they lead to.

One might also question whether any of this actually indicates *belief* in these conspiracy theories. Neil Levy and Robert Ross (2021) offer several reasons to be skeptical about what studies purporting to be about *belief* in conspiracy theories show (Levy 2020). The first is that people who don't follow the news closely may not actually have opinions about the topics on which they are asked, and yet feel pressure to answer if a study does not allow an answer of "I don't know," likely a common feeling among participants. This criticism obviously doesn't apply to the study above, which does include this answer, clearly a popular choice. Levy and Ross rightly point out that people who don't have prior convictions may use partisan heuristics to decide on what answer to give, for example agreeing to negative claims about politicians that they don't like (e.g. Republicans might decide to agree that Barack Obama lied about where he was born). Interestingly, the study above also seems to be immune from this criticism. It does not mention any particular party or politician. In fact, the satanic child-abusing politicians in the QAnon conspiracy are Democrats, but one would have to already know about the QAnon conspiracy to know this. Levy and Ross note, again correctly, that the claims people make or agree to can often be ways of expressing political allegiance rather than stating beliefs. (We will discuss this idea further in Chapter 6.) It is possible that this plays a role in the pattern of responses to the question about Satan-worshipping pedophiles. If Trump supporters are aware that this is a QAnon belief, and if they are also aware that Trump has said friendly things about QAnon, their allegiance to Trump may make them agree to this claim, or at least hesitate to reject it outright. It may well be, in fact, that many of those choosing "I don't know" as a response do so because they find the claim implausible, but out of loyalty to Trump they do not want to reject it.

It may be, then, that the results of this study tell us less about what people genuinely believe and more about what they are willing to say. But this is still immensely interesting. The fact that people are willing to entertain, in thought or speech, the idea that leading Democrats are Satan-worshipping pedophiles is a remarkable one. The rise of such willingness, it seems to me, could quite legitimately be referred to as a situation in which the QAnon conspiracy theory is on the rise.

Finally, the rise of wildly implausible and dangerous conspiracy theories *in public discourse* is significant, even if some of those propounding these theories don't actually believe them. Conspiracy theories like those discussed above have become an everyday part of our media ecosystem in a way that they did not used to be. Importantly, such conspiracy theories have become surprisingly common among elected politicians of the Republican Party. And the conspiracy theory holding that the 2020 election was stolen from Donald Trump has become nearly mandatory among Republican Party candidates for office. The Great Replacement Theory had been amplified by Tucker Carlson on Fox News over 400 times by May 2022 (Romano 2022). Republican politicians have continued to publicly support it, even in the aftermath of a mass shooting based on it (Smith 2022). This level of mainstream support for wildly implausible and dangerous conspiracy theories *is* new.

My claim, then, is not that there has been a rise in *belief in conspiracy theories in general*. Instead, my claim is that *wildly implausible and dangerous conspiracy theories* are playing a larger role *in our political discourse*. This is in fact consistent with Uscinski et al.'s findings, and in a separate paper Uscinski suggests that journalists may have taken conspiracist beliefs to be newer than they were because "the conspiracy theories adopted by

QAnon accused the establishment—mainstream media, political elites, and societal institutions—of either conspiring or covering up the conspiracy, so these were not common among people like mainstream journalists who were themselves engrained in the establishment" (Uscinski 2022: 555–6). In other words, these sorts of conspiracy theories were not a part of mainstream political discourse, and now they are. This is precisely the change I am interested in here.[18]

4. So, What Is New?

We have now surveyed the cases for and against various popular claims regarding a rise in lying, a rise in bullshit, a post-truth epistemic landscape, and a change or rise in conspiracy theorizing. It is time to take stock. It seems to me that the changes relevant to our discussion of public discourse are the following:

- Increased use of statements by prominent national politicians that are seen as *obviously* false by a large segment of the population, including statements of wildly implausible and dangerous conspiracy theories.
- Greatly reduced concern by prominent national politicians about a large segment of the population seeing them as propagating obvious falsehoods (and wildly implausible, dangerous conspiracy theories), and lack of career-ending consequences for this.[19]

This characterization is different from many others for two main reasons. First, it focuses on political discourse, not political belief. Second, it keeps firmly in mind the fact that the population is divided in the way that these claims are viewed.

There is, by now, an immense and growing literature on how this change was brought about. This literature is largely based on social science and epistemology, tracking the spread of the blatant falsehoods, the nature of the networks that they spread in, the psychology of those who find them appealing, and the ways that these connect with partisan politics. There has been very little attention to the words that are used in propagating these falsehoods. To some extent, this lack of attention is understandable. There are very large groups for whom the phrasing that is used does not much matter. Those who are already devoted to Alex Jones, Donald Trump, and QAnon don't need the sort of careful convincing that calls for particular rhetorical choices. The committed opponents of these conspiracy theorists will not be moved by the exact words that are used when discussing Hillary Clinton's alleged penchant for baby-eating—they will oppose these claims no matter how they are phrased.

None of this means, however, that those words and expressions don't matter. People aren't divided into these groups in a fixed way. At some point, people who previously didn't believe that Democrats were harvesting adrenochrome from children came to believe it. People who never before worried about tracking devices in vaccines started to worry about them. Some of those who didn't come to *believe* these things at least started to think that it was worth considering or investigating them. Many of these people would previously have mocked adherents to such theories, and dismissed out of hand a politician who seemed to take them seriously. Perhaps most crucially of all, many politicians ceased to feel the need to distance themselves from implausible conspiracy theories. My contention is that rhetoric does make a difference when it comes to these changes. It makes a difference because it matters to the people who are persuadable. They may not be persuaded, but they may become comfortable enough with the ideas that they think these ideas are worth discussing. And some of them will be persuaded. The words that are chosen, I will argue, make a difference to the comfort that allows these ideas to spread.

To return to the story with which I started the chapter: I was, of course, right to worry about the way the world was changing with regard to truth in political discourse. But that *Time* magazine cover was an exaggerated response—much like my desire to collapse on the floor of the airport. Reports of truth's death were greatly exaggerated.[20]

But our political discourse's relationship to truth is increasingly fraught. Baurmann and Cohnitz (2021) argue compellingly that widespread belief in implausible conspiracy theories is eroding trust in highly damaging ways: belief in such theories leads to an undermining of trust in the many epistemic and other authorities who reject these theories. This leads to believers being increasingly cut off from valuable sources of knowledge and expertise: "false conspiracy theories are dangerous levers to start a dynamic downward spiral...believers of conspiracy theories will often generalize their institutional mistrust and simultaneously restrict their epistemic trust to persons who are enforcing and stabilizing this mistrust" (Baurmann and

Cohnitz 2021: 346). It is natural to suppose that public prominence of these theories, bringing with them repetition of trust-undermining arguments and claims, contributes to this.

Chapter 5 explores linguistic mechanisms—once more, dogwhistles and figleaves—that have facilitated the worrying discourses described in this chapter.

5
Figleaves, Dogwhistles, and Falsehood

A current US member of Congress has referred to "a global cabal of Satan-worshiping pedophiles" (Funke 2021), and publicly floated a conspiracy theory about space lasers controlled by Jews causing wildfires (Chait 2021). Another—himself a doctor—suggested that the Omicron variant of COVID-19 was created by Democrats to aid in the midterm elections (Cillizza 2021). The Great Replacement Theory, which holds that elites are plotting to replace White people with people of color, has become a mainstream view among Republican politicians (Smith 2022). Wikipedia has an entire entry devoted to listing all of the conspiracy theories that were either created or promoted by the previous President of the United States, Donald Trump. And the list is long.

Not very long ago, claims like these would have been career-enders: the politician in question would have been mocked across the political spectrum, and their followers would have been reduced to a tiny number of fringe conspiracists. Very obviously, things have changed: as described in Chapter 4, claims like these have become increasingly mainstream. In this chapter, I suggest that dogwhistles and figleaves have both played a role in this. Briefly, the general picture will be this: figleaves serve to reassure those who may worry that a speaker is not being sufficiently truthful. Dogwhistles, specifically Overt Code dogwhistles, allow the coded transmission of messages that serve to spread conspiracy theories. Together these have contributed to a discursive environment that is rich in blatant falsehoods and wildly implausible conspiracy theories, and one in which politicians seem to pay little price for propagating these.

1. Background: The Norm of Truthfulness

The linguistic devices that will be our focus here are significantly parallel to those we saw in our discussion of the spread of blatant racism. And the framework within which they operate is parallel as well. Once more, we see a widely held but woolly norm, very open to interpretation.

The Norm of Truthfulness is at its heart a simple (indeed over-simple) one, and its form—like that of the anti-racism norm—reflects this: **be truthful.**[1] Much like the Norm of Racial Equality, this norm is both widely accepted and extremely open to interpretation. This is a part of the reason that we can find such strong parallels between the ways that people get around this norm and the ways that they get around the Norm of Racial Equality. However, the ways in which this norm is open to interpretation are somewhat different and well worth exploring.

1.1 Contextual Scope of Application

Those who subscribe to the Norm of Racial Equality generally think that it holds universally. While people offer lots of excuses for their behavior and are willing to accept justifications in order to convince themselves that apparently racist behavior isn't really racist, there is no mainstream line of thought holding that it's OK to be racist, but only under certain circumstances. This is very much not to deny that there are plenty of people who behave in racist ways under plenty of circumstances; my claim is just that there are not many people *who would say that racism is generally bad but fine under certain circumstances.*[2]

Importantly, this is a contrast with how (most) people feel about untruthfulness. It is very common to think that untruthfulness is generally bad, but fine under certain circumstances. The circumstances in which it is considered acceptable to be untruthful vary from person to person, but they tend to include things such as the following:

- Politeness: "What a delicious meal you've made!"
- Kindness: "I'm sure everybody's forgotten what you did at that party when you'd had too much to drink."
- Protection: "No, Mr. Axe Murderer, there's nobody in my basement."

This fact about the Norm of Truthfulness means that for any norm-violating utterance, then, there will always be the possibility of raising doubt over whether the context is one in which the norm applies. We will see that this makes for a number of very appealing and highly effective figleaves.

1.2 Meaning of "Truthfulness"

There is room for debate over the interpretation of "truthfulness," with some taking it to apply only to what is *said* and others assuming a broader understanding.

This fact makes available an alternative move for those who think the norm applies universally: those who think this can also maintain that the norm only applies to what is literally said, and not to what is communicated beyond this. Thus, they can still navigate exactly the same circumstances we just discussed by carefully misleading rather than lying:

- Politeness: "An unforgettable meal!" This only *says* that the meal is unforgettable. It suggests the meal was unforgettable because it was so good, but it would still be true if the meal was unforgettably terrible.
- Kindness: "Who would remember that?" This doesn't *say* that nobody remembers the embarrassing incident, because literally it is just a question. However, it does suggest that nobody remembers the embarrassing incident.
- Protection: "I saw him yesterday, but... [puzzled shrug]" This carefully phrased response to the axe murderer avoids saying that the intended victim is not in the basement, which would be a lie. However, it very clearly suggests that.

The vagueness of the injunction "be truthful" facilitates these sorts of maneuvers: some will take the norm to require conveying only truths, while others will take it to require merely that one does not *say* false things.[3]

1.3 Linguistic Scope of Application

There are also further uncertainties regarding the *linguistic* scope of application of the Norm of Truthfulness. Some people will take it to apply only to assertions, while others might think it applies to questions, commands, or other grammatical constructions.

It is tempting to suppose that, really, only assertions can be true or false and so only utterers of assertions can adhere to or deviate from the Norm of Truthfulness. However, it is actually quite natural in ordinary language to treat people as untruthful when they make other kinds of utterances (Viebahn et al. 2021):

- "How much money is Bill Gates making from the microchips in the vaccines?" This question clearly conveys, via presupposition, that there are microchips in the vaccines.
- "Quick—stop them from draining the babies' adrenochrome!" This imperative is based on the assumption that people are draining the babies' adrenochrome.
- "I wonder if Nancy Pelosi is the leader of the conspiracy or just a foot-soldier..." This presupposes that Pelosi is at least part of a conspiracy.

Utterances like these clearly communicate falsehoods, even though they don't make assertions. On the ordinary understanding of truthfulness, then, it is not at all clear-cut to insist that only assertions can be truthful or untruthful. This is important to understanding the way that the Norm of Truthfulness works. The ordinary norm does, arguably, apply well beyond assertions. However, uncertainty about what constructions it applies to can be exploited in order to bring about deniability: it makes room for people to convey falsehoods via speech acts that are not assertions, and then to insist that they have not violated the norm because they have not asserted anything false.

1.4 Violating the Norm of Truthfulness

One way of violating the Norm of Truthfulness is by saying something widely known to be false—like suggesting that Jewish space lasers cause wildfires (Chait 2021), that (deceased Venezuelan leader) Hugo Chávez helped to steal votes for Joe Biden (Sommer 2020), or that Democrats/Jews/elites are trying to replace White people with people of color (Rose 2022). That's one key reason that it's considered (by many of us) so outrageous when politicians assert things like these. Moreover, we may think that it's outrageous even if we think the politicians are saying what they believe to be true. And the Norm of Truthfulness—due in part to its looseness—can explain this. In addition to the falsehood of these claims, the politicians asserting them can also be seen as violating the Norm of Truthfulness by *not properly pursuing* truthfulness. Maybe they believe these claims, but they shouldn't. Rather than accepting such absurdities, this line of thought goes, politicians owe it to us to take their responsibilities seriously by properly vetting and fact-checking their claims, and deferring to appropriate experts. A politician who asserts these things may be seen as doubly violating the Norm of Truthfulness by saying something false, while also not taking sufficient care with their utterances.

In our discussion of the Norm of Racial Equality, we noted that despite its weakness it seems to have constrained public discourse in certain ways: very explicit expressions of racism were avoided in political discourse during the pre-Trump period when this norm held sway. Similarly, widespread acceptance of the Norm of Truthfulness led, before the Trump era, to certain constraints on public discourse as well. Certain kinds of very obviously false claims were simply not considered acceptable from a national politician. The two basic kinds of claims that were considered unacceptable were (1) claims that the politician clearly didn't believe, and (2) claims that were widely accepted as false by the mainstream media. Generally, the second sorts of claims were also those rejected by acknowledged experts.

In this chapter, we will be asking how it came to be so much more acceptable for politicians to say things starkly at odds with widely accepted truths, and how these claims became a mainstream part of public discourse. We will be trying to understand how it is that many people have been so much more tolerant than one would expect of shockingly implausible claims. We will explore how wildly implausible and dangerous conspiracist claims have come to be a part of our mainstream discourse. (In Chapter 6 we will be looking in more detail at how it became more acceptable for politicians to say things they clearly don't believe.)

2. Figleaves for Falsehood

Figleaves for falsehood are additional bits of speech (usually) which allow the speaker to convince the audience that the apparent norm violation is, after all, OK—not something which should spark distrust. Here's a general definition:

A falsehood figleaf F for an audience A and utterance F is a bit of speech which blocks A from *correctly* concluding that A's utterance of F does not respect the Norm of Truthfulness.

A key way to do this is by convincing the audience that the Norm of Truthfulness does not apply. This can take several forms, corresponding to the issues of interpretation just surveyed. One might maintain that the utterance is of a sort to which the norm simply cannot apply—either because of its structure or because of the context. Alternatively, one might insist that the norm is being adhered to even if falsehoods are being conveyed. As long as the audience can be induced to doubt whether the norm has been violated, trust is not destroyed in the way that it would be through a clear violation. Blatant falsehoods may thus be allowed to circulate more freely than they would otherwise. We will see in what follows that all of the interpretive issues about the Norm of Truthfulness yield corresponding figleaves. In addition, there is also the maneuver of simply denying that one is acting contrary to the Norm of Truthfulness. This maneuver also gives rise to many common figleaves.

Just like racial figleaves, falsehood figleaves may be either synchronic or diachronic. Although we will see that synchronic figleaves play a special role in our era of blatant falsehoods, diachronic figleaves have long been very important in politics. The reason for this is that, traditionally (and for obvious reasons), politicians have preferred to attempt convincing lies, rather than blatant falsehoods accompanied by figleaves. However, a convincing lie at one time turns into an obvious one as the truth is discovered. When this happens, figleaves become very important. Below, we will briefly discuss figleaves that are used for concealed falsehoods, before moving on to the more surprising terrain of figleaves for blatant falsehoods.

2.1 Concealed Falsehoods

False utterances by politicians, we have seen, are nothing new. Indeed, it is almost expected that politicians will not be truthful about everything. In most periods, however, the expectation has been that politicians would conceal the falsehood of their utterances—a practice commonly known as lying. One of the things that has been most striking about the Trump era is the willingness to make false utterances that are widely recognized as false. For utterances of concealed falsehoods, figleaves tend to occur most often diachronically, once the falsehood of the utterance has been revealed.

2.1.1 Literal Truth Figleaf
In our discussion of the Norm of Truthfulness, we saw that one interpretation allows one to be truthful by saying something which is technically true, even while one communicates a falsehood. This is a widely used tactic, but it seems to be especially popular with politicians. Famously, it was used by

Bill Clinton when his relationship with Monica Lewinsky was made public. When asked whether he was having a relationship with Ms. Lewinsky, he responded "there is not a sexual relationship."[4] Later, Clinton was confronted when it was made clear that there had indeed been a sexual relationship. Here is his response:

> It depends on what the meaning of the word "is" is. If the—if he—if "is" means is and never has been, that is not—that is one thing. If it means there is none, that was a completely true statement…Now, if someone had asked me on that day, are you having any kind of sexual relations with Ms. Lewinsky, that is, asked me a question in the present tense, I would have said no. And it would have been completely true.   (Noah 1998)

This response is many things. It is evasive. It is strangely phrased in the conditional. And it is also, arguably, a figleaf. Clinton is insisting that his response does count as truthful, because it was literally true—even though it was quite clearly misleading and rather obviously deliberately so. He is attempting to insist that he did not violate the Norm of Truthfulness by restricting the scope of that norm to what is literally said.

2.1.2 Norm Irrelevance Figleaf

As we have noted, the Norm of Truthfulness only applies in certain circumstances. If one's own safety or that of others requires deviation from this norm, most consider this to be acceptable. This fact is one of the reasons that probably the most famous example in discussions of deception is that of the person hiding potential victims from a rampaging murder. The view that lying is still forbidden[5] is widely considered extreme and implausible. In the case of political lying, it isn't surprising perhaps that one of the most commonly justified forms of dishonesty is dishonesty for the sake of national security. It is widely considered acceptable to deceive about matters such as where one is planning a crucial attack in a war, or where one's forces are most vulnerable. These sorts of lies to the enemy are considered a crucial part of wartime strategy. What shocked Hannah Arendt about what was revealed in the Pentagon papers was not that the United States had lied about a war. Lying about a war is absolutely standard. Arendt was shocked that there was no effort to conceal the truth *from the enemy*, and instead a very substantial effort to conceal the truth from the people of the United States. One reason this deception is so shocking is that, unlike the deception of the enemy, it is harder to justify in terms of national security.

It is not surprising, then, that assertions of national security, or of protecting the citizens more generally, are a common sort of figleaf for politicians. The Norm of Truthfulness is frequently not seeing as applying in circumstances like these. A very clear instance of asserting that the norm does not apply comes from the Kennedy administration's explicit claim that the government has a "right, if necessary, to lie to save itself" (Alterman 2020: 87). For those who agree that the norm does not apply where national security is at stake, this figleaf will be highly effective, convincing them that the Norm of Truthfulness has not been violated—because it does not apply. Although Kennedy-era Cold War deceptions are controversial, other uses of the national security figleaf are even more so.

Trump used this sort of protective, safety justification to explain why he insisted that COVID-19 was not very dangerous, even though he was well aware of its dangers. During the election campaign against Joe Biden, an interview that Trump had recorded with journalist Bob Woodward was released, in which Trump discussed his downplaying of COVID-19. Both in the interview and in response to criticism when it came out, Trump insisted that his dishonesty about COVID-19 was acceptable because it was to protect the public.

Trump, speaking to reporters Wednesday afternoon, said he'd been trying to avoid "panic" and was showing "leadership":

> "We have to show calm," he said. "Certainly I'm not going to drive this country or the world into a frenzy. We want to show confidence. We have to show strength."   (Gregorian 2020)

What Trump is doing is providing figleaves which suggest that this was a circumstance in which the Norm of Truthfulness didn't apply. This can be a very successful strategy for a politician, as people are aware that sometimes politicians need to keep truths from them. Preventing a panic can be a legitimate justification for falsehood. In this case, of course, that justification fell flat with much of the audience because the pandemic was clearly made so much more serious by Trump's insistence that it was no worse than the flu.

2.2 Blatant Falsehoods

Synchronic figleaves in politics have been relatively rare until recently. There's a good reason for this. In order to have a synchronic figleaf, there must be both (1) and (2):

(1) An utterance F which would otherwise be easily recognized as violating the Norm of Truthfulness.

(2) A figleaf of some sort providing cover for this by causing at least
some of the audience to doubt that F really violates the Norm of
Truthfulness.

These kinds of figleaves have been relatively rare in politics because traditionally politicians have tried to avoid utterances like F, which are readily
recognized as violating the Norm of Truthfulness. For good reason, they
have generally preferred to carefully deceive, and tried to bring it about that
their false utterances are not discovered. The Trump-era strategy of saying
openly false things but attempting to convince the audience that this is
acceptable is a relatively new one, at least in US politics. (Making openly
false utterances has a long history in authoritarian regimes, to be discussed
in Chapter 6.) One of the most important changes we've seen in the Trump
era is the use of synchronic figleaves for falsehood—needed only because of
a new willingness to make utterances that much of the audience will see as
obviously false.

Conspiracy theories like QAnon, and their key claims, are viewed as ludicrous and obviously false by the mainstream media and a large segment of
the population. They are viewed as important concealed truths by another
large and passionately committed segment of the population. The first
group will probably write off anyone putting forward QAnon or its key
claims. They will not vote for them, they will not share their tweets, and
they will discourage others from supporting anyone who puts forward these
sorts of theories. The second group, the passionate adherents, will obviously
behave very differently, believing the conspiracy theorists and purposefully
helping to disseminate their messages. Neither of these groups will have
their behavior affected by figleaves.

However, now consider the case of a politician who wants to gain the
support of QAnon adherents, since these are very important currently to
the Republican Party. This person will need to *signal support* for QAnon.
But at the same time, in most cases they will also need to retain at least
some support from those who reject QAnon. A figleaf can help them to
accomplish both of these goals. A conspiracist reference may be made, signaling support for QAnon. But if it is accompanied by a figleaf, this can
provide a license for non-QAnon adherents to stick with the politician, by
suggesting that they really do still adhere to the Norm of Truthfulness.

Another important role for figleaves comes in the spreading of wild conspiracy theories *by ordinary citizens*. Theories like QAnon have largely

spread through social media. In order to spread, they cannot remain confined to groups of people who are already passionately committed. But they are unlikely to be spread by people who are deeply opposed. What's needed is a way to allow these messages to spread to those who might be curious, and who might be drawn in. Figleaves can help to accomplish this: social media users can present conspiracist messages, but accompany them with reassuring caveats that make the not-yet-conspiracist people more likely to share these messages, and more likely to explore them further.

2.2.1 "Just Asking Questions"

As we have noted, there is room to interpret the Norm of Truthfulness as applying only to utterances which have the form of assertions. Some find it natural to suppose that questions can violate the norm, while others find it natural to insist, literal-mindedly, that a question cannot be true or false. This means that inserting or insinuating falsehoods in the form of a query can easily be defended as legitimate. The classic political trick of push polling takes advantage of this. A push poll purports to be a legitimate political poll. However, its point is not to study voters' answers but instead to make insinuations that the campaign does not want to openly assert. A classic example of this is the push poll used by the G. W. Bush campaign against John McCain in the 2000 presidential primary. It asked, "Would you be more or less likely to vote for John McCain... if you knew he had fathered an illegitimate black child?" This was obviously a tactic to spread a falsehood that the campaign expected to appeal to voters' racism. Openly asserting this falsehood was clearly considered a step too far, but the campaign was willing to insinuate it with this question.[6]

This is what gives rise to one of the most common figleaves for falsehood: *just asking questions*. Talk-show host Glenn Beck is famous for his use of "just asking questions." More specifically, he's famous for making wild allegations in the form of questions asking for the allegations to be disproved. He uses this technique so much that he's been satirized in an episode of *South Park* (Good 2009) and with the website GlennBeckRapedAndMurderedAYoungGirlIn1990.com (Brad 2009). Each of these satires focuses on the maneuver of presenting outrageous claims in the form of questions. This technique is a highly effective figleaf. While a high level of proof might be required in order to assert something, many would maintain that only curiosity is required in order to ask a question.

Gwyneth Paltrow made interesting use of this figleaf, in arguing that Conde Nast should not fact-check *Goop Magazine*, a very short-lived endeavor. (The refusal to allow fact-checking seems to have ended the partnership after two issues.) Goop's head of content explained that Goop did not require fact-checking because it was making no claims—just quoting others (a form of figleaf we will get to shortly) and asking questions (Wolfson 2018):

> She argued that they were interviewing experts and didn't need to check what they were saying was scientifically accurate. "We're never making statements," she said. Elise Loehnen, Goop's head of content, added that Goop was "just asking questions".

Another frequent user of this technique is podcaster Joe Rogan. In the quote below, he refers to Ivermectin. Ivermectin is a drug used for a variety of purposes (many veterinary), which has occupied a similar place to Hydroxychloroquine among Trump supporters, anti-vaccination activists, conspiracists (Elliott 2021), and even America's Frontline Doctors (discussed in Chapter 5), who sold and prescribed it online. However, it has not been shown to be effective against Covid (Szalinski 2021) and the large doses people take to fight Covid are known to be very dangerous (Varun 2022). Here is Joe Rogan:

> "This doctor was saying Ivermectin is 99 percent effective in treating Covid, but you don't hear about it because you can't fund vaccines when it's an effective treatment," he says on his podcast. "I don't know if this guy is right or wrong. **I'm just asking questions.**"
>
> (Dickson 2021, emphasis mine)

There are several notable features of this quotation. One of them is that he maintains he is just asking questions—a figleaf, but in fact he clearly is not just asking questions (in fact, nothing in this quotation is even in the form of a question). But Rogan also says that he is reporting what a doctor has said. This brings us to another figleaf, described below. (In fact, as we will see, this single quotation contains no fewer than three figleaves.)

2.2.2 Reported Speech
Reporting the speech of someone else can serve as a very effective figleaf.[7] This is because, of course, it is sometimes appropriate to report what other others have said; and it can be appropriate and truthful to do so even if what the others have said is false. These facts about reported speech mean that

reporting the speech of others can be an extremely effective way to insert falsehoods, even blatant falsehoods, into public discourse. Moreover, one can convince oneself and others that one is not violating the Norm of Truthfulness—because one isn't, at the level of what is said. However, falsehoods are being conveyed, and gaining currency in public discourse.

This is what someone like Joe Rogan does when he reports what a particular person has said, as he does in the previous passage, presented below with new emphasis:

> "**This doctor was saying Ivermectin is 99 percent effective in treating Covid, but you don't hear about it because you can't fund vaccines when it's an effective treatment,**" he says on his podcast. "I don't know if this guy is right or wrong. I'm just asking questions."
>
> (Dickson 2021, emphasis mine)

This sort of figleaf can make immensely important contributions to the circulation of false claims. People may feel very comfortable sharing reports of what others have said online, knowing that doing so is not an explicit endorsement. News organizations may find it appealing to report on ridiculous things that people have said—these can be a kind of clickbait—but doing so gives these claims greater prominence and keeps them in circulation. If news organizations can be induced to report on the ridiculous things that people have said, they may unwittingly become the accomplices of those who want to propel those ridiculous claims into mainstream discussions.

Benkler, Faris, and Roberts' *Network Propaganda* (2018) provides many examples of this (although they don't use the term "figleaf"). For example, they discuss the way that a narrative about the "Deep State" working to undermine Trump was introduced to non-fringe media discussions. Initial discussions of the story on Fox News always took the form of interviews with people who accepted it, with Fox itself expressing skepticism or neutrality about the claims. This allowed a story that even Fox might have hesitated to report as fact to become a familiar narrative before the organization endorsed it in response to Trump's support for it (Benker et al. 2018: 153).

Reposts on social media also function as a kind of reported speech, but one that is complicated in a way useful for bad actors (Rini 2017). Neri Marsili (2022), comparing reposts to gossip, writes:

> The problem with reposting is that it also comes with limited accountability. When you repost someone else's content, you don't really vouch for it

yourself, taking responsibility for its truth. As the popular disclaimer has established *ad nauseam*, a retweet is not an 'endorsement'. Like a rumour, it is a sort of second-hand report. It directs attention towards content that *someone else* has posted (and taken responsibility for).

Choosing to repost something rather than to put it into one's own words is, arguably, a kind of synchronic figleaf in and of itself.[8] The fact that it is a retweet conveys that it is someone else's speech, and directs attention to that person. As we have already noted, truthfully reporting someone else's saying of a false thing will often be seen as not violating the Norm of Truthfulness.[9] Moreover, this very clearly makes available a diachronic figleaf after the fact, when someone is criticized for what they have retweeted. Here is Marsili (2022) again, describing Trump's use of this maneuver (though not under the name "figleaf"):

> Trump, once again, illustrates this pattern egregiously. He has frequently retweeted conspiracy theories, fake news and blatantly false claims. Confronted publicly about his retweets, he's always brushed off the accusations with confidence. For instance, questioned about a retweet alleging that Marco Rubio was not eligible to run for president, he blurted: "Honestly, I've never looked at it. Somebody said he's not. And I retweeted it. I have 14 million people between Twitter and Facebook and Instagram, and I retweet things and we start dialogue and it's very interesting." Similarly, challenged to explain why he retweeted a message from a neo-Nazi account (containing made-up crime statistics regarding white people murdered by Afro-Americans): "Bill, am I gonna check every statistic? All it was is a retweet. It wasn't from me."

2.2.3 "A Lot of People Are Saying"

A somewhat more disreputable version of this is to vaguely gesture at the idea that a claim is in wide circulation, with a phrase like "a lot of people are saying." This method has become so popular and so important to the spread of conspiracy theories that it was used as the title for a book discussed in Chapter 4. The authors write, "if *a lot of people are saying it*, to use Trump's signature phrase, then it is true enough" (Muirhead and Rosenblum 2019: 3).[10] What I take "true enough" to mean here is *true enough to pass on to others*. This idea—that something can be passed on without worry if enough people are saying it—is a key part of what gives this sort of figleaf its power.

A further example of this comes from Trump's discussion of the conspiracy theory which holds that the Clintons killed Vince Foster, a friend of theirs who committed suicide. Here's what Trump said, when asked in an interview:

"I don't bring it up because I don't know enough to really discuss it," Trump said while bringing it up. "I will say there are people who continue to bring it up because they think it was absolutely a murder. I don't do that because I don't think it's fair."   (Johnson 2016)

Trump here distances himself just slightly from the claim that Foster was murdered, by discussing it as something that other people bring up. By noting that other people bring it up—and noting their sense of certainty about it—he lends credibility to the story. But the fact that he is reporting what other people say serves as a figleaf for his spreading of this conspiracy theory. Quite clearly, Trump does not have adequate justification to assert that Foster was murdered, let alone killed by the Clintons. But no justification of that sort might seem to be required for *the claim that people say* Foster was killed by the Clintons. For those who accept it, then, the figleaf serves to assuage the worry that Trump might be violating the Norm of Truthfulness.

Of course, this doesn't work with everyone. Like many others, Jenna Johnson, author of the *Washington Post* article in which this quote appears, has noticed (though not in the terminology of "figleaves") how Trump uses this figleaf as a method for spreading conspiracy theories:

Trump frequently couches his most controversial comments this way, which allows him to share a controversial idea, piece of tabloid gossip or conspiracy theory without technically embracing it.   (Johnson 2016)

But Trump is not, of course, the only culprit. Ted Cruz made very heavy use of a "people are saying" figleaf as he lent early support to Trump's claims of a stolen election. Rather than explicitly expressing agreement with these claims, Cruz presented them as needing to be investigated because *other people* believed them:

"Recent polling shows that 39 percent of Americans believe the election that just occurred, quote, was rigged," Cruz said. "You may not agree with that assessment. But it is nonetheless a reality for nearly half the country."

(Bump 2021)

Once more, this figleaf worked with some but not all. It gave just enough reassurance to worried Cruz supporters, who wanted to be able to tell themselves that Cruz wasn't actually supporting the conspiracy theory. But his call for investigation give an immense boost to those who did support the conspiracy theory and attacked the Capitol. Once more, then, we see how this figleaf can take advantage of, and enhance, the political divisions among the population.

Vague claims about what people are saying played a crucial role in the rise of the Pizzagate conspiracy theory that we discussed in Chapter 4. This kind of figleaf is likely to be especially important in introducing people to a conspiracy theory, which might initially sound too absurd to take seriously. Here are some examples of this sort of utterance, taken from Benkler, Faris, and Roberts (2018), which occurred in stories that their analysis shows to have played a crucial role in the spread of the Pizzagate theory (emphases mine):

> "Emails reveal that Podesta attended 'Spirit Cooking' event *that has been described as* Satanic." (226)
>
> "*Some are even linking* the spirit cooking revelation to claims that the Podesta emails contain 'code for child sex trafficking'..." (229)
>
> "*Theories and screenshots began to swirl, claiming tha*t bizarrely-worded emails about food were codes for child sex trafficking." (230)

This figleaf plays an important role in misinformation regarding the pandemic. Here is Naomi Wolf on Twitter discussing purported vaccine side effects:

> Well hundreds of women on this page say they are having bleeding/clotting after vaccination or that they bleed oddly being AROUND vaccinated women. Unconfirmed, needs more investigation. But lots of reports.[11]

In short, making vague claims of a message being in wide circulation is a highly effective and much-used figleaf for falsehood. It allows one to introduce a claim into public discourse, while avoiding accountability, all the while bestowing on it a feeling of importance that comes from the fact that *lots* of people are saying this thing.

Johnson also calls attention to the way this move functions once its maker is called out on the falsehoods that they are spreading. At this point, the diachronic figleaf often explicitly distances the speaker from responsibility for the spread of falsehood:

> If the comment turns out to be popular, Trump will often drop the distancing qualifier—"people think" or "some say." If the opposite happens, Trump can claim that he never said the thing he is accused of saying, equating it to retweeting someone else's thoughts on Twitter.
>
> (Johnson 2016)

2.2.4 "It's a Joke"

Humor figleaves are, we already saw, important in denials of racism. They are, unsurprisingly, also very popular figleaves for the spread of falsehood and wild conspiracism—after all, it would be unreasonable to expect jokes to be true. This kind of figleaf for falsehood, then, gets its plausibility from the fact that the Norm of Truthfulness does not apply to humorous utterances.[12]

Humor figleaves are very popular diachronically, to suggest that what seemed a serious utterance was not. During a press conference, Donald Trump infamously suggested that disinfectants might be useful against COVID-19:

> "I see the disinfectant that knocks it out in a minute, one minute," referring to disinfectants such as isopropyl alcohol that had previously been brought up at the briefing. "And is there a way we can do something like that by injection inside, or almost a cleaning? Because you see it gets inside the lungs and it does a tremendous number on the lungs, so it would be interesting to check that." (Blake 2020)

The suggestion that ingesting disinfectants could be useful was taken seriously by the large number of Americans who contacted poison control authorities to ask whether this would be a good idea (Elliott 2020). There was, understandably, a strong outpouring of criticism for this utterance. After that, Trump made use of a humor figleaf:

> "I was asking a question sarcastically to reporters like you just to see what would happen," Trump said. (Blake 2020)

Interestingly, Trump never *asserted*, as has often been reported, that people should inject bleach to prevent COVID-19. And he does note that he was asking a question—also a popular figleaf. But in addition Trump used a humor figleaf. This figleaf, for those it worked on, convinced people that the press conference—previously understood as a serious event—could well have been a venue for humor instead.

Importantly, the success of the figleaf does not require actually convincing its intended audience that the remarks were intended as humorous. Instead, what is required is merely a raising of doubt. If they become convinced that the remarks *might* have been joking, this can induce the desired hesitation, giving them a reason not to withdraw their trust. Moreover, the figleaf can even be effective—though in a different way—with respect to those who do not accept it. It becomes much harder to challenge an utterance that has been explicitly tagged as a joke. One runs the risk of appearing humorless and uncomprehending. This makes it much more difficult to correct falsehoods that have been flagged as jokes.

The joke emoji and its relatives are popular synchronic figleaves, used to suggest that one is only joking. The potential effectiveness of this figleaf is underscored by the 2014 verdict in the *Ghanam* v. *Does* case, in which according to Elisabeth Camp:

> the use of a ':P' emoticon to represent a face with its tongue sticking out, was judged to "make it patently clear" that the commenter was making a joke and so that "a reasonable reader could not view the statement as defamatory." (2022: 248)

2.2.5 Just a Performance

Closely related to a humor figleaf, but somewhat broader, is the idea that an utterance should not be taken seriously because it is part of a performance. The idea here is that in a performance one is not asserting but playing a character. The audience is in on a performance and does not take it seriously. Because of all this, the Norm of Truthfulness does not apply to such a performance. This move has also become remarkably popular among those putting forward patently false or wild conspiracist claims.

Alex Jones, propagator of many wild and dangerous conspiracy theories, has attempted to defend himself by using such a claim. In a child custody lawsuit, Jones's ex-wife claimed that his endorsement of wild conspiracies meant that his home was not a stable and appropriate one for their children. His lawyer insisted that all of those apparent endorsements were just pieces of performance art:

"He's playing a character," attorney Randall Wilhite said of Jones. "He is a performance artist." (Borchers 2017)

Although Alex Jones's use of this maneuver did not work, other uses have been more successful. For example, take the case of Tucker Carlson, whom we have already discussed as a leading proponent of the Great Replacement Theory. The judge in a defamation lawsuit ruled that Carlson's comments could not be taking as defamatory because no reasonable person would take him seriously. According to her:

"[The] 'general tenor' of the show should then inform a viewer that he is not 'stating actual facts' about the topics he discusses and is instead engaging in 'exaggeration' and 'non-literal commentary,'" the ruling said.

(Sheth 2020)

2.2.6 Ignorance Figleaves

One fascinating sort of figleaf is to appear to assert something, while backing off from the assertion by declaring a lack of knowledge about the topic. A nice example of this is a description of G. W. Bush campaign operatives discussing Bush's primary opponent John McCain:

A national correspondent covering Bush that year told me that campaign operatives, "in a very off-the-record setting, would say something like 'I don't know if this is true or not, but, of course, you know McCain just doesn't seem sane, does he?' They'd kind of plant the seeds that way."

(Gooding 2008)

We also see a figleaf of this sort in the figleaf-packed quotation from Joe Rogan that we have already discussed. Rogan not only says that he is just asking questions, and not only spreads falsehoods by attributing them to someone else, but adds on that he doesn't in fact know whether what this other person has said is true:

"This doctor was saying Ivermectin is 99 percent effective in treating Covid, but you don't hear about it because you can't fund vaccines when it's an effective treatment," he says on his podcast. "**I don't know if this guy is right or wrong.** I'm just asking questions." (Dickson 2021)

This kind of figleaf has been discussed in the philosophical literature on deception as a potential *proviso lie*—a lie in which one makes clear that one is not warranting the truth of what one says. If one knows the falsehood of what one is saying, Don Fallis (2009): 50 argues that one may still count as lying despite the addition of a proviso such as an ignorance figleaf (though not calling it a figleaf): "this case shows that you can be lying (when you say something that you believe to be false) even if you explicitly say that you are not warranting the truth of what you say."

2.2.7 Dissociation from Conspiracy/False Claim

One of the best-known racial figleaves is the phrase "I'm not a racist but…" It is perhaps not surprising, then, that very similar figleaves are used for conspiracy theories and other false claims that people might want to dissociate themselves from.

It is not at all uncommon for opponents of Covid vaccination (or indeed of other vaccines) to declare defensively that they are not anti-vaccine. For example, here's Tucker Carlson hosting Glenn Beck to discuss COVID-19 vaccination: "Nobody here is anti-vaccine, but…" Carlson began, before going on to give large amounts of airtime and credibility to antivaccination sentiment" (Media Matters Staff 2021). (Interestingly, he followed this up with an ignorance figleaf: "what do I know? I'm hardly a man of science…") Even John F. Kennedy Jr., a longtime leader of the anti-vaccination movement, insists, in an anti-vaccination documentary, "I'm not anti-vax…I am somebody who is skeptical of government and pharma, but I'm not anti-vax" (Pilkington 2019).

General Michael Flynn, a strong supporter of the QAnon conspiracy theory, employed a remarkable figleaf during his speech at a QAnon conference, insisting, "This is not a conspiracy theory."[13] Flynn's use of this figleaf, in this location, suggests that even adherents of this elaborate and wildly implausible conspiracy theory have some concerns about thinking of it *as a conspiracy theory*. To allay these concerns, Flynn offers reassurance via figleaf that it is *not* a conspiracy theory.

2.2.8 Julian Assange's Multiple Figleaves Regarding Seth Rich

In the summer of 2016, a large quantity of internal emails from the Hillary Clinton campaign was released by WikiLeaks, an organization run by Julian Assange. Also that summer, Seth Rich—an employee of the Democratic National Committee (DNC)—was shot in a mugging. It has now been firmly established that the emails came from Russian hackers. But at the time, Assange strongly suggested that they came from Seth Rich, thereby fueling a conspiracy theory—which was then picked up and promoted by Fox News—holding that the Clinton campaign had Rich murdered.

During an interview about the leaked emails (Kroll 2022), Assange noted that Wikileaks does not delay the release of materials because that would be a disservice to sources who risk their jobs and lives. He continued: "there's a twenty-seven-year-old who works for the DNC [who] was shot in the back, murdered just two weeks ago for unknown reasons as he was walking down the street in Washington." The interviewer asked what Assange was suggesting, and Assange said, "I'm suggesting that our sources take risks..." The interviewer asked if Rich was Assange's source, and Assange said that they don't comment on who their sources are. The interviewer pressed him: "Then why make the suggestion about a young guy being shot in the streets of Washington?"

> Assange repeated what he'd already said—that it was concerning to WikiLeaks's sources to know that a political aide had been gunned down in the middle of a contentious presidential campaign. The murder only underscored the "serious risks" those sources faced.
> Van Rosenthal [the interviewer] wasn't buying it. "But it's quite some-thing to suggest a murder," he said. "That's basically what you're doing."
> "Others have suggested that," Assange said. "We are investigating to understand what happened in that situation with Seth Rich. I think it is a concerning situation..."   (Kroll 2022: 51–2)

This collection of utterances from Assange is very carefully phrased. He never *says* that Rich was his source, or that Rich was murdered for provid-ing information to WikiLeaks. Instead, he crafts his utterances to suggest these claims—setting himself up for a literal truth figleaf if needed ("I never said that!"). But that's not all he does: he also uses a "lots of people are say-ing" sort of figleaf by uttering "others have suggested that" when asked if he's suggesting that Rich was murdered due to the dangers of being a source. And this was true: there were already people arguing that Rich was mur-dered by the Clintons, many (though not all) of them Bernie Sanders sup-porters. But once Assange made his carefully phrased and figleaved utterance, the conspiracy theory spread to Fox News, and from there it acquired astonishing spread and staying power (Kroll 2022).

3. Non-figleaf Use of Figleaf Phrases

One issue that frequently complicates discussion is that the very same phrase may be used both as a figleaf and *not* as a figleaf. This is, if anything, even more common with falsehood figleaves than with racial figleaves.

Consider, for example, the figleaf of reporting what someone else has said. To be more specific, let's take "Michael Flynn says." One user of this phrase might be a person who seeks to propagate falsehoods by repeating false utterances prefaced by this phrase over and over on social media. This person, let's assume, knows that the imbedded statements are false, and deliberately uses "Michael Flynn says" to avoid accountability and help the message to spread. Let's also assume that some of those who share these posts recognize the falsehood of Flynn's claims but reassure themselves that they are only spreading *the fact that Flynn has said these things*, not saying these things themselves. In this case, the phrase is clearly functioning as a figleaf.

Now consider the case of a reporter, perhaps reporting on Flynn's role in the QAnon conspiracy theory. This reporter is likely to make quite a few utterances including the phrase "Michael Flynn says." They then follow this up by assessing the truthfulness of Flynn's claims and criticizing them when appropriate. But we have no temptation to call this a figleaf. The reason here is that the reporter is not violating the Norm of Truthfulness: their goal is not the propagation of falsehoods, and this is obvious. So the phrase does not keep us from recognizing the reporter's violation of the Norm of Truthfulness.

However, let's turn now to a very different reporter. This reporter, like the previous one, reports what Flynn says. However, he does so uncritically, despite knowing that these claims are false. This reporter, then, is arguably violating the Norm of Truthfulness. Some of his audience is aware of the falsehood of Flynn's claims but reassure themselves that the reporter is only reporting, and not to blame for the circulation of the false claims. For these people, "says" functions as a figleaf. Of course, for others this figleaf will not succeed—they will criticize the reporter for uncritically spreading falsehoods. And yet others will be unaware of any violation of the Norm of Truthfulness. For these people there will be no need for a figleaf.

In short, it is always important to bear in mind that not all uses of common figleaves phrases are actually figleaves, and it can be difficult to sort out.

4. Dogwhistles and Wild Conspiracism

It is not just figleaves that are used to spread wildly implausible and dangerous conspiracy theories. Dogwhistles turn out to play a crucial role, which we will explore in this section. Coded messages were vital both to the initial spread of the QAnon conspiracy theory and to its continued popularity. As Mike Rothschild writes, "unseen by the media and unchecked by the social platforms, Q believers were developing a method of communication that was simple and clear to people who spoke the language, while being totally incomprehensible to outsiders" (2021: 146). In particular, they were urged to make memes that functioned as, in our vocabulary, Overt Code dogwhistles. "Q drops are full of exhortations to readers to make memes and disseminate them as a way of avoiding big tech censorship and algorithms" (2021: 147).

The cryptic nature of the Q memes and messages not only allows them to avoid restrictions on social media, but also makes for deniability. "Trump would routinely share Q memes and slogans, often acting like he had no idea what they were about." (2021: 149). One nice example of this included both a dogwhistle winking at QAnon followers and an ignorance figleaf:

> Even in early March 2020, as COVID-19 panic began to settle over the country, Trump responded to the chaos and fear not with a speech or rhetorical exhortation for Americans to socially distance, but with a meme—of him playing a fiddle with the text "MY NEXT PIECE IS CALLED...NOTHING CAN STOP WHAT'S COMING", with Trump himself adding, "Who knows what this means, but it sounds good to me!"
> (2021: 149)

"Nothing can stop what's coming" is a QAnon slogan, used to refer to the "coming storm"[14] of rounding up all the famous people who have been kidnapping children to drain their adrenochrome. To the uninitiated, however, it reads as merely overly dramatic tweeting. In what follows, we'll work through a few further examples of the ways that dogwhistles function as part of the QAnon movement.

4.1 "WWG1WGA"

To an outsider who does not know about QAnon codes, "WWG1WGA" means nothing. However, it stands for the crucial QAnon phrase "where we go one we go all." Use of this phrase indicates that one is a QAnon adherent, and use of "#WWG1WGA" plays an important role in helping QAnon posts to go viral, aiding in the spread of QAnon messaging. In addition to the concealment that comes from use of the coded phrase, use of this hashtag on Instagram is also often visually concealed from those who view Instagram on their phones:

> Very recently, a number of Instagram influencers using the stylised "design look" popular on the platform—light earth tones, single dominant colours, loopy fonts, and low-detail imagery, all employing filters and all aligned with the bland aesthetics of an Ikea living room or hipster coffee shop—have embraced the conspiracy theory. The aesthetics and the subjects—family, food, and fun—are therefore familiar and anodyne, but the accompanying text and hashtags use themes familiar to QAnon, such as "WWG1WGA"...Given the specific affordances of Instagram as a platform and their users' device usage, few viewers will see the full text of a post as they "heart" a given photo: full textual content is only accessible by clicking the "More" link, so hashtags appended at the end of a post will be hidden from view by casual scrollers. The result is that these influencers gain exposure to their cause by people who upvote a photo, but who do not themselves necessarily see the text. QAnon adherents, however, interact with the post's text, clearly understanding its intent.
>
> (Drainville and Saul, forthcoming)

Putting all of these together, we get an extremely effective dogwhistle, which allows the message of QAnon to be spread by people who have been deceived into thinking that they are just sharing an image that they like. Influencers may even use the hashtag simply as a way of gaining more followers. (That is, for some of them it may be an unintentional Overt Code dogwhistle.) At the same time, the QAnon followers are watching use of the hashtag spread, and identifying (apparent) fellow travelers. All of this contributes to the spread of the wildly false and implausible conspiracy theory.

4.2 Anti-vax Emojis

Anti-vaccination activists and conspiracy theorists have found it increasingly difficult to spread their messages due to social media crackdowns on misinformation. This has led them to use emojis as visual dogwhistles, which seems to have been an effective technique for evading post removal:

Pizza slices, cupcakes, and carrots are just a few emojis that anti-vaccine activists use to speak in code and continue spreading COVID-19 misinformation on Facebook. (Belanger 2022)

Bloomberg reported that Facebook moderators have failed to remove posts shared in anti-vaccine groups and on pages that would ordinarily be considered violating content, if not for the code-speak. One group that Bloomberg reviewed, called "Died Suddenly," is a meeting ground for anti-vaccine activists supposedly mourning a loved one who died after they got vaccines—which they refer to as having "eaten the cake."

4.3 "#Save the children"

Save the Children is the name of a long-standing and perfectly respectable international organization. Many people support this organization simply because they care about child welfare. However, "save the children" is also a slogan and a hashtag that has been enthusiastically adopted by QAnon followers. As such, it has become a very interesting Overt Code dogwhistle. Some uses of "save the children" are completely innocent references to the long-standing organization. Others are QAnon code. The situation on Twitter is similarly entangled, as the hashtag is used not only by the organization, but also by QAnon followers. The deniability offered by use of "save the children" serves many purposes.

Because a group devoted to *Save the Children* might be QAnon but also might be legitimate, social media organizations that have committed to shutting down QAnon groups are hesitant about shutting down "save the children" groups:

"Save the Children" is a fuzzier area for platform enforcers, because it can be difficult to tell who is genuinely concerned about child exploitation and who is taking advantage of those concerns to sow misinformation. That vagueness has helped QAnon believers avoid a total crackdown, and has given them venues to discuss their theories that aren't as vulnerable to being taken away. (Roose 2020)

The innocent appearance of the phrase "save the children" has also offered a wonderful recruitment tool. People who have a genuine concern with child welfare may click on posts or follow hashtags that pull them, gradually, into the QAnon conspiracy.

4.4 New Age Q Dogwhistles

The QAnon movement has been remarkably successful at spreading to New Age and wellness communities. Within these communities, slogans are adopted that fit well into previous discourse, and can thereby help to normalize and spread the theory—as well as, of course, achieving some degree of deniability.

This content uses coded language, talking of "awakening," "enlightenment," and "seeking one's own truth." It appears alongside posts about veganism, meditation, and acupuncture. Users bypass content moderation efforts by tech companies by adapting their language, making them difficult to dislodge, and giving themselves an air of semi-plausible deniability (Guerin 2021).

This shows a fascinating case in which terms already present in a linguistic community are then adopted as dogwhistles. It provides insight into the ways that wild conspiracist ideas can make inroads by adopting the right coded terminology for the right groups.

4.5 "Cofveve"

In May 2017, Donald Trump sent out one of his strangest tweets, almost certainly the result of a typo on the word "coverage": "Despite the constant negative press covfefe." Several hours passed without another tweet, during which time this tweet stayed up and speculation about it went viral. Much of this speculation was, of course, humorous. The tweet became even more famous, however, when Trump insisted that it was not a mistake. His press secretary took questions on the subject:

Reporter: Do you think people should be concerned that the president posted somewhat of an incoherent tweet last night, and that it then stayed up for hours?
Spicer: Uh, no.
Reporter: Why did it stay up so long? Is no one watching this?

Spicer: No, I think the president and a small group of people knew exactly what he meant.   (Galluci 2017)

Spicer was, in fact, claiming that "covfefe" was, in our terms, an Overt Code dogwhistle. There is little evidence that it actually was anything but a typo. However, some QAnon supporters have, as a result of this incident, attempted to theorize its true meaning (Roose 2021). This is an interesting development due to the inevitable uncertainty about whether a phrase is an Overt Code dogwhistle or not. Previously, we discussed instances in which a term was used as an Overt Code dogwhistle, but the uncertainty allowed for denials. In this case we have a term which probably isn't an Overt Code dogwhistle, but which is *thought* to be one. Nonetheless, the nonsensical tweet—by being interpreted as a dogwhistle—helps to perpetuate the key QAnon idea that Trump is communicating in code.

4.6 QAnon Letter/Number Codes

QAnon letter and number codes are another interesting case of something which appears to be an Overt Code dogwhistle, but which may not be. Along with some very clear utterances, and some clearly coded utterances, QAnon also posts strings of letters and numbers. These are taken to be codes, and followers devote an enormous amount of time and energy to decoding them. This collaborative, communal activity is an important way in which members bond, an element of the conspiracy theory community that is thought to be crucial to the theory's power and longevity. A recent analysis, however, has argued that the sequences involved in these codes are most likely the result of random typing:

"These are not actual codes, just random typing by someone who might play an instrument and uses a qwerty keyboard," Mark Burnett, a security consultant who has analyzed millions of passwords over the course of more than a decade, wrote on Twitter after studying the codes. Burnett said he noticed a pattern in the codes: "almost all the characters" in the codes alternate between the right and left hand or are close to each other in a normal QWERTY keyboard. Imagine someone's hands resting on a regular keyboard. According to Burnett, QAnon is likely simply typing keys randomly with his left hand and right hand where they rest, resulting in a combination of characters alternating between one group of keys on the right side of the keyboard, and one group of keys on the left side of the keyboard.   (Franceschi-Biccierai 2018)

If this is right, then we have the deliberate creation of strings of letters and numbers which are meant to appear to be Overt Code dogwhistles accessible to insiders. Although they are probably not actually codes, they nonetheless serve an important function in the spread and maintenance of the QAnon conspiracy theory. In this indirect way, then, these pseudo-dogwhistles contribute to the spread of falsehood.

5. Dogwhistles, Figleaves, and the Rise of Wild Conspiracism

Coded dogwhistles have helped wilder and wilder conspiracy theories to spread and gain greater prominence. First, and most obviously, they help the conspiracy theories to grow and acquire more followers. Equally important, they help to normalize conspiracist discourse—the use of coded language has helped these discourses to seem less strange.

Figleaves have done yet more to normalize conspiracist discourse. In the case of racial figleaves, we saw an effect on the interpretation of the Norm of Racial Equality. Here, what we see is parallel: an effect on the interpretation of the Norm of Truthfulness. Not long ago, the realm of politics was viewed as a place for carefully considered speech: not one for jokes, and not one for ideas far outside the mainstream consensus. The Norm of Truthfulness applied in such a way that a politician could not defend themself by saying that they were only joking—except in clearly designated humorous contexts, like the annual Washington Correspondents' Dinner. Moreover, politicians were expected to follow an agreed-upon basis of facts, those accepted by the consensus of mainstream experts and mainstream media. Figleaves have been used to repeatedly introduce wildly implausible conspiracy theories into political discourse. As this has happened over and over again, some have begun to shift away from the idea that politicians should be relying on an accepted body of mainstream facts and experts. In short, a broader interpretation of the Norm of Truthfulness has been eroded.

Together, these two developments have had a devastating effect on our public discourse. They have played a role in creating what Neil Levy (2021) calls "epistemically polluted environments," which make successful individual cognition much more difficult than it would otherwise be. They give spread and respectability to ideas that should have been weeded out, but which exert an undeniable appeal. The proliferation of implausible conspiracy theories has a disorienting effect, making it difficult to arrive at clear convictions about facts, and leaving people even more vulnerable (than they would otherwise be) to charismatic authoritarians—which we will explore in Chapter 6.

6

Obvious Falsehoods without
Deniability

So far, my focus throughout this book has been largely on utterances that involve an element of deniability.[1] We have seen how both dogwhistles and figleaves are used in order to obtain deniability for racist, false, and conspiracist utterances. Nonetheless, this deniability is not always present. Sometimes the problematic element is just blatant, with no cover at all. And this gives rise to a question. How can such blatantly troubling utterances succeed? How can politicians who make them get elected and remain popular? In some sense, we can understand how there might be people who are untroubled by blatant racism—they are racists themselves, and perfectly comfortable supporting somebody else whom they see as racist. So the function of blatantly racist utterances is not hard to understand. (Indeed, these can easily be made sense of as we have done throughout this book by looking at the divided population.) But the blatantly false utterances, and the obvious lack of concern with truth, are much more puzzling. Could there really be people who are comfortable supporting someone who spouts blatant falsehoods, who engages in what has been seen by so many as bald-faced lying? Someone who doesn't even seem to think about whether their utterances are true? How could such a politician not just survive, but seemingly thrive, despite this? Nonetheless, two populist leaders at the same time seemed to do just that: Boris Johnson and Donald Trump.

In this chapter, we will tackle the question of how bald-faced lies and obvious lack of concern for truth could be a successful political strategy. This chapter will explore how we might make sense of this phenomenon. Once more, the key will be to pull apart different audiences and their different interests, to examine how they are being manipulated. We will see that the pattern which emerges is one very familiar from the study of authoritarianism. Although this chapter is not about the role played by dogwhistles and figleaves, it represents an important piece of the puzzle of how blatant falsehoods and conspiracism thrive in the public discourse of a deeply divided society.

We will start with a small terminological note. A bald-faced liar is generally understood as someone who utters a falsehood, knowing that it is so obviously false that it is very unlikely their audience will believe them (Kenyon 2003; Sorensen 2007). A bullshitter is traditionally understood as a person who speaks without regard to the truth or falsehood of what they are saying (Frankfurt 2005). In a recent paper, Tim Kenyon and I have argued that making sense of current political figures requires careful attention to the relatively unexplored category of bald-faced bullshitters, who (roughly speaking) make it obvious that they are unconcerned about the truth or falsity of what they are saying (Kenyon and Saul 2022).[2] Both bald-faced liars and bald-faced bullshitters share the trait of making it obvious that they are not following the Norm of Truthfulness.

1. Puzzling Examples

In thinking about the puzzling phenomenon of political success despite bald-faced lies and bald-faced bullshit, it will be good to have some examples to hand.

1.1 Boris Johnson's Brexit Column

Throughout the Brexit campaign and after, Boris Johnson enjoyed extraordinary levels of support from large segments of the UK population, despite being widely thought of as uninterested in being truthful. One might suppose that this was because Johnson supporters were largely single-issue pro-Brexit voters, and they were unconcerned with whatever Johnson might say about anything else. However, it was in fact widely known that Johnson did not decide to back the Brexit campaign until the very last minute. Johnson, who at the time wrote a newspaper column, was known to have written two columns—one in favor of Brexit and one against. At the last possible minute, Johnson decided to publish the pro-Brexit column and join the Brexit campaign. They cannot, then, have thought that Johnson had a genuine and deep pro-Brexit conviction. Instead, most people thought of Johnson as an opportunist who joined the side that he thought would be best for him. Johnson, then, was seen as someone who says what is convenient for him without regard to its truth. (Johnson is a highly plausible example of a bald-faced bullshitter.) He is definitely not thought of as someone who respects the Norm of Truthfulness—his lying is very much out in the open. As former Tory politician Rory Stewart said in 2022, "People have known that Boris Johnson lies for 30 years" (Lyall 2022). And it is puzzling that people can trust and support someone who seems so obviously to have this kind of character. And yet he was elected Prime Minister. (What finally eroded his popularity was not lying, but—first—that he had several parties during Covid lockdowns, and—second—his support for a politician who had committed sexual harassment.)

1.2 Boris Johnson's Bus-Making Hobby

While he was running for Prime Minister, Boris Johnson gave a remarkable interview. Johnson was asked an easy question: what does he like to do to relax? A normal politician would use the opportunity to present himself as a sympathetic man of the people by talking about getting together with friends and family, or watching football. Johnson's answer, which really cannot be fully appreciated except by watching a video,[3] was a rambling, halting story about making buses out of old wine crates. The manner in which he told the story was unquestionably the manner of someone making it up as he went along. The story was pretty much universally received as obviously false. Some speculated that there must be armies of interns at Downing Street hastily manufacturing buses out of boxes in order to back up the story, but in fact no effort was made to support it. Although there was widespread amusement, it was not widely seen as a problem that Johnson was clearly not telling the truth.[4]

1.3 Trump Inauguration Photo and Weather Lie

Famously—and as we have already discussed—Barack Obama's inauguration was much better attended than Donald Trump's, and photos make this difference very clear. Nonetheless, Donald Trump and his supporters insist that Trump's inauguration photo shows more people than Obama's. They even insist upon this with the photos in front of them, clearly showing the relative audience sizes. Trump also insists that there was beautiful weather and a shining sun all through his inauguration speech, despite the footage showing rain, umbrellas, and people in raincoats. These are remarkable examples of clear bald-faced lies: everyone can see that the claims are false, and yet Trump persists in making them. Adding to the bafflement, they are not even lies on important topics. Why on earth would someone lie about the weather? As Masha Gessen (2021) notes, "the weather is a simple, safe basis of shared reality. To lie about the weather, one would have to be a strange kind of liar." And when someone does lie about something like this, why are people willing to trust and support him? Don't they, one might wonder, feel resentful that they are being lied to?

1.4 Hurricane Map

In 2019, hurricane Dorian was approaching the United States. Hurricane forecasters had mapped out its probable course, and this course did not include Alabama. However, Trump tweeted out that Alabama was in the path of the storm. Falsehoods about the course of a hurricane can, of course, be dangerous and expensive, leading the wrong people to evacuate and the wrong state governments to take action. Accordingly, the national weather service issued a statement making it clear that Alabama was not in the storm's path. Trump then held a briefing, displaying a National Hurricane Center map showing the likely course of the hurricane. This likely path was indicated with a white loop, and it did not include Alabama. However, an additional loop, clearly drawn on by hand with a black sharpie (Trump's favorite writing instrument) *did* include Alabama. This was not a clever deception, or skilled alteration of the image. There was no attempt whatsoever to make this believable. And yet, the President presented it as the truth. It was an utterly bald-faced lie, on a matter of urgent significance (Smith 2019).

2. True Believers in Echo Chambers?

It is important to remember that, no matter how implausible and bald-faced a lie seems to many, there may well be others who genuinely believe it. This would be one group of people who do not need figleaves for falsehood, because they do not see blatantly false claims as false. These people are, to name a few, the committed conspiracy theorists. They genuinely believe, for example, that Hillary Clinton runs a cabal of Satan-worshipping pedophiles out of a pizza shop. Perhaps, then, there's not much really in need of explanation: the people who support makers of blatantly false claims *don't see them as blatantly false.* There's nothing all that mysterious about people who believe false things supporting people who say those very same false things. The only puzzle might be how they sustain these false beliefs.

One popular thought is that these false beliefs are sustained by the existence of what Thi Nguyen (2020) calls "epistemic bubbles"—communities of like-minded people who share a large number of beliefs. (Often these are called "echo chambers," but, as Nguyen argues, echo chambers are an importantly different phenomenon.) Simply as a result of this uniformity, the shared beliefs go unquestioned. An old-fashioned paradigm case of such a community might be a closed-off society, perhaps on an isolated island without Internet. A more up-to-date paradigm case would be people who spend all their time conversing online with others who share their beliefs. And, indeed, many of the people with wild conspiracist beliefs do spend large amounts of time in online spaces with like-minded folk. An oft-proposed remedy for epistemic bubbles is to work to bring it about that people are exposed to a wider variety of views, by trying to add new voices to these communities. Exposure to new views would lead to reinvigorated discussions and questioning, and people would work collaboratively across their differences to get to the truth together.

But "epistemic bubble" isn't actually the best characterization of their situation. They are not, for the most part, in isolated communities without exposure to people who don't share their beliefs. They are well aware of the existence of other ways of thinking, and indeed they may even hate-watch segments of speeches by those they disagree with, like Anthony Fauci and Joe Biden. The problem is not that followers of these conspiracy theories are unaware of the existence of alternative views. It is that these views are dismissed as products of a deceitful mainstream media and of political elites who are a part of the conspiracy. In other words, the problem is that believers in these conspiracies are in what Nguyen (following Jamieson and Cappella 2008) call *echo chambers*, which are much more difficult to penetrate. In echo chambers, opposing views need not be absent. What makes for an echo chamber is the conviction that anyone who holds opposing views is to be reviled. Decades of concerted effort by right-wing talk radio figures like Rush Limbaugh helped to create echo chambers, by building a core of followers who believed that the mainstream media were corrupt and deceitful (Jamieson and Cappella 2008; Rosenwald 2019). Donald Trump built upon this foundation, using anti-media rhetoric over and over, up to the point of calling the mainstream media "the enemy of the people." Similarly, distrust in academia was carefully built over the years, in part by painting academics as left-wing indoctrinators and in part by setting up parallel institutions to undermine expert consensus (O'Connor and Weatherall 2019; Levy 2021). This meant that actual expert researchers, with knowledge and credentials, came pre-discredited. In these echo chambers, then, mainstream news organizations and knowledgeable experts are viewed as fundamentally untrustworthy. An important consequence of this is that claims which seem clearly false to those who follow mainstream media or expert opinion do not seem clearly false to members of these echo chambers. Good examples of claims like this would be the claim that Trump won the 2020 election, that Covid vaccines are dangerous and unnecessary, and that Hillary Clinton runs that pedophile ring.

However, this explanation founders when it comes to certain claims. It's not just the mainstream media suggesting that Obama's inauguration crowd was larger than Trump's, that it was in fact raining at Trump's inauguration, or that Boris Johnson is inventing his bus-making hobby—it's the evidence of one's own eyes. We can't explain people's willingness to go along with this simply by talking about echo chambers, because this isn't just a matter of choosing whose testimony to accept and whose to dismiss. The evidence of falsehood isn't just testimonial—sometimes it's direct. And it's obvious. So the question remains: how can people be so tolerant of, even enthusiastic about, political leaders demonstrating so very clearly that they do not care about the Norm of Truthfulness?

3. People Not Seeking Truth?

One reason that people might not care about politicians manifestly disrespecting the Norm of Truthfulness is that they are not seeking politicians who care about this norm. After all, people don't *always* care about this norm. Although it's hard to imagine how somebody could completely fail to care about the norm, *across every area of their life*, there are in fact times when people don't care about it—when seeking entertainment, for example. If politics is viewed as a form of entertainment, there's no reason to care about whether politicians respect the Norm of Truthfulness. This fits well into a recently advocated explanation—already touched upon in Chapter 4—for the willingness of Trump supporters to assert obvious falsehoods, like those about inauguration crowds: they are not seeking to say true things, but rather just to show support for their team. This phenomenon is known as "expressive responding" in the literature—subjects use the opportunity to express a view as a way of indicating their loyalties, rather than focusing on saying what is true (Schaffner and Luks 2018; E. Anderson 2021; Hannon 2021; Levy and Ross 2021). Engaging in such behavior builds loyalty further, and the sense of alienation from those who insist on the falsehood of one's claims only stokes the Us versus Them mentality.

A recent study (Schaffner and Luks 2018) suggests strongly that this is sometimes the case. This study made use of photos from Obama's and Trump's inaugurations. It asked some participants which photo had more people, and other participants which photo was from Trump's inauguration. The study found that politically engaged Trump supporters were far more likely than any other group to incorrectly identify both which photo went with which inauguration (a question which requires a bit of knowledge), and which photo showed more people (a question whose answer should be obvious just at a glance). Giving the wrong answer about which photo contains more people—an obvious fact—is puzzling unless we posit that they actually *do* know which one is Trump's inauguration photo but want to show support for Trump. It's the more engaged supporters who will know this, and it's they who give wrong answers to both of these questions. Shaffner and Luks therefore conclude that expressive responding is the best explanation. In this case, quite plausibly, these people are themselves engaging in bald-faced bullshitting, or possibly bald-faced lying. They cannot possibly believe that the experimenters will accept their claims as true, but this does not matter to them because that is not their primary concern. Their primary concern is to demonstrate the fervency of their support for Trump—a matter of allegiance rather than belief.

Importantly, the pattern of responses we see is also consistent with thinking of politics as entertainment, much like sports. It is perhaps a notable fact that both Johnson and Trump rose to public prominence *as entertainers*. Johnson built much of his fame by appearing on humorous news quiz shows, and Trump through tabloid and radio shock jock appearances. It seems clear that a good deal of Trump's early media coverage in his campaign for the Republican nomination was due to viewing him as an unserious figure doing such outrageous things that he provided entertainment. Indeed, the *Huffington Post* initially covered him in its entertainment section rather than in politics or news (Borchers 2015). As late as 2020, even pundits who opposed Trump admired him as an entertainer (Rosenberg 2020):

> The theatrics of the State of the Union normally rely on the president's delivery and the audience's response. Trump's greatest innovation was to

turn himself less into a monologuing actor and more into a sort of reactionary Oprah Winfrey, sprinkling giveaways and surprise guests throughout the evening... If the president gets those four more years Republicans cheered for, it will be because he is unusually deft at seizing control of that canvas and filling it up with vivid images and moments. Americans may not be able to agree on whether that work is a masterpiece or a moral disaster. But either way, we won't be able to look away.

If an increasingly cynical public looks to politics not for truth or for solutions, but for entertainment, one can see how falsehoods might not be a problem. There is something outrageous and entertaining about a person presented with the two inauguration photos insisting on a manifest falsehood. And there is definitely something mesmerizing about Boris Johnson's bus-making monologue. Such cases can seem like harmless light entertainment.

But it is more difficult to see how some of the other key examples could be seen as harmless. People really do need to know the actual path of a hurricane, and—when deciding whom to support—British voters needed to know what Boris Johnson actually thought about Brexit, not just which column he chose to publish. Obfuscating these with falsehoods surely can't be seen as simply light entertainment.

4. Bald-Faced Lies Not So Bad

It is something of a commonplace that politicians are not to be trusted. The idea that all politicians lie is extremely widespread. If one holds this view, then it is absolutely no surprise to catch a politician lying. Indeed, the bald-faced liar may be seen as a welcome relief from the normal course of events, if one takes the normal course of events to be politicians deliberately and successfully deceiving the public.

Roy Sorensen (2007), in the first philosophical paper to discuss bald-faced lies under that name, argues that there is nothing wrong with bald-faced lies precisely because no one is deceived and no one intends to deceive. Both of these reasons can serve as a justification for supporting a politician who is a bald-faced liar. When Trump drew on the hurricane map with a sharpie, this line of thought goes, nobody actually took him seriously—they couldn't possibly do so. If he had made the alteration in a skillful manner, intending to actually deceive people, it might have done harm. But, according to this way of thinking, the lie was rendered harmless by its obviousness. The fact bald-faced lies are harmless can help to explain some of the support for the bald-faced liar.

Some even argue that bald-faced lies are not really lies. On Ishani Maitra's (2018) view, for example, bald-faced lies are more akin to the utterances of an actor than they are to assertions. Just as it would be inappropriate to see an actor as lying when they say their lines on stage, it is inappropriate to see a bald-faced liar as lying. Maitra does not conclude from this that there is no room for moral condemnation of a bald-faced liar, but we can well imagine that some might take a different view. They might think that precisely because they have concluded the bald-faced liar is not actually lying, what they are doing is not so bad.

Teresa Marques (2020) has argued that a view like Maitra's is not ultimately satisfying, and she gives two reasons. First, one who accuses an actor of lying is seen as hopelessly confused about what's going on. But this is not so for one who accuses a bald-faced liar of lying. Marques's second objection, however, is even more powerful. If we see bald-faced liars like Trump and Johnson as merely doing something like what actor actors do, we cannot make sense of the profoundly damaging effect that they have on public discourse and those attempting to engage with it. She writes that bald-faced lies are powerful devices for gaslighting: people who encounter regular bald-faced lies, especially from their leaders, can come to doubt what they previously thought they knew, or to doubt their capacities as knowers. This can't be explained on the view which holds that bald-faced liars are like actors.

My contention is that each of these views captures something important about how bald-faced lies function in a diverse and divided community. Some people see the lies as harmless because obvious, and may even see them as something like an actor's performance. It is likely that some of these people are among those who view the bald-faced liar as an entertainer. Maitra's description of how she takes bald-faced lies to function captures what is happening with this group.

However, Marques is right about what bald-faced lies do with respect to two other groups. One audience is unsettled by the bald-faced lies, caused to doubt their previous certainties, perhaps even gaslit. Anne Applebaum (2022) notes astutely that when people "fear that they can't know something, or [have] the impression that it's impossible to know something," this is "useful to autocratic regimes because... they lead people to feel that they're powerless."

Yet another audience is enraged by the bald-faced lies, calling them out as lies and disagreeing with them vehemently. Bald-faced lies further deepen the divisions between already divided groups. Those who think bald-faced lies are harmless lash out against critics as oversensitive. Those who see the harm that bald-faced lies do become increasingly frustrated and enraged. This anger is then pointed to in order to increase the sense of threat among the supporters of the bald-faced liar: the accusation is that critics are unreasonably angered by something utterly harmless, and that this indicates how unhinged and dangerous these critics are.

5. Authoritarianism, Power Lies, and Compliance Lies

Obvious lies have a long history at the center of authoritarianism. Megan Hyska (2022) calls lies of this sort "hard propaganda." Hyska argues that they serve at least three important functions, each of which we will delve into further with examples:

- Authoritarian leaders tell deliberate and obvious falsehoods as a display of their power: the fact that they can get away with this shows how powerful they are.
- The telling of these falsehoods demonstrates what loyal subjects should do—they should say whatever the leader wants them to, even if it is false.
- When loyal subjects do this, it is degrading and humiliating. This serves as a means of subordination.

The obvious lies told by authoritarian leaders are what Tim Kenyon and I have previously called "power lies," and their repetitions by subordinates are what we have called "compliance lies" (Kenyon and Saul 2022).

5.1 Lies as Authoritarian Power Display

A key reason that authoritarian leaders tell obvious lies is to demonstrate that they have the power to do so. The move is not unlike Trump's declaration that he could shoot a man in the middle of Fifth Avenue and get away with it. Masha Gessen puts it like this:

The Trumpian lie is…The power lie, or the bully lie. It is the lie of the bigger kid who took your hat and is wearing it—while denying that he took it. There is no defence against this lie because the point of the lie is to assert power, to show I can say what I want when I want to.   (2021: 106)

An authoritarian bald-faced liar is demonstrating that they can declare something obviously false and have others fall in line. Marques describes it well:

It is because bald-faced lies are assertions made 'with utter confidence and without trying to conceal' their falsehood that they impose asserted false-hoods on context. Getting away with a bald-faced lie is a form of dominat-ing conversational contexts.   (2020: 256)

Getting away with a bald-faced lie is, as Marques explains, a way of domi-nating others. If this is in a small group conversation, it's a domination of the conversation. But if it's a leader speaking to the country, the domination is much broader. Displays of power are traditionally extremely important to authoritarian leaders. That's why they so favor large-scale military parades. Bald-faced lies are another important way of displaying power. In what fol-lows, we look at why power lies are so effective.

5.2 Power Lies as Attractive

One theory has it that power, even clearly malign power, is in itself appeal-ing. Steve Bannon, Trump's advisor, clearly holds this view:

Darkness is good. Dick Cheney. Darth Vader. Satan. That's power.
(Steve Bannon, quoted in Snyder 2018)

But it's not at all obvious that this is really the case. Darth Vader is in some sense a popular figure, and Satan is certainly a compelling one. But Dick Cheney? It's not clear that Bannon's view on this matter is widespread.

More explanation is needed than this. One compelling explanation begins from noticing that, despite his many obvious lies, Trump is fre-quently described by supporters as authentic. At first blush, this seems baffling. But an important recent psychology paper offers some insight.

(Hahl, Kim, and Sivan 2018) use experimental data to show that there are certain circumstances under which a "lying demagogue" comes to be seen as authentic and appealing. A bald-faced liar comes to be seen as authentic precisely because they are seen as violating an established norm—(that which I call) the Norm of Truthfulness. The demagogue is seen as authentic and appealing in such circumstances because he successfully presents himself as "an authentic champion of those who are subject to social control by the established political leadership." He gains support as brave and authentic because he is "willing to sacrifice his acceptance by the establishment" (Hahl et al. 2018: 6) by violating important establishment norms—thus showing that he is *genuinely* anti-establishment. This sacrifice of establishment acceptance becomes especially appealing when there is a *crisis of legitimacy.* Such a crisis can be brought on by a group feeling either that they are not being represented by those with power, or that their power is slipping away. And it seems that a key motivator for Trump voters has been a fear that they are losing status (Mutz 2018).

5.3 Compliance Lies

Power lies are also used to extract what Kenyon and Saul (2022) call "compliance lies." These are the lies told by subordinates, which echo the leader's bald-faced lies. The subordinates tell these lies in full knowledge of their obvious falsehood. They serve as both a loyalty display and a form of humiliation, further evidence of the authoritarian leader's domination. We will look at an example from Republican senator Ted Cruz, who was in the Capitol as the insurrection occurred, both witnessing it and fleeing from the violent intruders.

Immediately after the January 6 insurrection, Ted Cruz condemned it in very strong terms:

> The attack at the Capitol was a *despicable act of terrorism and a shocking assault on our democratic system.* The Department of Justice should vigorously prosecute everyone who was involved in these *brazen acts of violence.* I thank the brave men and women of the U.S. Capitol Police and all other law enforcement agencies who responded to restore peace.
>
> (Holmes 2022, emphases mine)

As late as a full year after the event, Cruz continued to criticize it, calling it a violent terrorist attack:

We are approaching a solemn anniversary this week, and it is an anniversary of a *violent terrorist attack* on the Capitol.

(Holmes 2022, emphasis mine)

By the time of this last utterance, however, it had become clear that Trump had retained his dominance of the Republican Party and that Republican politicians were expected to fall in line behind his version of what happened on January 6. This version, starkly at odds both with what was seen on national TV and with what politicians like Cruz personally experienced, was that the event was non-violent, except perhaps for antifa (Cohen 2021): "These were peaceful people, these were great people," Trump said.

Cruz came under fire for his description of the interaction as a violent terrorist attack. To quell these criticisms, Cruz abased himself by completely contradicting what he had already said and describing the events in a way deeply at odds with what he knew to be true:

On January 6, 2021, you had tens of thousands of people *peacefully protesting*, and yet the corporate media and Democrats slander them with the made-up term "insurrectionist."   (Holmes 2022, emphasis mine)

By doing this, Cruz showed a willingness to contradict himself and to tell a story that he knew was false. It was a demonstration that he valued loyalty to Trump above truth. As such, it was a clear and effective compliance lie.

5.4 Bald-Faced Lies Both Unite and Divide

Figleaves and dogwhistles exploit, build on, and deepen the divisions between groups. Bald-faced lies also do precisely this. Interestingly, a part of the way that they do it is to further unite the group that supports the bald-faced liar. Once people have subordinated themselves to a leader with compliance lies and committed to a worldview that they know is false, it becomes even more important to keep that leader in charge. Timothy Snyder quotes Charles Clover discussing this dynamic: "Putin has correctly surmised that lies unite rather than divide Russia's political class. The greater and the more obvious the lie, the more his subjects demonstrate their loyalty by accepting it..." (2018: 163).

Of course, in a divided country, those who oppose the bald-faced liar react differently. They attempt to correct the falsehoods, over and over. They criticize the liar for lying. But as they see that the liar's support is not diminishing, and the falsehoods are still being believed, even as they grow more implausible, this group becomes increasingly frustrated. Divisions between these two groups are heightened by this dynamic. Such divisions are heightened yet further if the liar's supporters are also enjoying the spectacle of the opponents' anger. And of course, in Trump's America, they are. This is an important method for "owning the libs"—deliberately provoking angry reactions from people on the left (Robertson 2021). It is also well known and often practiced by other authoritarians. Timothy Snyder chronicles the way that Vladimir Putin uses this technique. Snyder (2018) describes Putin as practicing a deliberately *implausible* deniability:

> By denying what everyone knew, Putin was creating unifying fictions at home and dilemmas in European and American newsrooms.

Putin, according to Snyder, uses bald-faced lies to both unite the Russian public and befuddle journalists abroad, who are used to presenting "both sides." This is very much what we see from Trump: the use of bald-faced lies to unite Republicans and cement their support, while creating a situation that mainstream journalists are highly ill-equipped to deal with, as described below.

5.5 Bald-Faced Lies Confuse the Media

Dogwhistles, figleaves, and bald-faced lies are all difficult for journalists to deal with when fighting falsehood. In the case of dogwhistles, they must be willing to point out a coded message or a surreptitious influence that not everyone will be aware of—and that will be stridently denied. This is difficult because it risks accusations of unjustified and biased reporting. In the case of figleaves, journalists must contend with the very tricky fact that a figleaf can make an utterance true despite the fact that it remains immensely misleading. If lots of people are saying that Hillary Clinton sacrifices babies, then "lots of people are saying that Hillary Clinton sacrifices babies" is true. Nonetheless, reporting this fact risks spreading falsehood and perpetuating a very dangerous conspiracy theory.

Bald-faced lies present a different problem. Long-standing journalistic conventions dictate that objectivity should be demonstrated by offering both sides of any story that presents a controversy. As Timothy Snyder writes:

> "I am lying to you openly and we both know it" is not a side of the story. It is a trap. In such a situation, the normal approach seems inadequate.

"Trump says his inauguration crowd was bigger than Obama's, but others disagree" seems like precisely the wrong way to deal with such a demonstrable fact.   (2018: 164)

When an utterance is obviously false, journalists must choose between sacrificing their training to point out the falsehood, or presenting an obvious falsehood as just one of the sides available.

This is further complicated by taboos, and sometimes even rules, against designating anything clearly as a lie. In the UK Parliament, politicians are absolutely forbidden from accusing one another of lying. The pressure against such an accusation is also quite strong for journalists, including US journalists. The Trump era has put pressure on the convention of never using the term "lie," and prompted a move toward very prominent fact-checking. This allows reporters to evaluate the truth or falsehood of politicians' claims, rather than just interviewing people who disagree. However, even this turns out to be an inadequate response.[5] As Masha Gessen notes, the lies are repeated over and over while the fact checks generally occur only once, becoming swamped by the lies. Even for those who do see the fact checks, they may fail to function as intended:

...the fact checking articles themselves, appearing soon after the lie is uttered in public or on Twitter, serve as a gateway for the lie's entrance into public consciousness. Worse still, this particular gateway has a way of placing the lie and the truth side by side, as though the facts were a matter of debate. Then one of the sides drops the conversation while the other continues pounding the subject.   (Gessen 2021: 115–16)

The very fact that journalists are ill-equipped to deal with this strategy is a source of joy to supporters, for whom "owning the libs" has become an important goal and strategy. This strategy has been openly embraced, with right-wing podcast host Dan Bongino saying "My entire life right now is about owning the libs" (Robertson 2021).

5.6 Bald-Faced Lies Cause Breakdown in Trust

Bald-faced lies and obvious bullshitting play an important role in a deliberate strategy that Steve Bannon calls "flooding the zone with shit" (Illing 2020). Regina Rini describes the strategy clearly:

By flooding the channels of public discourse with falsehood, then allowing citizens to know that this has happened, anti-democrats make it reasonable for us to trust no one, least of all our co-citizens. That is the story of how weaponized skepticism slices through democratic culture—not down some dark alley, but out in the open where everyone can watch it happen.

(2021: 32)

The idea that one can profit by being obvious about one's falsehoods is a startling one. But it helps perhaps to take a step back, and ask whether we can imagine profiting from inducing a state of confusion in others, or profit by making people distrust information which would be helpful to them—or information that would be harmful to oneself. It is not at all difficult to imagine that one may profit by succeeding in these endeavors. If the public sphere is filled with obviously false or contradictory statements, and if authority figures like politicians, or people claiming to be scientists or doctors, are also making obviously false or contradictory statements, it's no longer at all clear whom to trust. It's understandable that people might give up entirely on trusting authorities such as journalists or scientists. And this can be exploited.

Who would profit from that loss of trust? People who fear what journalists or scientists might reveal. There have been deliberate, multi-decade campaigns to undermine trust in scientists by tobacco companies, fossil fuel companies, and the politicians supported by these companies (Oreskes and Conway 2010; O'Connor and Weatherall 2019; Levy 2021). In the past, these campaigns took the form of cherry picking or manufacturing what might appear to be scientific evidence. But a broad-spectrum distrust in what should be epistemic authorities will accomplish much the same thing, and more. If people don't trust scientists or journalists, they won't trust scientists or journalists who tell them that they should worry about global warming.

The generalized distrust is also damaging because of what it does to democratic accountability—which is why it is such a useful tool for authoritarians. If people don't trust journalists, they won't trust journalists to say that Trump tried to steal the 2020 election. If journalists cannot reveal the truth and be believed, it is difficult for there to be accountability when leaders engage in wrongdoing. This is why general confusion about what is true, and loss of trust in epistemic authorities is—and long has been—immensely useful to autocratic leaders. A confused and distrustful populace is a populace that can easily be controlled. Such a state of affairs is described well by

Hannah Arendt, who of course was talking about the effect of Nazi propaganda on Germans:

> In an ever-changing, incomprehensible, world the masses had reached the point where they would, at the same time, believe everything and nothing, think that everything is possible and that nothing was true...Mass propaganda discovered that its audience was ready at all times to believe the worst, no matter how absurd, and did not particularly object to being deceived because it held every statement to be a lie anyhow. (1976: 382)

In this portion of the book, I have worked to address the question of how it is that saying things widely known to be false, even making wild conspiracist claims, has come to be so much more acceptable in our political discourse. In Chapter 5, I argued that dogwhistles play a crucial role in concealing such claims while allowing them to spread, while figleaves serve to make them seem just a little bit more acceptable, giving them more purchase in mainstream communication. In this chapter, though, I turned to the puzzling issue of people who don't need any of these stealthy maneuvers—people who see these claims as bald-faced lies and yet support the bald-faced liars. I argued that there really are such people, and that there really is something troubling to explain here. Once more, the explanation requires noticing that different things are true of different groups. Some people simply view politics as something akin to sports, and go along with false claims because that is how to support their team. Others admire a leader who makes false claims precisely because that leader is so openly flouting establishment norms, and that is what they want to see. Authoritarian leaders make obviously false claims because these are a great way to maintain power—in part because the ability to make such claims is itself a demonstration of power, and in part because such claims leave the population confused and powerless. Many will go along with such claims from the powerful, precisely because they have been left uncertain about what is true, or about their ability to resist. All of these groups and their motivations come together to yield a situation in which there is a shocking quantity of support even for claims which are recognized as obviously false, and for the leaders who make such claims.

7

Dogwhistles, Figleaves, and the Fight against Racism and Blatant Falsehood

This book began by reflecting on the rise of explicit racism and blatant false-hood in public discourse, a rise that many have found disorienting and even baffling. Politicians have been shockingly successful, despite blatantly racist utterances and open adherence to stunningly unlikely conspiracy theories. The sorts of claims that were once confined to the *Daily Stormer* and the *Weekly World News* have now become normal discussion-fodder in main-stream venues. In this book, I have tried to offer a partial explanation of these changes, looking closely at linguistic devices that have facilitated them. We have seen two key moves, both of which lend deniability to norm-violating utterances. Yet they work in very different ways. Dogwhistles work by concealing their controversial content, either from all of the audience or from part of it. This concealment allows for the spread of messages that might otherwise be rejected, and for the priming of socially unacceptable (e.g. racist) responses. Figleaves are generally added onto a message that would normally be recognized as unacceptable, working by raising doubt about the unacceptability of the message or the attitudes behind it. In so doing, they can change how messages like these are seen, helping to normalize them. These two devices work in tandem, spreading messages (or influencing people) surreptitiously and mainstreaming the more overt messages. Together, they have proved a dangerous combination, leading to the spread and increasing acceptability of blatant racism and wild conspiracism. We have seen that they also play upon and heighten divisions between groups, stoking the tensions that have fueled fears of a "new civil war," and building the sort of divided populace that fascist leaders everywhere have found useful (Stanley 2018).

Given the dangerous changes enabled by these devices, it is natural to want to know what we can do about them. Is there a way to fight the perni-cious messages transmitted by dogwhistles, either keeping them from spreading or neutralizing their power? And what of figleaves? Is there anything we can do about the reassurance that they seem to provide to people about previously unacceptable messages? In this chapter, I will explore the state of our knowledge regarding what to do about dogwhistles and figleaves, and I will suggest directions for future efforts and research.

Perhaps disappointingly, but certainly unsurprisingly, I will not be offering an easy solution to these problems. Instead, I will be drawing out some important lessons that need to be borne in mind as we seek ways of responding to dogwhistles and figleaves. My focus here will be squarely on these two communicative devices. That is, I will not be attempting to engage with the extensive and important literature that exists on combatting racism and wild conspiracy theorizing more broadly. However, history has shown us how racism has evolved—through periods of more and less overt expression, and through an ever-changing variety of dogwhistles and devices. Throughout these changes, racism has survived and even thrived. Developing successful techniques to combat particular linguistic devices is, I think, urgent and important. But we should not overestimate what it would mean. Not only would there still be plenty of racism still left to fight, but there would be new *linguistic* devices to fight. We would still need to keep up with these innovations and find ways to deal with them. This does not mean the fight is pointless. The fight is far from pointless, and is in fact of the utmost importance. But it will undoubtedly be, as Kate Norlock (2018) puts it, a "perpetual struggle."

It's important to be aware at the outset of some limitations of our knowledge. As I write this, there has been substantial research on how to fight racist dogwhistles, though (as we'll see) the landscape has changed quickly enough that it's not clear how useful this now is. There has, to my knowledge, been no research on how to fight racial figleaves. Moreover, there has been no research that I know of on how to fight conspiracist dogwhistles or conspiracist figleaves. We can make some inferences from what we know about racist dogwhistles and figleaves, and what we know about combatting the spread of falsehoods. As we will see, however, even in the best-researched areas we unfortunately have more questions at this point than answers.

Despite this, I will argue that we should not despair. Learning about these devices has helped us to a new understanding of key ways that blatant racism and wild conspiracism spread. Understanding their working gives us clear directions for what questions we should ask next and what we should think about trying—as citizens, as policy-makers, or as researchers. We cannot make progress in combatting these powerful manipulation techniques until we recognize and come to understand them. This chapter will help us to do that. In the following sections, I will work through various approaches in turn.

1. Revealing the Norm Violation

1.1 Covert Effect Racist Dogwhistles

Once upon a time, not that long ago, it looked like there was a fairly simple solution for Covert Effect racist dogwhistles: call attention to what is really going on. As we saw in Chapter 2, this is what Jesse Jackson did, back at the time of the Willie Horton ad. He pointed out, loudly and clearly, that the ad was racist. Although this was very dismissively received in the mainstream media, it was also remarkably effective. Tali Mendelberg (2001) found that as soon as Jackson started talking about this on the mainstream news, the correlation between racial resentment level and intention to vote for Bush began to fall away. Many White people, despite their levels of racial resentment, very much seemed not to want to violate the Norm of Racial Equality. Causing them to reflect on the possibility of racism in the ad made the dogwhistle stop working. This observation formed a key foundation for Mendelberg's claim that dogwhistles of this sort need to operate outside of consciousness.

This solution, however, is not as promising as it once seemed. Explicitness about race does not seem to be viewed as unfavorably as it used to be. Valentino, Neuner, and Vandenbroek (2018) conducted studies during the Obama era, very similar to the studies that were previously done of Covert Effect dogwhistles. The studies presented participants with issues or candidate commercials or news stories, which discussed race either explicitly or in dogwhistle terms. They then tested for correlations between subjects' racial attitudes and their attitudes toward these issues. Previous studies would have predicted a correlation when dogwhistle terms were used, but *not* when racially explicit terms were used—because with racially explicit terms people would self-monitor and not let their racial attitudes influence their judgments. This is not what was found. Instead, there was no difference in effectiveness between the ads with dogwhistles and those with explicitly racial words.

In Chapter 2, we saw evidence that that making racial content explicit will cause the kind of self-monitoring that keeps people from being influenced by Covert Effect dogwhistles. This no longer seems to be the case. Valentino et al. (2018) believe that this is in part an ironic effect of Barack

Obama's election: Obama's election led many White people to believe that racism was a thing of the past, something they didn't need to worry about so much—or even that now it's appropriate to worry instead about racism against White people. This led to a decline in the felt need to self-monitor for racism, and it also seems to have led to a rise in the thought that White people are a group under threat. All of this meant that more explicit reference to race became more socially acceptable.[1]

Valentino et al. (2018) also found something else that is very important. In previous studies of Covert Effect dogwhistles, the correlation between policy preferences and racial attitudes was present *only* after a message involving a Covert Effect dogwhistle. It did not occur with an explicitly racial message, because subjects engaged in self-monitoring. But it also did not occur in the control condition, in which there was no racialized message presented at all. In their more recent study, however, policy preferences were correlated with racial attitudes *even in the control condition*. The prevailing explanation of this seems to be that Obama's election, and the backlash against it, made race so constantly salient and ever-present that there ceased to be non-racialized issues.[2]

In fact, of course, we should not have needed an empirical study at this point to tell us that calling attention to the racism of a politician's rhetoric no longer has quite the effects that it once did. We have, after all, lived through Trump's campaign, presidency, and post-presidency. We have seen incident after incident clearly and explicitly described as racist, by news media and even by his Republican colleagues—with no loss to the effectiveness of his rhetoric. Here are two prominent examples of *Republicans* clearly condemning Trump's racism:

- "[Republican] House Speaker Paul Ryan delivered a harsh rebuke of the recent comments made by presumptive Republican presidential nominee Donald Trump about an Indiana-born judge with Mexican heritage who is presiding over a lawsuit about Trump University. Ryan said he 'disavows' Trump's comments and that they are 'the textbook definition of a racist comment"' (DeBonis 2016)
- "[Donald Trump is] a race baiting, xenophobic religious bigot," [Republican Senator Lindsey] Graham says in the clip, adding, "You know how you make America great again? Tell Donald Trump to go to Hell" (Pitofsky 2020)

At many points along the way, there were predictions that Trump's 2016 campaign was doomed due to his racist comments. These predictions were, quite clearly, not borne out. And the very Republicans who condemned Trump's racism in the quotes above became Trump supporters as time went on. Clearly, calling attention to racism is not nearly as damaging as it once was.

1.2 Overt Code Racist Dogwhistles

One might also expect that making the content of an *Overt Code* dogwhistle explicit would ruin its effectiveness. After all, a code that ceases to be secret is no longer much of a secret code. So perhaps this method would be effective to counter Overt Code dogwhistles?

It is certainly true that a revealed Overt Code dogwhistle can no longer serve the function of allowing for secret communication, understood only by the in-group. However, a new code can always be created for that purpose. And the no-longer-secret code may still be quite useful. Despite the absence of total secrecy, the code can still be used to communicate in a deniable manner. As we saw in Chapter 2, this deniability can be very politically effective. Paul Ryan, for example, was able to use the term "inner city" and then deny that he meant anything racial by it. This denial created uncertainty for some and for others served as a reason to simply accept that he did not mean anything racial. The fact that many people did recognize the racial dogwhistle was easily exploited to heighten divisions and stoke the concern that the woke left is trying to silence ordinary and innocent speech.

A further potential problem, already suggested by our discussion of Covert Effect dogwhistles, is that accusations of racism are no longer so damaging. If that's right, then maybe revealing the Overt Codes will not be so damaging—even when these are the codes used by White supremacists. And this is a terrifying thought. Is it now, one might wonder, completely socially acceptable to be blatantly racist, even an avowed White supremacist? As we will see below, this doesn't actually seem to be the case. Once more, fully understanding our situation requires reflecting upon differences between groups.

1.3 Extremist Responses to Revealing the Dogwhistles

Part of the problem with the strategy of revealing the dogwhistles is that extremists now expect this, and know how to exploit it. Trump and Republicans more generally have become increasingly expert at turning any mention of racism against those who call attention to it. One way this happens is through the well-established figleaf of racism accusation, accusing the person who makes a racism accusation of being the real racist. But, as we have noted in passing several times, the strategy goes further than this. Because it is very difficult to convince someone of the presence of a dog-whistle if they are not already disposed to suspect racism in an utterance, accusations of dogwhistling are always subject to uncertainty. Deniability, in other words, is ever-present. This deniability allows for the dogwhistler and their allies to insist that *they* are merely calm and reasonable people who are not jumping to conclusions. This means they can paint their opponents as unreasonable people who do jump to conclusions. Most important of all, they can add to the sense of White people under threat by insisting that unreasonable racism accusations are being hurled against people who make perfectly innocent comments.

This strategy, like all of those that we have discussed in this book, relies crucially on the divided audience. Ian Haney López writes that "Trump especially innovated by shifting racial appeals decisively into the audible range—but for his critics, not for his base" (2019a: 31). The idea is to play upon the racial resentments of one group (that which Haney López called his base) without their full awareness that this is happening. This group is able to convince themselves that what is happening is not really racism. At the same time, Trump and his allies are very well aware that their opponents will see the racism extremely clearly. They seek out this dynamic, as it both creates a battle which commands media attention and fuels the sense that Trump supporters are an embattled group being unfairly attacked. Haney López writes:

> …rather than seeking to use dogwhistles to keep race below the surface, Trump repeatedly stoked heated debates about his racial demagoguery. Trump was still dogwhistling, using coded phrases that triggered racial stereotypes without directly communicating a message of raw racism *to his base*. But he no longer obscured his racial appeals from the engaged political center. (2019a: 32-3)

The mainstream condemnation of Trump's speech, then, worked in Trump's favor with these voters. The one thing I would add to this picture is that Trump's use of racial rhetoric was also very clearly seen by those who *reject* the Norm of Racial Equality and embrace racism. These people were, and are, definitely part of his base—and the racial appeal is very much not concealed from them. In fact, López gives a very clear example of this:

After the white-power riots in Charlottesville in August 2017, Trump blamed "many sides" for the violence and urged the country to respect our "history" and "heritage". Though he was superficially communicating a condemnation of the violence, white supremacists instead heard something very different: the clasped hand of a warm endorsement. "Trump comments were good. He didn't attack us. He just said the nation should come together. Nothing specific against us," the neo-Nazi website *Daily Stormer* chuffed. "Really, really good. God bless him". (2019a: 39)

Communicating in this way with the explicit proud racists also helped fuel the explosive environment that Trump was stoking, ratcheting up both the racism of this group and the strength and vehemence of the opposition to Trump. Again, Trump was able to use this to help convince White people somewhere in the middle that they were under threat from the "woke."

All of this adds up to serious problems for the strategy of revealing and pointing to the racism. On the other hand, ignoring the racism seems like at least as large a mistake. Letting language like this go unchecked and unremarked on only normalizes it, and many decades of research on genocide show us the potential consequences of such normalization. One of the earliest writers on this topic was Victor Klemperer, a Jewish linguist who survived the Nazi era. Famously, he described how linguistic changes gradually laid the groundwork for the Holocaust:

Words can be like tiny doses of arsenic: they are swallowed unnoticed, appear to have little effect, and then after a little time the toxic reaction sets in after all. (Klemperer 2000: 15–16)

Lynne Tirrell has developed this metaphor, carefully exploring in a series of papers the ways that toxic speech infects the populace and brings about great social harms (Tirrell 2012, 2017, 2021). Allowing racist speech to go unchallenged runs the risk of it being smoothly accommodated and thereby normalized (McGowan 2009, 2019; Maitra 2012; Langton 2018). Ignoring such speech, then, cannot be the right response.

2. Anything Goes?

We have already discussed experimental results from Valentino et al. (2018). These indicate that explicit racial language *is* more acceptable in politics than it once was. For the items they tested, whether an explicit or dogwhistle term was used did not make a difference to subjects' responses. Their conclusion from this is quite a strong one:

> …the substantial power of racial attitudes in mainstream American politics no longer varies according to the ways in which race is discussed.
>
> (Valentino et al. 2018: 758)

Taken literally, this suggests that *any* racial references at all are now acceptable—even the very worst slurs. In fact, I doubt that they mean their claim to be quite that strong. I strongly suspect they don't mean to include slurs as one of the "ways." Nonetheless, the Trump era has led to a widespread sense that all taboos around racial language have now vanished. If that's right, then revealing the presence of dogwhistles truly does seem like a useless move.

But, despite the changes of the Trump era, it does *not* seem that anything goes. That's one reason this book contains so many Trump-era utterances which *include* deniability devices like dogwhistles and figleaves. For further indicators, it's worth considering the evidence which Haney López (2019a) has amassed, showing that political racial discourse in the United States is still constrained by something like the Norm of Racial Equality, and that Trump voters, in large part, have managed to see him as *not racist*, despite his rhetoric.

Haney López provides a valuable contrast between Trump's rhetoric and that of 2016 Tennessee congressional candidate Rick Tyler. Where Trump said, "Make America *Great* Again," Tyler explicitly said "Make America *White* Again." He advocated "a moratorium on nonwhite immigration and the abolition of policies that subsidize nonwhite birthrates" (Haney López 2019a: 25–6). Although Trump's rhetoric rarely appears subtle, it does in comparison to Tyler's. And indeed Tyler's message was clearly and unequivocally condemned by Republicans. Similarly, former KKK leader David Duke was soundly defeated in his 2016 congressional bid by the very same voters who supported Trump and gave him a landslide victory in that district. Haney López writes, " 'Make America *Great* Again is a winning message among a majority of white voters and some voters of color as well, 'Make America *White* Again is a loser's lament' " (2019a: 26–7).

As we already saw in Chapter 3, Haney López considers Trump's use of figleaves to be vital to his success (although his terminology is different since he does not distinguish these from dogwhistles). Haney López maintains that for many voters, these provide convincing reassurance that Trump is not racist. He notes that a 2016 poll found 87 percent of Trump voters said that Trump was not racist, while only 5 percent of them said that he was (2019a: 27). Though López does not discuss this, it is worth noting that these responses are not entirely reliable guides to what people believe. If someone respects the Norm of Racial Equality, they will not be comfortable *saying* that they support a candidate who is racist. Some of the 87 percent, then, might actually think that Trump is racist, but not want to say this. Even if this is right, though, it's nonetheless significant that they are not comfortable saying this, as it is some indication of enduring power for the Norm of Racial Equality. Haney López argues, and I agree, that this lingering power, and the need for figleaves, should be a source of hope: there is much more potential for fighting racism if it is making people uncomfortable than if it is not.

3. Challenges for Moderation/Banning

Dogwhistles pose particular difficulties for any efforts to automate moderation or for banning of problematic terminology. First, they quickly evolve. In particular, once an Overt Code dogwhistle becomes known, a new code word is found. This poses difficulties for attempts to detect such speech online. Searching for a particular well-known and clearly hateful term (such as the n-word) is relatively easy. For a constantly evolving and changing set of terms, it is significantly more difficult.

The challenge becomes even more serious once we consider the fact that dogwhistles are almost always terms which also have a wholly innocent meaning. Any attempt to detect dogwhistle terms will yield a large number of false positives, because the number 88 is not only a way of saying "Heil Hitler" but also a number. "Heritage" occurs in many innocuous discussions of history, important landmarks, and the like. These facts make it obviously problematic to contemplate banning or removing certain terms from social media as an effective means of combatting the spread of hate. We would not want all occurrences of these terms to be prevented. (Think of the unfortunate person having an 88th birthday, or who has a business at street number 88.) Similarly for conspiracist terms that function as dogwhistles. These include "the storm," "patriot," "breadcrumbs," and even "save the children" (Rothschild 2021). Each of these terms or phrases has entirely innocuous meanings which pose problems for any effort to automatically detect them.

Yet each of them is also a dogwhistle to the extravagantly implausible and dangerous QAnon conspiracy theory. Moreover, Save the Children is a genuine and valuable charitable organization that does great work in the world. There would be significant additional ethical problems with restricting the use of this phrase.

Considering dogwhistles, then, shows us the limits of certain automated approaches to hateful speech online.

4. Challenges for Nudging

Some online interventions have been shown to have great potential for diminishing the extent to which people share false news stories. For example, Gordon Pennycook and colleagues have shown in a series of studies (Pennycook et al. 2020; Pennycook and Rand 2022), that nudges or prompts which cause users to think about accuracy—even if these prompts are relatively brief and unconnected to false news stories—bring about a reduction in willingness to share false news stories. Pennycook's work seems to show that people are fairly good at differentiating between false and true news stories, but often prioritize other matters when deciding what to share on social media. Prompts to reflect on accuracy can help to overcome this.[3]

Importantly, the items used in these studies have been stories that are simply false, and unaccompanied by figleaves. This matters because of the way that figleaves interact with the Norm of Truthfulness—when they work, they convince people to be less worried that this norm is being violated. An obviously false story does not seem so obviously false if it's prefaced by "people are saying" or "just wondering." Indeed, the post genuinely is no longer a literally false one if people are really saying it or wondering about it, because the post only says that people are talking about the false claim—it doesn't assert the claim. There is good reason to suspect, then, that an accuracy nudge might no longer work. Given the apparent widespread use of such figleaves, this seems like something that very much merits investigation.

5. Inoculation against Dogwhistles and Figleaves

One of the most promising solutions currently being explored seems especially well suited to combatting the influence of dogwhistles and figleaves. Nicely building on the metaphor of toxicity,[4] this solution is sometimes known as inoculation. It is motivated by the very substantial evidence showing how difficult it is to effectively respond to hateful or wild conspiracist speech after the fact.[5] In brief: such responses may come too late, may be ignored, and may even serve to reinforce what they are attempting to combat. Continuing with the toxicity model, it may not be possible to effect a cure once the pathogen has been ingested. An inoculation before the fact, however, has the potential to keep the toxicity or the pathogen from taking hold. As we are now all too well aware, inoculation is not a perfect solution to an outbreak, but it is a crucial part of an effective solution. And research on inoculation against racist and wild conspiracist speech bears out this idea.[6]

"Inoculation" in this context refers to a collection of techniques that involve exposing people to weakened forms of the problematic speech against which researchers are trying to protect them, combined with something like an antidote to such speech. For example, experimenters working to combat Islamophobic indoctrination trained subjects with a brief video "explaining rhetorical techniques used by extremists." Those who were inoculated in this way turned out to be less susceptible to radicalization than control subjects who were not (Lewandowsky and Van der Linden 2021: 16). This sort of technique has also proven effective against conspiracist speech. Exposing subjects to "anti-conspiratorial information which foreshadowed the arguments that conspiracy theorists might make against vaccinations" had the remarkable result that "they were no longer adversely affected by subsequent conspiratorial rhetoric" (Lewandowsky and Van der Linden 2021: 15). Subjects in the control condition were much more affected by the anti-vaccination rhetoric. Crucially, many of these inoculation campaigns consist of education and training regarding manipulative rhetorical techniques. Such a campaign for dogwhistles and figleaves, then, does not seem out of the question.

5.1 Dogwhistle Inoculation

Inoculation against dogwhistles might involve several different approaches. The most obvious would be to expose subjects to particular known dogwhistles in the context of an explanation of what dogwhistles are and how they are used to manipulate people. Dogwhistles, as they've traditionally been used, are designed not to be noticed. Just noticing the existence of a dogwhistle and understanding what it is doing, then, is a very significant challenge. (Think here of the situation you were in before you learned that

"88" can be a dogwhistle.) This particular challenge needs to be met through the production and dissemination of detailed knowledge regarding the workings of racist speech. And there are many hard at work on this, including academics, journalists, and activist organizations like the Southern Poverty Law Center and the Anti-Defamation League, which maintains a hate symbols database. Getting this knowledge into the right hands, and getting people to take it seriously, is an important and difficult task. Adding to this challenge is the fact that the knowledge needs constant updating. Where Overt Code dogwhistles are intended to be genuinely secret, they evolve quickly once discovered.

This clearly needs to be at least part of what is done. Those who don't want any part in spreading racist[7] thought need to know, for example, that the number 88 or what seems to be an interesting image of a sun might in fact be a White supremacist dogwhistle. If they know this, they may think twice before sharing texts or images containing these. But that is really the easiest part of the battle. As we have seen, dogwhistles are ever-changing. As one code becomes well known, another rises up to take its place.

So the inoculation needs to be substantially broader. There needs to be education about the ways that dogwhistles can work. People need to be taught both about Overt Code dogwhistles and about Covert Effect dog-whistles. This difference needs to be a crucial part of what is taught. People need to realize that White supremacists and wild conspiracists deliberately use innocent-seeming code words to communicate with each other (as in Overt Code dogwhistles). But they also need to know that they themselves might be affected, outside of their awareness, by words that have acquired certain cultural associations (as in Covert Effect dogwhistles). And they need to know about the ways that this technique can be used in attempts to manipulate them. Fortunately, research by Lewandowski and colleagues shows the efficacy of education about rhetorical techniques. Hopefully, these can make headway in combatting dogwhistles.

5.2 Figleaf Inoculation

The issue with figleaves is somewhat different. There is nothing particularly concealed about the figleaves. The phrases are obvious, and not in any kind of code. Moreover, those who engage with them frequently reflect upon them consciously—thinking, for example, "he said some of the Mexicans are good people. That's not the sort of thing a racist would say..." What's concealed with figleaves is their potential for damage. The way that a figleaf works is by convincing people not to worry about something that they would otherwise have recognized as clearly racist. This is an immensely dangerous effect to have. As I argued in Chapter 3, racial figleaves are powerful devices for shifting our norms against racism in precisely the wrong direction: making us more comfortable with utterances we would previously have judged to be unacceptable.

Figleaves, however, are so far relatively unknown—not much warned against, or even discussed or remarked upon. Many people who worry about racism or conspiracism are even reassured by them. A racist post accompanied by a figleaf seems less dangerous than one without a figleaf. But this is a very profound mistake, as figleaves render the posts *more* dangerous: figleaves are precisely the devices that allow for the dangerous shifting of norms. An important thing we need, then, is raising of awareness about what figleaves are and the damage that they do. When figleaves are encountered, people should be not reassured but rather on guard.

5.3 How to Teach about Dogwhistles and Figleaves

Inoculation techniques will, of course, need to be carefully developed and tested. However, it's worth reflecting on some general principles which are likely to be useful.

One of the most basic, recurrent problems one faces upon encountering a racist dogwhistle or a figleaf is the nearly irresistible question of whether or not the racism was intentional. This is not an accident: it is a key reason that dogwhistles and figleaves are such appealing and successful techniques. They work because they provide deniability, and what is deniable is usually whether or not the racism was intentional. The irresistibility of this question arises in part from the widespread White Folk Theory of Racism (discussed in Chapter 1). On the White Folk Theory, as we have seen, in order to be racist something must be intentional. Those who adhere to it focus almost exclusively on the mental states of possibly racist people. As I have argued throughout this book, the White Folk Theory plays a crucial role in laying the groundwork for deniably racist utterances, providing handy and appealing reasons to doubt that almost anyone or anything is really racist. It also distracts us into discussions of intentions and away from a focus on damaging effects.

If we reject this theory, however, we make room for sometimes judging words or utterances to be racist, regardless of intentions. And this is surely right and important for understanding dogwhistles. To take a very simple example, consider people who are unaware that "George Soros" is an anti-Jewish dogwhistle, who retweet a message claiming that George Soros supports Covid vaccination. For those in the know, the message will be understood as both an anti-Jewish and an anti-vaccination message, and it will have predictably anti-Jewish and anti-vaccination effects—regardless of the benign intentions of the retweeters. If we focus exclusively on the retweeters' innocent intentions, we miss this very important fact about what is actually happening. The White Folk Theory of Racism, with its exclusive focus on intentions, is thus a dangerous distraction from some of what we need to do to understand and combat the spread of racism. One important thing to do, then, is to resist the impulse to always and exclusively focus on intentions. If we want to understand the spread of a dangerous phenomenon, it is far more useful to focus on effects. But I should also note an important caveat.

Although I have warned against the danger of an exclusive focus on intentions, it is worth noting that sometimes we should care about intentions. Imagine, for example, that a dating app matches you with someone who seems otherwise perfect except for the fact that they are standing in front of a street number that happens to be 88. When trying to decide whether to date or even meet this person, you will very reasonably care a great deal about whether this 88 was intentionally included or not. Intentions matter enormously in this case because you are considering a personal relationship with this person.[8] Similarly, if you encounter a photograph of a politician who happens to be standing in front of the street number 88, you will quite rightly seek evidence of whether this was intentional or not. Intentions matter here too, because you're considering voting to give this person political power. In both cases, you will look for other clues—things they have said or done, symbols that are or are not present in other photographs, and so on. You'll care about each of these in their own right, possibly, but you will also be crucially concerned with what they show you about the person's intentions. In cases like these, intentions matter because what kinds of things that person intends is important to a decision that you're making. But when considering *methods for spreading racism*, intentions are not nearly so important. *Effects* are, for that purpose, where your focus should be.

All too often, popular discussions of problematic speech fall into an unproductive debate over whether we should focus on intentions or effects. My hope is that careful education about dogwhistles and figleaves will allow people to see that both matter, and both need attending to, though for different purposes.

6. Conclusion

Dogwhistles and figleaves are small communicative devices, which may at first have seemed a strange subject for a book-length treatment. I hope to have convinced the reader that these devices very much repay careful study. Separately and together, they serve to conceal, to excuse, and to deny racist and wild conspiracist speech, helping to fuel the extremist public discourse that now surrounds us. They exploit and play upon divisions between groups, and they work extremely effectively to heighten these divisions yet further. These devices are dangerous in their own right, and this alone is reason to study them. However, they also serve as a kind of case study in the ways that divisions are exploited and strengthened, very much to our detriment. My hope is that recognizing and reflecting on these mechanisms in detail will help to lay the groundwork for better combatting them in the future. This can, I hope, form a useful part of the much larger project of fighting racism and misinformation.

Afterword

A Note for the Curious—Other Dogwhistles, Other Figleaves

My focus here has been on dogwhistles and figleaves for racism and falsehood. But these are emphatically not all the dogwhistles and figleaves there are. Whenever people want to communicate in norm-defying ways, these methods are likely to be used. In other work I have discussed figleaves for sexism (Saul 2021), and there are almost certainly figleaves for any socially unacceptable prejudice (see Kenyon 2022b on violence figleaves). Figleaves for anti-trans attitudes are currently being used very frequently by opponents of trans rights—think of all the writings that include the phrase "I'm not anti-trans" or that tell the reader about a trans friend before going on to argue that trans people should be denied the rights they need to live in a society. Moreover, anti-trans prejudice is a central part of the far-right authoritarianism that also includes the blatant racism and obvious falsehood discussed in this book. Anti-trans figleaves are deserving of their own longer study, which I hope to carry out soon.

Similarly, dogwhistles can be used by many different groups who wish to communicate in a coded manner or to influence people beyond their awareness. Donald Trump and Mike Pence seem to have used Kentucky Fried Chicken as a visual Overt Code dogwhistle, referencing a sexist joke about Hilary Clinton (Hod 2016). And arguably "women's rights" has in some circles sadly become an Overt Code dogwhistle for anti-trans views.

Importantly, these techniques are not confined to the nefarious: they come in handy whenever a norm is being violated, and sometimes this happens in a good cause. People engaging in resistance against oppressive powers often communicate via dogwhistles for their own safety (Witten 2014; Saul 2018; Drainville and Saul, forthcoming). Finally, dogwhistles and figleaves are used by protest movements of all kinds, as they serve important needs in terms of covert planning, recruitment, and reassurance—both with respect to insiders and outsiders (Saul 2023). Again, this is something that I plan to explore in future work.

Notes

Introduction

1. I'm very grateful to an anonymous referee for calling this sketch to my attention.
2. To watch the sketch, see "Election Night-SNL," 2016. Retrieved March 3, 2023, from https://www.youtube.com/watch?v=SHG0ezLiVGc.
3. There was, however, evidence that this could successful in certain regions (Hutchings and Jardina 2009).
4. This phrase originated with a Simpson's episode, but has become a popular meme (https://knowyourmeme.com/memes/the-quiet-part-loud).
5. There have also been significant rises in blatant misogyny, homophobia, and transphobia. However, these bear a somewhat different relationship to widespread norms. I will not be focusing on them here, though I plan to explore them in future work.
6. It builds upon work in Saul (2018, 2019a, b); and Drainville and Saul (forthcoming).
7. I previously called these simply "overt." (In an early draft of a paper, which some have quoted, I used the term "explicit.")
8. I previously called these simply "covert." (In an early draft of a paper, which some have quoted, I used the term "implicit.")
9. Figleaves have, in fact, long been used, but recently they have been especially important to the facilitation of blatant racism.

Chapter 1

1. This very much parallels parts of what sociologist Eduardo Bonilla-Silva (2002) calls the ideology of Color-Blind Racism, which includes avoidance by White people of "direct racial language" (2002: 41), and especially precludes "saying things that sound or can be perceived as racist" (2002: 42).
2. I discuss this more in Saul (2017, 2019a, b, 2020). In Chapters 2 and 3, I show how dogwhistles and figleaves are used to convince people that the norm is not being violated.
3. Hill also uses the term "personalist ideology" more broadly, to refer to views of language that focus on speaker beliefs and intentions.
4. Hill does not explicitly note that the beliefs or intentions must be conscious, but this requirement is clear from her examples and discussion.

5. Hill also suggests that racists are seen as in need of education and assistance, which could help them to overcome the racism. This points to a difference between the kind of monstrousness taken to be involved in racism and that which Emerick and Yap discuss, but nonetheless racists are generally seen as monstrous prior to such reeducation.

6. Brison's point here is about how this blocks recognition of rape as gender-based violence, and I agree. But this isn't my focus here.

7. Kate Manne also discusses this, referring to "a mistaken idea about what rapists must be like: creepy, uncanny, and wearing their lack of humanity on their sleeve" (2018: 198).

8. See, for example, Garcia (2001), Glasgow (2009), Headley (2000), Levy (2016), Philips (1984), and Shelby (2002).

9. See, for example, Mills (2007) and Taiwo (2022).

10. Many thanks to an anonymous referee for pressing me on this point.

11. See, for example, https://www.merriam-webster.com/dictionary/racist.

Chapter 2

1. https://www.merriam-webster.com/words-at-play/dog-whistle-political-meaning

2. https://www.dictionary.com/browse/dog-whistle

3. https://www.urbandictionary.com/define.php?term=dog%20whistle

4. This linkage was itself misleading, since the program was created by Dukakis's Republican predecessor.

5. Horton himself always went by "William." Atwater chose to use the name "Willie." Horton, interviewed, remarked, "My name is not 'Willie'. It's part of the myth of the case. The name irks me. It was created to play on racial stereotypes: big, ugly, violent, black 'Willie'. I resent that". (Rodricks 1993).

6. Horton maintains his innocence. For more, see Keller (2015).

7. Another difference between Haney López's account and mine is that Haney López requires that dogwhistles "stoke widely condemned social hostilities" (2019a: 41). Many of the dogwhistles that are my focus in this book do that, but on my view not all dogwhistles do.

8. For monolithic models, see Khoo (2017), Henderson and McCready (2018), Quaranto (2022), Santana (2022), and Stanley (2015). For a paper which further develops the bifurcated model given here, see Torices (2021).

9. In previous work I called these simply "overt" and "covert" dogwhistles.

10. This is slightly oversimplified: later in this chapter, we will see that a dogwhistle that is more widely known can actually have particular utility in fomenting division. Sometimes this may be the goal.

11. Though this example also shows the way that states' rights can be used by either side: individual states have used states' rights arguments to contest the federal protection established by *Obergefell* v. *Hodges*.

12. Reactions to dogwhistles by people who are not White have not been studied as much, probably because the focus has been on understanding White racism. For an important exception to this, however, see the work of Ismail White (2007).

13. For an excellent discussion of the complexities of the non-target audience, see Torices (2021).

14. https://files.integrityfirstforamerica.org/14228/1614109097-832-2-expert-report-of-k-blee-and-p-simi.pdf, 9.

15. Ibid., 11.

16. Ibid.

17. Ibid., 26.

18. Of course, programmers are hard at work on finding ways to differentiate between the hateful and non-hateful meanings of these words (Pearson 2017).

19. I am not actually Jewish, but my father was. For those who are anti-Jewish, that is generally sufficient to count as Jewish, so my name would be enclosed in triple parentheses.

20. This particular experiment is also one of very few to examine the effect of this sort of messaging on African-Americans. Fascinatingly, it found that for African-Americans the explicit racial language was more effective at activating racial attitudes than the covert dogwhistle language needed for White people.

21. Indeed, Wetts and Willer (2019) experimentally confirmed that this sort of dog-whistle works only on racially resentful White liberals.

22. This is confirmed in Hutchings et al. (2009).

23. These definitions focus on dogwhistles as norm-violating. In Drainville and Saul (forthcoming), our focus is on parallels with visual art, so we use a broader definition to explore these.

24. For an interesting discussion of the speech act pluralism these distinctions require, see Lewiński (2021).

25. In Austin's terminology (Austin 1976) this is a perlocutionary act, a speech act picked out by its effects. More specifically, it is a *covert* perlocutionary act. A covert perlocutionary act, also discussed by Bach and Harnish (1982), is one that does not succeed if the intention behind it is recognized. For more on these, see Saul (2018).

26. My thanks to Anna Klieber, for bringing this example to my attention.

27. https://www.salon.com/2023/03/27/this-is-not-a-dog-whistle-waco-rally-called-out-as-blaring-air-horn-to-extremists_partner/.

28. For an account that makes deniability central to the definition of "dogwhistle," see Santana (2022).

29. Indeed, as we will see in Chapter 6, what Timothy Snyder calls *implausible* deni-ability can be especially damaging in certain ways.

30. "Open Letter to the LSA," July 6, 2020. Retrieved March 5, 2023, from https://docs.google.com/document/d/17ZqWl5grm_F5Kn_0OarY9Q2jlOnk200PvhM5e3isPvY/edit.

31. It's also true, though less crucial, that some dogwhistles are covert effect dogwhistles. I say this is less crucial simply because it's unclear what kind of dogwhistle "urban" is without further study.

32. It is possible that within a localized academic community, a term which is usually a dogwhistle may not have its usual effect. But this would need to be specifically shown. Merely stating its widespread use in an academic community is not enough.

33. https://twitter.com/cpc_hq/status/1422165410410008578

34. https://files.integrityfirstforamerica.org/14228/1614109097-832-2-expert-report-of-k-blee-and-p-simi.pdf, 9.

35. https://twitter.com/justin_ling/status/1427662834578644995

36. It is worth noting, however, that at the same time the Conservative Party released an alternative version of the slogan that was *not* 88 characters: This one is not 88 characters: "Canada's Recovery Plan will secure the future for you, your children and your grandchildren." However, it is still 4 words and still closely resembles David Lane's "14 Words."

37. https://mobile.twitter.com/justin_ling/status/1427662834578644995

38. https://files.integrityfirstforamerica.org/14228/1614109097-832-2-expert-report-of-k-blee-and-p-simi.pdf, 41.

39. Personal correspondence.

Chapter 3

1. The focus on *sending* may also be a dogwhistle to the Great Replacement Theory.

2. It's perhaps worth noting another consequence of this functional definition of "figleaf": a figleaf need not be intended to function in this way to be a figleaf. What matters is what it does.

3. For discussions of other figleaves, see Saul (2017, 2019a, b, 2021).

4. See also Bonilla-Silva (2018: 81–2).

5. https://www.bbc.com/news/av/uk-42830165

6. See also Bonilla-Silva (2018: 81–2).

7. https://files.integrityfirstforamerica.org/14228/1614109097-832-2-expert-report-of-k-blee-and-p-simi.pdf, 26.

8. Ibid., 42.

9. For an interesting argument that the use of humor *in recruitment* should not be seen as a figleaf, see Adams (2023). Adams suggests that it's important for those being recruited to *recognize* the racism, while at the same time being given something positive to associate with that, hence sugar-coating. My view is that it may still be important at an early stage to have figleaves creating uncertainty over the presence of racism. This is entirely compatible with sugar-coating as the later mechanism.

10. One particular form of this occurs within trolling culture. For more on trolling, see Barney (2016) and Connolly (2022).
11. https://files.integrityfirstforamerica.org/14228/1614109097-832-2-expert-report-of-k-blee-and-p-simi.pdf, 27.
12. For more on this move, see Boogaart, Jansen, and van Leeuwen (2022).
13. For an argument that retweets are not endorsements, see Marsili (2021).
14. https://anth1001.files.wordpress.com/2014/04/enoch-powell_speech.pdf
15. Haney López classifies this as a dogwhistle, but as I argue later in this chapter I think it is better to call it a figleaf and distinguish it from a dogwhistle.
16. See, for example, Hinton (2020).
17. For a discussion of third-party figleaves, see Turri (2022).
18. For a discussion of the way that *contradictory figleaves* can be used, see Kenyon (2022).
19. https://files.integrityfirstforamerica.org/14228/1614109097-832-2-expert-report-of-k-blee-and-p-simi.pdf

Chapter 4

1. For an illuminating taxonomy and history of kinds of political deception, see also Novaes and De Ridder (2021).
2. I'm using a relatively recent case study. But obviously there are much older ones available. For example, Wright (2021) has an excellent discussion of the anti-Jewish falsehoods propagated concerning the murder of William of Norwich in 1144.
3. He also objects to the phrase because it is difficult to define. This problem, however, strikes me as common to pretty much all terminology.
4. This section of the book draws heavily on Kenyon and Saul (2022). See that paper for more detail on these ideas.
5. In fact, on the view developed in Kenyon and Saul (2022), bald-faced lies are a subspecies of bullshit. But this classificational point is not relevant to my argument here.
6. For a fuller argument to this effect, see Kenyon and Saul (2022).
7. See, for example, Kunda (1990) and Sides, Tesler, and Vavreck (2018).
8. My thoughts on conspiracy theorizing owe an enormous debt to the wonderful virtual reading group on conspiracy theories that met early on in the Covid lockdown period. I am especially grateful for Brian Montgomery's wise insistence that we not just read *about* conspiracy theories, but watch and discuss conspiracist videos.
9. For an illuminating discussion of the variety of ways that conspiracy theories are understood, see Napolitano and Reuter (2021).

10. Although I am discussing a wildly implausible anti-vaccination conspiracy theory, I think it's important to note that not all opposition to vaccination has this sort of origin. Maya Goldenberg has made a powerful case that a great deal of vaccine hesitancy results from a deeply problematic history that has led to distrust of medical authorities (Goldenberg 2021).

11. I'm very grateful to Mirelle Martin for discussion of this group and conspiracy.

12. https://www.americasfrontlinedoctors.com, consulted March 24, 2021. Now unavailable.

13. https://www.americasfrontlinedoctors.com/wp-content/uploads/2020/09/White-Paper-on-HCQ-2020.2.pdf, consulted March 24, 2021. Now unavailable.

14. Levy (2021) has an excellent discussion about the many campaigns against scientific consensus that involve setting up professional-looking alternative institutions that *look* like legitimate scientific experts but are not.

15. https://www.americasfrontlinedoctors.com/wp-content/uploads/2020/09/White-Paper-on-HCQ-2020.2.pdf, consulted March 24, 2021. Now unavailable.

16. The Satanic Panic of the 1980s did not involve claims about high-level officials conspiring, and instead was mostly focused on childcare centers, heavy metal music, and Dungeons and Dragons players. None of these groups are very powerful forces in society.

17. Uscinski and colleagues do note that there are higher levels of belief in key elements of QAnon than in a theory named as "QAnon."

18. One might well point to the Satanic Panic of the 1980s as a precursor which shows the current state of things to be not so anomalous. Certainly, this involved some very implausible conspiracist claims. However, at the time it was taken extremely seriously not just by conspiracy theorists but by the mainstream media and police—that is, the experts of the day. By the standards of the time, then, it was not wildly implausible. This makes it very different from QAnon or the Great Replacement, which are roundly rejected by current experts and mainstream media (Yuhas 2021).

19. Here I am assuming an understanding of "obvious falsehood" roughly like that used by Ashton and Cruft: "A claim or idea is 'obviously false' when facts that falsify it are widely known" (Ashton and Cruft 2021: 12).

20. I am here drawing on a line that is (fittingly) a famous misquote of Mark Twain: https://www.mentalfloss.com/article/562400/reports-mark-twains-quote-about-mark-twains-death-are-greatly-exaggerated.

Chapter 5

1. This is very much *not* meant to be any of the well-worked-out norms philosophers have discussed, such as Grice's Maxim of Quality (Grice 1975) or those discussed in the norms of assertion literature (for an overview, see Pagin and Marsili

(2007)). It is crucial that this is a much woollier, more ordinary notion, which each person can understand in their own way.

2. A referee has pointed out that jokes said to be "racist but funny," and "justifiable" racial profiling might count against this claim. I think these examples are complex, and can't make up my mind about them. However, it may well be that these are indeed cases where people think racism is OK under certain circumstances. If that's right, the Norm of Racial Equality and the Norm of Truthfulness are even more parallel than I take them to be here.

3. I discuss these sorts of tactics at length in Saul (2012).

4. https://www.youtube.com/watch?v=XBzHnZiSv7U

5. Generally attributed to Kant, but with some dissenters such as Varden (2010).

6. For more on insinuation, see Camp (2018).

7. For an interesting extended discussion of this move, though not under the name "figleaf," see Boogaart et al. (2021).

8. It's worth noting that if one wants to treat this as a figleaf, that will require a modification to the definition, since it is not an additional bit of speech.

9. Indeed, it will often genuinely not be a violation, a complication we will discuss.

10. As discussed in Chapter 4, I disagree with some of how these authors understand the current rise in conspiracy theorizing. However, they make many valuable observations, and one of them concerns the use of this phrase.

11. https://twitter.com/naomirwolf/status/1383973370501337092

12. For an excellent extended discussion of these, though not under the name "figleaf," see Camp (2022).

13. Episode 6, *The Coming Storm Podcast*, 35 minutes.

14. In 2020, the Texas Republican Party even adopted "we are the storm" as its slogan—a clear use of this QAnon dogwhistle (Rosenberg and Haberman 2020).

Chapter 6

1. Many of the ideas in this chapter are drawn from Kenyon and Saul (2022), and developed more fully there.

2. In fact, we argue for somewhat different definitions of "bald-faced bullshitting" and "bald-faced lying," which turns out on our view to be a subcategory of bald-faced bullshitting. But these arguments and more precise definitions are not relevant to this chapter.

3. https://www.youtube.com/watch?v=gLcCZjDoWTQ

4. Some interesting explanations have been offered for Johnson's decision to tell the story. One is that it was designed to distract from news stories about the police investigating a domestic violence incident at his flat (https://inews.co.uk/news/politics/boris-johnson-model-buses-paint-make-london-bus-interview-talk-radio-true-306883). Another is that it was designed to game the search

engine results for "Boris Johnson bus," which would otherwise result in stories about the false claims on the side of the famed Brexit bus (https://www.wired.co.uk/article/boris-johnson-model-google-news). Importantly, both of these explanations involve goals that have nothing to do with truthfulness.

5. For more on the inadequacy of fact checking, see Uscinski and Butler (2013) and Lewandowsky and Van Der Linden (2021).

Chapter 7

1. It is worth noting, however, that the kinds of racial references studied by Valentino and colleagues were nowhere near as crudely or blatantly racist as those uttered by Trump.

2. It's not certain that this is the case, however, as the study focused exclusively on healthcare, which may have been particularly linked to Obama and therefore to racialized attitudes.

3. Worryingly, however, this effect may be confined to Democrats (Rathje et al. 2022).

4. For much more on this, see Tirrell (2017, 2021).

5. For good overviews of these difficulties, see Lepoutre (2021) and Lewandowski and Van der Linden (2021).

6. This sort of approach is also called "diachronic counterspeech" by Lepoutre (2021).

7. Obviously, those who *do* want to spread racism will not be moved by this sort of education. The sort of education they need is beyond the scope of this book.

8. Dogwhistles add a new layer of complexity to the dating strategy remarked on by the fictional Bridget Jones: "It's amazing how much time and money can be saved in the world of dating by close attention to detail. A white sock here, a pair of red braces there, a gray slip-on shoe, a swastika, are as often as not all one needs to tell you there's no point in writing down phone numbers and forking out for expensive lunches because it's never going to be a runner" (Fielding 2016: 13).

Bibliography

Adams, K. K. J. (2023). "A Spoonful of Sugar Makes the Hate Speech Go Down: Sugar-Coating in White Nationalist Recruitment Speech." *Topoi* 42: 459–68.

Aisch, G., J. Huang, and C. Kang (2016). "Dissecting the #PizzaGate Conspiracy Theories." *New York Times*.

Alexander, M. (2020). *The New Jim Crow: Mass Incarceration in the Age of Colorblindness*. New York: The New Press.

Alterman, E. (2020). *Lying In State: Why Presidents Lie—And Why Trump is Worse*. Basic Books.

Anderson, D. E. (2021). *Metasemantics and Intersectionality in the Misinformation Age: Truth in Political Struggle*. Cham: Springer Verlag.

Anderson, E. (2021). "Epistemic Bubbles and Authoritarian Politics." In E. Edenberg and M. Hannon (eds.), *Political Epistemology*. Oxford: Oxford University Press, 11–30.

Appiah, K. A. (2020). "The Case for Capitalizing the *B* in Black." *The Atlantic*.

Applebaum, A. (2022). "Transcript: Ezra Klein Interviews Anne Applebaum". *New York Times*.

Arendt, H. (1972). "Lying in Politics." *Crises of the Republic*, New York: Mariner Press, 1–48.

Arendt, H. (1976). *The Origins of Totalitarianism*. New York: Harcourt.

Ashton, N. and R. Cruft (2021). *Shaping Democracy in the Digital Age: Interim Report of the "Norms for the New Public Sphere" Project*.

Associated Press (2020). "The Bizarre Story of How Internet Conspiracy Theorists Convinced Themselves Wayfair Is Trafficking Children."

Associated Press (2022). "Confederate Flag-Toting Man, Son Convicted in Jan. 6 Riot." *NBC News*.

Austin, J. L. (1976). *How to Do Things With Words*. Oxford Paperbacks [Originally lectures in 1955].

Bach, K. and Harnish, R. (1982). *Linguistic Communication and Speech Acts*. MIT Press.

Barbaro, M. (2016). "Donald Trump Clung to 'Birther' Lie for Years, and Still Isn't Apologetic." *New York Times*.

Barney, R. (2016). "[Aristotle] On Trolling", *Journal of the American Philosophical Association* 2 (2): 193–5.

Basham, L. and M. Dentith (2016). "Social Science's Conspiracy Theory Panic: Now They Want to Cure Everyone." *Social Epistemology Review and Reply Collective* 5(10).

Baurmann, M. and D. Cohnitz (2021). "Trust No One?" In S. Bernecker, A. K. Flowerree, and T. Grundmann (eds.), *The Epistemology of Fake News*. Oxford: Oxford University Press, 334–57.

BBC (2017). "Brexit: Article 50 Has Been Triggered-What Now?"

BBC (2020). "Coronavirus: Outcry after Trump Suggests Injecting Disinfectant as Treatment."

Belanger, A. (2022). "Anti-Vaccine Groups Avoid Facebook Bans by Using Emojis." *Ars Technica.*

Bendix, A. (2021). "How a Group With Right-Wing Ties Duped Tens of Thousands of Americans into Buying Covid-19 Drugs that Don't Work." *Business Insider.*

Benkler, Y., R. Faris, and H. Roberts (2018). *Network Propaganda: Manipulation, Disinformation, and Radicalization in American Politics.* New York: Oxford University Press.

Blake, A. (2020). "'Trump's Ridiculous Defense of His Comments about Injecting Disinfectants." *Washington Post.*

Blake, J. (2020). "Trump Called Him 'My African American'. His Life Hasn't Been the Same Since." *CNN.*

Boland, J. (2018). "Iraq 15 Years On: The Birthplace of Post-Truth." *Politics.Co.UK.*

Bonilla-Silva, E. (2002). "The Linguistics of Color Blind Racism: How to Talk Nasty about Blacks without Sounding 'Racist'." *Critical Sociology* 28(1–2): 41–64.

Bonilla-Silva, E. (2018). *Racism without Racists: Color-Blind Racism and the Persistence of Racial Inequality in America.* Lanham, MD: Rowman & Littlefield.

Bonilla-Silva, E. and T. A. Forman (2000). "'I Am Not a Racist But...': Mapping White College Students' Racial Ideology in the USA." *Discourse and Society* 11(1): 50–85.

Boogaart, R., Jansen, H., and van Leeuwen, M. (2021). "I was only quoting": Shifting viewpoint and speaker commitment". In L. Horn (ed.) *From Lying to Perjury: Linguistic and Legal Perspectives on Lies and Other Falsehoods 2022 Vol. 3.* Berlin, Germany: De Gruyter, 113.

Borchers, C. (2015). "Huffington Post Took Donald Trump Out of the Entertainment Section. Has Anything Changed?" *Washington Post.*

Borchers, C. (2017). "Alex Jones Should Not Be Taken Seriously, According to Alex Jones's Lawyers." *Washington Post,* https://knowyourmeme.com/memes/glenn-beck-rape-murder-hoax

Brad (2009). "Glenn Beck Rape and Murder Hoax." *Know Your Meme,* https://knowyourmeme.com/memes/glenn-beck-rape-murder-hoax

Breitman, K. (2015). "Poll: Half of Republicans Still Believe WMDs Found in Iraq." *Politico,* https://www.politico.com/story/2015/01/poll-republicans-wmds-iraq-114016

Brison, S. J. (2006). "Justice and Gender-Based Violence." *Revue internationale de philosophie* (1): 259–75.

Bump, P. (2021). "Ted Cruz's Electoral Vote Speech Will Live in Infamy." *Washington Post,* https://www.washingtonpost.com/politics/2021/01/06/ted-cruzs-electoral-vote-speech-will-live-infamy/

Camp, E. (2018). "Insinuation, Common Ground, and the Conversational Record." In D. Fogal, D. W. Harris, and M. Moss (eds.), *New Work on Speech Acts.* New York and Oxford: Oxford University Press, 40–66.

Camp, E. (2022). "Just Saying, Just Kidding: Liability for Accountability-Avoiding Speech in Ordinary Conversation, Politics and Law." In L. Horn (ed.), *From Lying to Perjury: Linguistic and Legal Perspectives on Lies and Other Falsehoods.* Berlin, Germany: De Gruyter, 227–60.

Carless, W. (2023). "Trump Holding His Next Rally in Waco, Texas, Sends a Message to the Far Right, Experts Say." *USA Today*.

Cassam, Q. (2019). *Conspiracy Theories*. Cambridge, UK and Medford, MA: Polity Press.

Cassam, Q. (2021). "Bullshit, Post-truth, and Propaganda." In E. Edenberg and M. Hannon (eds.), *Political Epistemology*. Oxford: Oxford University Press, 49–63.

Chait, J. (2021). "Marjorie Taylor Greene Blamed Wildfires on Secret Jewish Space Laser." *New Yorker Magazine*.

Chow, K. (2016). "'Politically Correct': The Phrase Has Gone from Wisdom to Weapon." *NPR: Code Switch*, https://www.npr.org/sections/codeswitch/2016/12/14/505324427/politically-correct-the-phrase-has-gone-from-wisdom-to-weapon

Cillizza, C. (2016). "Why the 'Lyin' Ted' Attack Works So Well for Donald Trump." *Washington Post*.

Cillizza, C. (2021). "Have You Heard the New Republican Conspiracy Theory about the Omicron Variant?" *CNN: The Point*, https://www.cnn.com/2021/11/29/politics/omicron-ronny-jackson/index.html

Cohen, D. (2021). "Trump on Jan. 6 Insurrection: 'These Were Great People'." *Politico*, https://www.politico.com/news/2021/07/11/trump-jan-6-insurrection-these-were-great-people-499165

Connolly, P. J. (2022). "Trolling as Speech Act", *Journal of Social Philosophy* 53(3): 404–20.

Cortada, J. W. and W. Aspray (2019). *Fake News Nation: The Long History of Lies and Misinterpretations in America*. Lanham, MD: Rowman & Littlefield.

DeBonis, M. (2016). "Ryan Says Trump's Attacks on Judge Fit 'the Textbook Definition of a Racist Comment'." *Washington Post*, https://www.washingtonpost.com/news/powerpost/wp/2016/06/07/ryan-says-trumps-attacks-on-judge-fit-the-textbook-definition-of-a-racist-comment/

Delgado, H. N. (2020). "Far-Right 'Boogaloo' Movement Is Using Hawaiian Shirts to Hide its Intentions." *The Conversation*, https://theconversation.com/far-right-boogaloo-movement-is-using-hawaiian-shirts-to-hide-its-intentions-142633

Dickson, E. J. (2021). "How Joe Rogan Became a Cheerleader for Ivermectin." *Rolling Stone*.

Drainville, R. (2016). The Visual Propaganda of the Brexit Leave Campaign, *Hyperallergic*.

Drainville, R. and J. Saul (forthcoming). "Visual and Linguistic Dogwhistles." In L. Anderson and E. Lepore (eds.), *Oxford Handbook of Applied Philosophy of Language*. Oxford: Oxford University Press.

Draper, R. (2020). "Colin Powell Still Wants Answers." *New York Times*.

Driesbach, T. (2021). "How Extremists Weaponize Irony to Spread Hate." *NPR*, https://www.npr.org/2021/04/26/990274685/how-extremists-weaponize-irony-to-spread-hate.

Eligon, J. (2019). The "Some of My Best Friends Are Black" Defense. *New York Times*, https://www.nytimes.com/2019/02/16/sunday-review/ralph-northam-blackface-friends.html

Elliott, J. (2020). "Poison Control Calls Spike after Trumps Talks of Disinfectant to Fight Coronavirus." *Global News*, https://globalnews.ca/news/6871768/coronavirus-donald-trump-disinfectant-poison/

Elliott, J. (2021). "Anti-Vax Activist Dies of Covid-19 amid QAnon Demands for Ivermectin." *Global News*, https://globalnews.ca/news/8186493/veronica-wolski-anti-vax-qanon-ivermectin-covid-19/

Emerick, B. (2016). "Love and Resistance: Moral Solidarity in the Face of Perceptual Failure." *Feminist Philosophy Quarterly* 2(2): 1–21.

Emerick, B. and A. Yap (forthcoming). *Not Giving Up on People*, Rowman and Littlefield.

Enders, A. and J. Uscinski (2020). "Is QAnon Taking Over America? Not So Fast." *The Guardian*.

Fallis, D. (2009). "What Is Lying?" *Journal of Philosophy* 106(1): 29–56.

Farber, B. (2020). "Anti-Semitic Dogwhistles Have Abounded for Centuries. Now, Add George Soros to the List", AntiHate.Ca, https://www.antihate.ca/antisemitic_dog_whistles_have_abounded_for_centuries_now_add_george_soros_to_the_list

Fielding, H. (2016). *Bridget Jones's Diary: A Novel*. London: Pan MacMillan.

Forbes, S. (2008). *Boogie Man: The Lee Atwater Story*.

Fox, M. (2021). "The Long List of Marjorie Taylor Greene's Anti-Semitic, Anti-Muslim Conspiracy Theories." *Haaretz*.

Franceschi-Biccierai, L. (2018). "Password Analyist Says QAnon's 'Codes' Are Consistent With Random Typing." *Vice*, https://www.vice.com/en/article/9km87z/qanon-codes-are-random-typing

Frankfurt, H. G. (2005). *On Bullshit*. Princeton, NJ: Princeton University Press.

Funke, D. (2021). "What Marjorie Taylor Greene Has Said about Conspiracy Theories." *Tampa Bay Times*.

Galluci, N. (2017). "Sean Spicer Weighs in on 'Covfefe', Continues to Baffle America." *Mashable*, https://mashable.com/article/sean-spicer-covfefe-tweet

Garcia, J. L. (2001). "Racism and Racial Discourse," *Philosophical Forum* 32(2): 125–45.

Gessen, M. (2021). *Surviving Autocracy*. New York: Riverhead Books.

Glasgow, J. (2009) "Racism as Disrespect", *Ethics* 120: 64-93.

Goldenberg, M. J. (2021). *Vaccine Hesitancy: Public Trust, Expertise, and the War on Science*. Pittsburgh, PA: University of Pittsburgh Press.

Good, C. (2009). "South Park Does Glenn Beck." *The Atlantic*.

Gooding, R. (2008). "The Trashing of John McCain." *Vanity Fair*.

Gregorian, D. (2020). "Trump Told Bob Woodward He Knew in February that Covid-19 Was 'Deadly Stuff' but Wanted to 'Play It Down'." *NBC News*, https://www.nbcnews.com/politics/donald-trump/trump-told-bob-woodward-he-knew-february-covid-19-was-n1239658

Grice, H. P. (1975). "Logic and Conversation." In P. Cole and J. L. Morgan (eds.), *Speech Acts*. Leiden: Brill, 41–58.

Guerin, C. (2021). "The Yoga World Is Riddled with Anti-Vaxxers and QAnon Believers." *Wired*.

Habgood-Coote, J. (2019). "Stop Talking about Fake News!" *Inquiry* 62(9–10): 1033–65.

Hahl, O., M. Kim, and E. W. Z. Sivan (2018). "The Authentic Appeal of the Lying Demagogue: Proclaiming the Deeper Truth about Political Illegitimacy." *American Sociological Review* 83(1): 1–33.

Haltiwanger, J. (2019). "Trump Said 'I Don't Have a Racist Bone in My Body' As He Slammed Criticism of His Racist Tweets." *Business Insider*.

Haney López, I. (2014). *Dog Whistle Politics: How Coded Racial Appeals Have Reinvented Racism and Wrecked the Middle Class*. Oxford and New York: Oxford University Press.

Haney López, I. (2019a). *Merge Left: Fusing Race and Class, Winning Elections, and Saving America*. New York: The New Press.

Haney López, I. (2019b). "Why Do Trump's Supporters Deny the Racism that Seems So Evident to Democrats?" *Los Angeles Times*.

Hannon, M. (2021). "Disagreement or Badmouthing? The Role of Expressive Discourse in Politics." In E. Edenberg and M. Hannon (eds.), *Political Epistemology*. Oxford: Oxford University Press, 297–318.

Headley, C. (2000). "Philosophical Approaches to Racism: A Critique of the Individualistic Perspective," *Journal of Social Philosophy* 31: 223–57.

Henderson, R. and E. McCready (2018). *How Dogwhistles Work*. Cham, Springer International Publishing.

Hill, J. H. (2008). *The Everyday Language of White Racism*. Chichester, UK and Malden, MA: Wiley-Blackwell.

Hinton, A. (2020). "What White Power Supporters Hear Trump Saying." https://www.sapiens.org/language/white-power-dog-whistles/

Hod, I. (2016). "Are Trump-Pence's KFC Pics a Dog-Whistle to a Sexist Clinton Joke?" *Yahoo News*, https://news.yahoo.com/trump-pence-kfc-pics-dog-whistle-sexist-clinton-221947842.html?guccounter=1&guce_referrer=aHR0cHM6Ly93d3cuZ29vZ2xlLmNvbS8&guce_referrer_sig=AQAAAAiyQF3sYqqaNr2hsLHboxnb_FhK5-pVWQtD_h6Q4Ncp6GLCG7WQFnQRUpzgO4E-mDMEu8XsKF8HLRRf-FAaTNn7ZZKEP_64OlGRFjlA_8TsLBFMqys5W5B9neoXWnE08mtDWpvkqF8PwXruYVljmUBWl4G-dOiLi0w08Qh_GKH9

Holmes, J. (2022). "Wow, Ted Cruz's Take on January 6 Sure Has Evolved!" *Esquire*.

Hurwitz, J. and M. Peffley (2005). "Playing the Race Card in the Post–Willie Horton Era: The Impact of Racialized Code Words on Support for Punitive Crime Policy." *Public Opinion Quarterly* 69(1): 99–112.

Hutchings, V. L. and A. E. Jardina (2009). "Experiments on Racial Priming in Political Campaigns." *Annual Review of Political Science* 12: 397–402.

Hyska, M. (2022). "Against Irrationalism in the Theory of Propaganda." *Journal of the American Philosophical Association* 9(2): 1–15.

Illing, S. (2020). "'Flood the Zone with Shit': How Misinformation Overwhelmed Our Democracy." *Vox*, https://www.vox.com/policy-and-politics/2020/1/16/20991816/impeachment-trial-trump-bannon-misinformation

Jamieson, K. H. and J. N. Cappella (2008). *Echo Chamber: Rush Limbaugh and the Conservative Media Establishment*. Oxford and New York: Oxford University Press.

Jerde, S. (2015). "Trump: I Don't Like What Scalia Said about Affirmative Action." *The Hill*, https://thehill.com/blogs/ballot-box/presidential-races/263074-trump-scalia-affirmative-action/

Johnson, J. (2015). Trump Calls for "Total and Complete Shutdown of Muslims Entering the United States." *Washington Post*.

Johnson, J. (2016). " 'A Lot of People Are Saying' ... How Trump Spreads Conspiracies and Innuendos." *Washington Post.*

Kates, J., J. Tolbert, and A. Rouw (2022). "The Red/Blue Divide in Covid-19 Vacciation Rates Continues: An Update." *KFF,* https://www.kff.org/policy-watch/the-red-blue-divide-in-covid-19-vaccination-rates-continues-an-update/#:~:-text=The%20current%20gap%20of%2013.2,9%20percentage%20points%20last%20June

Katrowitz, A. (2016). "Racist Social Media Users Have a New Code to Avoid Censorship." *BuzzFeed News,* https://www.buzzfeednews.com/article/alexkantrowitz/racist-social-media-users-have-a-new-code-to-avoid-censorship

Keller, B. S. a. B. (2015). "Willie Horton Revisited." *The Marshall Project,* https://www.themarshallproject.org/2015/05/13/willie-horton-revisited

Kenyon, M. (2022). "An Apology, a Joke, and a Warning to the Left Walk into a Bar: The politics of layering racial figleaves," *Canadian Philosophical Association* (virtual meeting), May 2022.

Kenyon, T. (2003). "Cynical Assertion: Convention, Pragmatics, and Saying 'Uncle'." *American Philosophical Quarterly* 40(3): 241–8.

Kenyon, T. and J. Saul (2022). "Bald-Faced Bullshit and Authoritarian Political Speech: Making Sense of Johnson and Trump." In L. Horn (ed.), *From Lying to Perjury: Linguistic and Legal Perspectives on Lies and Other Falsehoods.* Berlin, Germany: De Gruyter, 165–94.

Khoo, J. (2017). "Code Words in Political Discourse." *Philosophical Topics* 45(2): 33–64.

Kinder, D. R. and D. O. Sears (1981). "Prejudice and Politics: Symbolic Racism versus Racial Threats to the Good Life." *Journal of Personality and Social Psychology* 40(3): 414.

Klemperer, V. (2000). (translated by M. Brady) *The Language of the Third Reich: LTI, Lingua Tertii Imperii—A Philologist's Notebook.* London and New Brunswick, NJ: Athlone Press.

Klieber, A. (2023). "Conversational Silence, Reconsidered". Under review.

Know Your Meme, "The Quiet Part Loud." https://knowyourmeme.com/memes/the-quiet-part-loud

Krieg, G. (2016). "It's Official: Clinton Swamps Trump in Popular Vote." *CNN,* https://www.cnn.com/2016/12/21/politics/donald-trump-hillary-clinton-popular-vote-final-count/index.html

Kroll, A. (2022). A Death on W Street: The Murder of Seth Rich and the Age of Conspiracy. New York: Public Affairs.

Kunda, Z. (1990). "The Case for Motivated Reasoning." *Psychological Bulletin* 108(3): 480–98.

Langton, R. (2012). "Beyond Belief: Pragmatics in Hate Speech and Pornography." In I. Maitra and M. K. McGowan, *Speech and Harm: Controversies over Free Speech.* Oxford: Oxford University Press, 72–93.

Langton, R. (2018). "The Authority of Hate Speech." *Oxford Studies in Philosophy of Law* 3: 123–52.

Lauwers, A. S. (2019). "Is Islamophobia (Always) Racism?" *Critical Philosophy of Race* 7(2): 306–32.

Lavin, T. (2018). "Conspiracy Theories about Soros Aren't Just False. They're Anti-Semitic." *Washington Post.*

Lee, B. (2016). "Maria Abramović Mention in Podesta Emails Sparks Accusations of Satanism." *The Guardian.*

Lepoutre, M. (2021). *Democratic Speech in Divided Times.* Oxford and New York: Oxford University Press.

Levy, N. (2016). "Am I a Racist? Implicit Bias and the Ascription of Racism ", *The Philosophical Quarterly*, Volume 67, Issue 268, July 2017, 534–51.

Levy, N. (2020). "Partisan Worlds." *Institute ot Art and Ideas News*, https://iai.tv/articles/partisan-worlds-auid-1548

Levy, N. (2021). *Bad Beliefs: Why They Happen to Good People.* New York: Oxford University Press.

Levy, N. and R. M. Ross (2021). "The Cognitive Science of Fake News." In M. Hannon and J. de Ridder (eds.), *The Routledge Handbook of Political Epistemology.* New York and London: Routledge, 181–91.

Lewandowsky, S. and S. van der Linden (2021). "Countering Misinformation and Fake News through Inoculation and Prebunking." *European Review of Social Psychology* 32(2): 348–84.

Lewiński, M. (2021). "Illoctionary Pluralism", *Synthese* 199: 3, 6687–714.

Lewis, D. (1979). "Scorekeeping in a Language Game." *Journal of Philosophical Logic* 8(3): 339–59.

Liao, S.-Y. (2016). "How Racists Are Made into Unicorns." *Medium.*

Lima, C. (2016). "Trump: 'I Have So Many African-American Friends that Are Doing Great'." *Politico*, https://www.politico.com/story/2016/09/donald-trump-african-american-friends-doing-great-227666

Loubriel, J. (2017). "4 Racial Dog Whistles Politicians Use (While Pretending They're Not Racist)." *Everyday Feminism*, https://everydayfeminism.com/2017/05/politicians-racial-dog-whistles/

Lovett, S. (2021). "Tory MP Says 'People Have Lost Sense of Humour' Over 'Blacking Up' as James Brown Fancy Dress Photo Emerges." *The Independent.*

Lowery, W. (2014). "Paul Ryan, Poverty, Dog Whistles, and Electoral Politics." *Washington Post.*

Lyall, S. (2022). "Boris Johnson's Lies Worked for Years, Until They Didn't." *New York Times.*

Macpherson, W. (1999). *The Stephen Lawrence Inquiry.* UK government report, https://assets.publishing.service.gov.uk/government/uploads/system/uploads/attachment_data/file/277111/4262.pdf

Madva, A. (2016). "A Plea for Anti-Anti-Individualism: How Oversimple Psychology Misleads Social Policy." *Ergo: An Open Access Journal of Philosophy* 3: 701–28.

Maitra, I. (2012). "Subordinating Speech." In I. Maitra and K. McGowan (eds.), *Speech and Harm: Controversies over Free Speech.* Oxford: Oxford University Press, 94–120.

Maitra, I. (2018). "Lying, Acting, and Asserting." In E. Michaelson and A. Stokke (eds.), *Lying: Language, Knowledge, Ethics, and Politics.* Oxford: Oxford University Press, 65–82.

Manne, K. (2018). *Down Girl: The Logic of Misogyny*. New York: Oxford University Press.

Margalit, Y. (2019). "Economic Insecurity and the Causes of Populism, Reconsidered." *Journal of Economic Perspectives* 33(4): 152–70, 10457–83.

Marques, T. (2020). "Disagreement with a Bald-Faced Liar." *Ratio* 33(4): 255–68.

Marsili, N. (2021). "Retweeting: Its Linguistic and Epistemic Value", *Synthese* 198.

Marsili, N. (2022). "Sharing Bullshit on Social Media." https://blogs.cardiff.ac.uk/openfordebate/sharing-bullshit-on-social-media/

Mathiesen, K. and D. Fallis (2016). "The Greatest Liar Has His believers: The Social Epistemology of Political Lying." In E. Crookston, D. Killoren, and J. Trerise (eds.), *Ethics in Politics*. New York: Routledge, 35–54.

McGowan, M. K. (2009). "Oppressive Speech." *Australasian Journal of Philosophy* 87(3): 389–407.

McGowan, M. K. (2012). "On 'Whites Only' Signs and Racist Hate Speech: Verbal Acts of Racial Discrimination." In I. Maitra and K. McGowan (eds.), *Speech and Harm: Controversies over Free Speech*. Oxford: Oxford University Press, 222–50.

McGowan, M. K. (2019). *Just Words: On Speech and Hidden Harm*. Oxford: Oxford University Press.

McIntosh, J. (2020). "Introduction: The Trump Era as a Linguistic Emergency." In J. McIntosh and N. Mendoza-Denton (eds.), *Language in the Trump Era: Scandals and Emergencies*. Cambridge: Cambridge University Press, 1–44.

Media Matters Staff (2021). "Tucker Carlson Hosts Glenn Beck to Question Covid-19 Vaccines." *Media Matters*, https://www.mediamatters.org/tucker-carlson/tucker-carlson-hosts-glenn-beck-question-covid-19-vaccines

Medina, J. (2013). *The Epistemology of Resistance: Gender and Racial Oppression, Epistemic Injustice, and the Social Imagination*. Oxford: Oxford University Press.

Meibauer, J. (2016). "Aspects of a Theory of Bullshit." *Pragmatics Cognition* 23(1): 68–91.

Mendelberg, T. (2001). *The Race Card: Campaign Strategy, Implicit Messages, and the Norm of Equality*. Princeton, NJ: Princeton University Press.

Mercieca, J. (2016). " 'Just Saying': Trump's Favorite Get-Out Clause." *Newsweek*.

Messing, S., Jabon, M., and Plaut, E. (2016). "Bias in the Flesh: Skin Complexion and Stereotype Consistency in Political Campaigns." *Public Opinion Quarterly* 80(1): 44–65.

Mills, C. (2007). "White Ignorance." In S. Sullivan and N. Tuana (eds.), *Race and Epistemologies of Ignorance*. New York: State University of New York Press, 11–38.

Mills, C. W. (2017). *Black Rights/White Wrongs: The Critique of Racial Liberalism*. New York: Oxford University Press.

Modood, T. and T. Sealy (2022). "Beyond Euro-Americancentric Forms of Racism and Anti-Racism." *Political Quarterly* 93(3): 433–41.

Moody-Adams, M. M. (1994). "Culture, Responsibility, and Affected Ignorance." *Ethics* 104(2): 291–309.

Moorman, T. (2020). "Watch Out, 'Super-Predator' Rhetoric Is Alive and Well." *Columbus Underground*.

Morin, W. (1988). "Behind the Numbers: Confessions of a Pollster." *Washington Post*, https://www.washingtonpost.com/archive/opinions/1988/10/16/behind-the-numbers-confessions-of-a-pollster/3523c065-11b5-42ba-9986-c317bdecf2dd/

Mounk, Y. (2018). "Americans Strongly Dislike PC Culture." *The Atlantic*.

Muirhead, R. and N. L. Rosenblum (2019). *A Lot of People Are Saying: The New Conspiracism and the Assault on Democracy*. Princeton, NJ, Princeton University Press.

Mutz, D. C. (2018). "Status Threat, Not Economic Hardship, Explains the 2016 Presidential Vote." *Proceedings of the National Academy of Sciences* 115(19): E4330–9.

Nagourney, A. (2016). "4 Key Trump Moments at the Final Debate." *New York Times*.

Napolitano, M. G. and K. Reuter (2023). "What Is a Conspiracy Theory?" *Erkenntnis* 88: 2035–62.

Newhouse, A. and N. Gunesch (2020). "The Boogaloo Movement Wants to Be Seen as Anti-Racist, But It Has a White Supremacist Fringe." *Center on Terrorism, Extremism, and Counter-Terrorism*, https://www.middlebury.edu/institute/academics/centers-initiatives/ctec/ctec-publications/boogaloo-movement-wants-be-seen-anti-racist-it

Nguyen, C. T. (2020). "Echo Chambers and Epistemic Bubbles." *Episteme* 17(2): 141–61.

Noah, T. (1998). "Bill Clinton and the Meaning of 'Is'." *Slate*, https://slate.com/news-and-politics/1998/09/bill-clinton-and-the-meaning-of-is.html

Norlock, K. J. (2018). "Perpetual Struggle." *Hypatia* 34(1): 6–19.

Novaes, C. D. and J. de Ridder. (2021). "Is Fake News Old News?", eds. S. Bernecker, A. Floweree, and T. Grundmann, *The Epistemology of Fake News*, OUP, 156–79.

O'Connor, C. and J. O. Weatherall (2019). *The Misinformation Age*. New York: Yale University Press.

Okrent, D. (2004). "Weapons of Mass Destruction? Or Mass Distraction?" *New York Times*.

Onley, D. (2018). "George H.W. Bush's Willie Horton Ad Remains Flashpoint in Dog-whistle Politics." *The Grio*.

Oreskes, N. and E. M. Conway (2010). *Merchants of Doubt: How a Handful of Scientists Obscured the Truth on Issues from Tobacco Smoke to Global Warming*. New York: Bloomsbury Press.

Pagin, P. and N. Marsili (2021). "Assertion", *The Stanford Encyclopedia of Philosophy*, Edward N. Zalta (ed.).

Palmeri, T. (2017). "Trump Fumes over Inaugural Crowd Size." *Politico*.

Partee, B. (2020). "My Response to the Pinker Petition." *Medium*.

Pearson, J. (2017). "AI Can Now Identify Racist Code Words on Social Media." *Vice*.

Pennycook, G. and D. G. Rand (2022). "Nudging Social Media toward Accuracy." *The ANNALS of the American Academy of Political and Social Science* 700(1): 152–64.

Pennycook, G., J. McPhetres, Y. Zhang, J. G. Lu, and D. G. Rand (2020). "Fighting COVID-19 Misinformation on Social Media: Experimental Evidence for a Scalable Accuracy-Nudge Intervention." *Psychological Science* 31(7): 770–80.

Perlstein, R. (2012). Exclusive: Lee Atwater's Infamous 1981 Interview on the Southern Strategy. *The Nation*.

Pettigrew, T. F. (2017). "Social Psychological Perspectives on Trump Supporters." *Journal of Social and Political Psychology* 5(1): 107–16.

Philips, M. (1984). "Racist Acts and Racist Humor." *Canadian Journal of Philosophy* 14 (1984): 75–96.

Phillips, A. (2017). "'They're Rapists.' President Trump's Campaign Launch Speech Two Years Later, Annotated." *Washington Post.*

Pilkington, E. (2019). "Release of Vaxxed Sequel Prompts Fears Dangerous Propaganda Will Spread Again." *The Guardian.*

Pine, D. W. (2017). "Is Truth Dead? Behind the *Time* Cover." *Time.*

Pitofsky, M. (2020). "GOP Group Touts Graham's Past Praise of Biden, Criticism of Trump in New Ad." *The Hill,* https://thehill.com/blogs/blog-briefing-room/news/502494-gop-group-touts-grahams-past-praise-of-biden-criticism-of-trump/

Plant, E. A. and P. G. Devine (1998). "Internal and External Motivation to Respond without Prejudice." *Journal of Personality and Social Psychology* 75(3): 811–32.

Pohlhaus Jr, G. (2012). "Relational Knowing and Epistemic Injustice: Toward a Theory of Willful Hermeneutical Ignorance." *Hypatia* 27(4): 715–35.

Politico Staff. (2017). "Transcript of White House Press Secretary Statement to the Media." *Politico,* https://www.politico.com/story/2017/01/transcript-press-secretary-sean-spicer-media-233979

Pomerantsev, P. (2019). *This Is Not Propaganda: Adventures in the War against Reality.* New York: Public Affairs.

Quaranto, A. (2022). "Dog Whistles, Covertly Coded Speech, and the Practices that Enable Them." *Synthese* 200(4): 330.

Rathje, S., J. Roozenbeek, C. S. Traberg, J. J. Van Bavel, and S. van der Linden (2022). "Letter to the Editors of Psychological Science: Meta-analysis Reveals that Accuracy Nudges Have Little to No Effect for US Conservatives: Regarding Pennycook et al. (2020)." *Psychological Science,* https://journals.sagepub.com/page/pss/letters-to-the-eds

Reilly, K. (2016). "Read Hillary Clinton's 'Basket of Deplorables' Remarks about Donald Trump Supporters." *Time.*

Reimann, N. (2020). "Some Americans Are Tragically Still Drinking Bleach as a Coronavirus 'Cure'." *Forbes,* https://www.forbes.com/sites/nicholasreimann/2020/08/24/some-americans-are-tragically-still-drinking-bleach-as-a-coronavirus-cure/

Rini, R. (2017). "Fake News and Partisan Epistemology." *Kennedy Institute of Ethics Journal* 27(2): E-43–64.

Rini, R. (2021). "Weaponized Skepticism: an Analysis of Social Media Skepticism as Applied Politica Epistemology." In E. Edenberg and M. Hannon (eds.), Political Epistemology. Oxford: Oxford University Press, 31–48.

Robertson, D. (2021). "How Owning Libs Became the GOP's Core Belief." *Politico,* https://www.politico.com/news/magazine/2021/03/21/owning-the-libs-history-trump-politics-pop-culture-477203

Roche, D. (2021). "Cop Sentenced to Prison for Posting Photo of Hitler's Favorite Food." *Newsweek.*

Rodricks, D. (1993). "Trying to Find the Real Willie Horton." *Baltimore Sun.*

Rogers, K. and N. Fandos (2019). "Trump Tells Congresswomen to 'Go Back' to the Countries They Came From." *New York Times.*

Romano, A. (2022). "Poll: 61% of Trump Voters Agree with Idea behind 'Great Replacement' Conspiracy Theory." *Yahoo News,* https://uk.news.yahoo.com/hed-poll-61-of-trump-voters-agree-with-idea-behind-great-replacement-conspiracy-

theory-090004062.html?guccounter=1&guce_referrer=aHR0cHM6Ly93d3cuZ29v
Z2xlLmNvbS88&guce_referrer_sig=AQAAAAiyQF3sYqqaNr2hsLHboxnb_FhK5-
pVWQtD_h6Q4Ncp6GLCG7WQFnQRUpzgO4E-mDMEu8XsKF8HLRRf-
FAaTNn7ZZKEP_64OlGRFjlA_8TsLBFMqys5W5B9neoXWnE08mtDWpvkqF8
PwXruYVljmUBWl4G-dOiLi0w08Qh_GKH9

Roose, K. (2020). "How 'Save the Children' Is Keeping QAnon Alive." *New York Times*.

Roose, K. (2021). "A QAnon 'Digital Soldier' Marches On, Undeterred By Theory's Unravelling." *New York Times*.

Rose, J. (2020). "Even If It's 'Bonkers', Poll Finds Many Believe QAnon and Other Conspiracy Theories." *NPR*, https://www.wbur.org/npr/951095644/even-if-its-bonkers-poll-finds-many-believe-qanon-and-other-conspiracy-theories?ref=postingthroughit.com

Rose, S. (2022). A Deadly Ideology: How the "Great Replacement Theory" Went Mainstream. *The Guardian*.

Rosenberg, A. (2020). "Trump's Address Proved He Is a Genius Entertainer. Democrats Ought to Worry." *Washington Post*.

Rosenberg, M. and M. Haberman (2020). "The Republican Embrace of QAnon Goes Far Beyond Trump". *New York Times*.

Rosenwald, B. (2019). *Talk Radio's America: How an Industry Took Over a Political Party that Took Over the United States*. Cambridge, MA: Harvard University Press.

Rothschild, M. (2021). *The Storm Is Upon Us: How QAnon Became a Movement, Cult, and Conspiracy Theory of Everything*. Brooklyn, NY: Melville House.

Safire, W. and W. Safire (2008). *Safire's Political Dictionary*. Oxford and New York: Oxford University Press.

Santana, C. (2022). "What's Wrong with Dogwhistles." *Journal of Social Philosophy* 53(3): 387–403.

Sarna, J. (2021). "A Scholar of American Anti-Semitism Explains the Hate Symbols Present during the US Capitol Riot." *The Conversation*.

Saul, J. (2019a). "Immigration in the Brexit Campaign: Protean Dogwhistles and Political Manipulation." In C. Fox and J. Saunders (eds.), *Media Ethics, Free Speech, and the Requirements of Democracy*. London and New York: Routledge, 21–37.

Saul, J. (2019b). *What Is Happening to Our Norms against Racist Speech?* Aristotelian Society Supplementary Volume. Oxford: Oxford University Press.

Saul, J. (2020). "The Republican National Convention: Even More Dangerous than 4 Years Ago." *The Conversation*, https://theconversation.com/the-republican-national-convention-even-more-dangerous-than-4-years-ago-145149

Saul, J. (2021). "Racist and Sexist Figleaves." In J. Khoo and R. Sterken (eds.), *The Routledge Handbook of Social and Political Philosophy of Language*. New York and London: Routledge, 161–78.

Saul, J. (2023). "Dogwhistles, Figleaves, and Social Movements." *Eastern Division Conference of the American Philosophical Association*, Montreal.

Saul, J. M. (2012). *Lying, Misleading, and What Is Said: An Exploration in Philosophy of Language and in Ethics*. Oxford: Oxford University Press.

Saul, J. M. (2017). "Racial Figleaves, the Shifting Boundaries of the Permissible, and the Rise of Donald Trump." *Philosophical Topics* 45(2): 97–116.

Saul, J. M. (2018). "Dogwhistles, Political Manipulation, and Philosophy of Language." In D. Fogal, D. Harris and M. Moss (eds.), *New Work on Speech Acts*. New York and Oxford: Oxford University Press, 360–83.

Schaffner, B. F. and S. Luks (2018). "Misinformation or Expressive Responding? What an Inauguration Crowd Can Tell Us about the Source of Political Misinformation in Surveys." *Public Opinion Quarterly* 82(1): 135–47.

Schwarcz, J. (2021). "Back Away From 'America's Frontline Doctors'." https://www.mcgill.ca/oss/article/covid-19-critical-thinking-pseudoscience/back-away-americas-frontline-doctors

Scott, E. (2015). "Trump Hits Scalia Over Comments on Black Students." *CNN*, https://theconversation.com/the-republican-national-convention-even-more-dangerous-than-4-years-ago-145149

Selley, C. (2021). "Canada's Pandemic Failures Are Systemic, Not Ideological." *National Post*.

Shear, M. D. (2018). "'I'm Not a Racist', Trump Says in Denying Vulgar Comment." *New York Times*.

Shelby, T. (2002). Is racism in the "heart"?. *Journal of Social Philosophy*, 33(3), 411–20.

Sheth, S. (2020). "Fox News Won a Court Case by 'Persuasively' Arguing that No 'Reasonable Person' Could Take Tucker Carlson Seriously." *Business Insider*.

Sides, J., M. Tesler, and L. Vavreck (2018). *Identity Crisis: The 2016 Presidential Campaign and the Battle for the Meaning of America*. Princeton, NJ: Princeton University Press.

Smith, C. (2021). "Ruminating over Conservative Leader Erin O'Toole's Tag Line." *The Georgia Straight*.

Smith, D. (2019). "Trump Shows Fake Hurricane Map in Apparent Bid to Validate Incorrect Tweet." *The Guardian*.

Smith, D. (2022). "'Replacement Theory' Still Republican Orthodoxy Despite Buffalo Shooting." *The Guardian*.

Snyder, T. (2017). "The Test of Nazism that Trump Failed." *New York Times*.

Snyder, T. (2018). *The Road to Unfreedom: Russia, Europe, America*. New York: Tim Duggan Books.

Sommer, W. (2020). "Here's How Hugo Chavez, Dead since 2013, Became Responsible for Trump's Election Loss." *The Daily Beast*, https://www.thedailybeast.com/heres-how-hugo-chavez-dead-since-2013-became-responsible-for-trumps-election-loss

Sommers, S. R. and M. I. Norton (2006). "Lay Theories about White Racists: What Constitutes Racism (and What Doesn't)." *Group Processes and Intergroup Relations* 9(1): 117–38.

Sorensen, R. (2007). "Bald-Faced Lies! Lying without the Intent to Deceive." *Pacific Philosophical Quarterly* 88(2): 251–64.

Stanley, J. (2012). "Speech, Lies and Apathy." *New York Times*.

Stanley, J. (2015). *How Propaganda Works*. Princeton, NJ and Oxford: Princeton University Press.

Stanley, J. (2018). *How Fascism Works: The Politics of Us and Them*. New York: Random House.

Stanley, J. and D. Beaver (forthcoming). *Politics of Language*. Princeton: Princeton University Press.

Staples, B. (2021). "How the White Press Wrote Off Black America." *New York Times*.

Stebbing, L. S. (1961). *Thinking to Some Purpose*. Harmondsworth: Pelican.

Suskind, R. (2004). "Faith, Certainty and the Presidency of George W. Bush." *New York Times*.

Swift, Jonathan. (2004). *A Modest Proposal and Other Prose*. Barnes & Noble Publishing.

Szalinski, C. (2021). "Fringe Doctors' Groups Promote Ivermectin for Covid Despite a Lack of Evidence." *Scientific American*.

Táíwò, O. (2022). Elite Capture: How the Powerful Took Over Identity Politics (And Everything Else), Pluto.

Tirrell, L. (2012). "Genocidal Language Games." In I. Maitra and M. K. McGowan (eds.), *Speech and Harm: Controversies over Free Speech*. Oxford: Oxford University Press, 174–221.

Tirrell, L. (2017). "Toxic Speech: Toward an Epidemiology of Discursive Harm." *Philosophical Topics* 45(2): 139–61.

Tirrell, L. (2021). *Discursive Epidemiology: Two Models*. Aristotelian Society Supplementary Volume. 95 (1): 115–42.

Topolski, A. (2018). "The Race-Religion Constellation: A European Contribution to the Critical Philosophy of Race." *Critical Philosophy of Race* 6(1): 58–81.

Turri, J. (2022). Figleaves Right and Left: A Case-Study of Viewpoint Diversity Applied to the Philosophy of Language. *Controversial Ideas*, 2(1).

Torices, J. R. (2021). "Understanding Dogwhistle Politics." *THEORIA: An International Journal for Theory, History and Foundations of Science*, 36(3): 321–39.

Uscinski, J., A. Enders, C. Klofstad, M. Seelig, H. Drochon, K. Premaratne, and M. Murthi (2022). "Have Beliefs in Conspiracy Theories Increased over Time?" *PloS one* 17(7): e0270429.

Uscinski, J. E. (2018). "Almost 60 Percent of Americans Believe in Conspiracy Theories about JFK. Here's Why That Might Be a Problem." *LSE Blogs*, https://blogs.lse.ac.uk/usappblog/2018/11/22/almost-60-percent-of-americans-believe-in-conspiracy-theories-about-jfk-heres-why-that-might-be-a-problem/

Uscinski, J. E. (2022). "Getting QAnon Wrong and Right." *Social Research: An International Quarterly* 89(3): 551–78.

Uscinski, J. E. and R. W. Butler (2013). "The Epistemology of Fact Checking." *Critical Review* 25(2): 162–80.

Valentino, N. A., V. L. Hutchings, and I. K. White (2002). "Cues that Matter: How Political Ads Prime Racial Attitudes during Campaigns." *American Political Science Review* 96(1): 75–90.

Valentino, N. A., F. G. Neuner, and L. M. Vandenbroek (2018). "The Changing Norms of Racial Political Rhetoric and the End of Racial Priming." *Journal of Politics* 80(3): 757–71.

Van Dijk, T. A. (1993). *Elite Discourse and Racism*. Newbury Park, CA: Sage.

Varden, H. (2010). "Kant and Lying to the Murderer at the Door…One More Time: Kant's Legal Philosophy and Lies to Murderers and Nazis", *Journal of Social Philosophy* 41: 4, 403–21.

Varun (2022). "Taking Large Doses of Ivermectin to Treat Covid-19 Is Dangerous and Can Cause Serious Harm." https://www.logically.ai/factchecks/library/630ec263

Viebahn, E., Wiegmann, A., Engelmann, N., and Willemsen, P. (2021). "Can a Question Be a Lie? An Empirical Investigation", *Ergo an Open Access Journal of Philosophy* 8: 7.

Walsh, C. (2021). " 'Taxpayer Dollars': The Orgins of Austerity's Racist Catchphrase." *Mother Jones.*

Wetts, R. and Willer, R. (2019). "Who is called by the dog whistle? Experimental evidence that racial resentment and political ideology condition responses to racially encoded messages". *Socius*, 5, https://doi.org/10.1177/2378023119866268

White, I. K. (2007). "When Race Matters and When It Doesn't: Racial Group Differences in Response to Racial Cues." *American Political Science Review* 101(2): 339–54.

Wills, V. (2016). "Bad Guys and Dirty Hands." *The Critique.*

Wilson, C. (2020). "Pete Evans Is Now Posting Neo-Nazi Symbols and the Far-Right Love It." *Gizmodo*, https://gizmodo.com.au/2020/11/pete-evans-is-now-posting-neo-nazi-symbols-and-the-far-right-love-it/

Withers, R. (2018). "George H. W. Bush's 'Willie Horton' Ad Will Always Be the Reference Point for Dog-Whistle Racism." *Vox.*

Witten, K. (2014). "Dogwhistle Politics: The New Pitch of an Old Narrative." Unpublished manuscript.

Wolfson, S. (2018). "Gwyneth Paltrow Didn't Want Conde Nast to Fact-Check Goop Articles." *The Guardian.*

Womick, J., T. Rothmund, F. Azevedo, L. A. King, and J. T. Jost (2019). "Group-Based Dominance and Authoritarian Aggression Predict Support for Donald Trump in the 2016 US Presidential Election." *Social Psychological and Personality Science* 10(5): 643–52.

Wood, M. (2019). "More Extremists Are Getting Radicalized Online. Whose Responsibility Is That?" *Marketplace*, https://gizmodo.com.au/2020/11/pete-evans-is-now-posting-neo-nazi-symbols-and-the-far-right-love-it/

Wright, S. (2021). "The Virtue of Epistemic Trustworthiness and Re-Posting on Social Media", (eds.) S. Bernecker, A. Floweree, and T. Grundmann, *The Epistemology of Fake News*, Oxford University Press, 245–64.

Yuhas, A. (2021). "It's Time to Revisit the Satanic Panic." *New York Times.*

Index

For the benefit of digital users, indexed terms that span two pages (e.g., 52–53) may, on occasion, appear on only one of those pages.